Teaching Young Gifted Children in the Regular Classroom

Identifying,
Nurturing, and
Challenging
Ages 4–9

Joan Franklin Smutny
Sally Yahnke Walker
Elizabeth A. Meckstroth

Edited by Marjorie Lisovskis

free spirit
PUBLiSHiNG

Works
for kids

Library of Congress Cataloging-in-Publication Data

Smutny, Joan F.
        Teaching young gifted children in the regular classroom : identifying, nurturing, and challenging ages 4–9 / Joan Franklin Smutny, Sally Yahnke Walker, and Elizabeth A. Meckstroth.
            p.   cm.
        Includes bibliographical references (p.   ) and index.
        ISBN: 1-57542-017-1
        1. Gifted children—Education (Preschool)—United States. 2. Gifted children—Education (Primary)—United States. 3. Gifted children—Education—United States—Curricula. 4. Gifted children—United States—Identification. 5. Early childhood education—parent participation—United States. 6. Classroom management—United States. I. Walker, Sally Yahnke, 1942–   . II. Meckstroth, Elizabeth A. III. Title.
LC3993.218.S68   1997
371.95—dc21   96-46737
                                                                                                          CIP

Index compiled by Eileen Quam and Theresa Wolner
Supervising editor: Pamela Espeland

10 9 8 7 6 5 4 3 2

Printed in the United States of America

Free Spirit Publishing Inc.
400 First Avenue North, Suite 616
Minneapolis, MN 55401-1730
(612) 338-2068
help4kids@freespirit.com

Dedication

To Susan Winebrenner, who inspired this book through her own text,
Teaching Gifted Kids in the Regular Classroom.

And to all the teachers, administrators, and parents of bright young children
whose talents and abilities deserve to be recognized and nurtured.

And to our own children, who are our original and continual inspirations:
Cheryl, Elizabeth, Sarah, Amy, Karen, and Anne.

Acknowledgments

This book was made possible by integrating the work, ideas, and ideals of
many treasured colleagues with our own decades of experience in gifted and
early childhood education. We appreciate and honor the thousands of professionals, parents, and children who have touched our lives and enriched us in
developing the ideas and activities within these pages. Thank you.

Contents

List of Tables and Figures

List of Reproducible Pages

Introduction

*"A beetle has a real short life, but that's okay.
After it's born, it mates and lays eggs,
and the rest is free time."*

"I feel microscopic in the crowded hallways."

*"I wasn't playing on the roof—
I was seriously on the roof."*

Sound familiar? Who hasn't delighted in hearing the wisdom of bright, creative young children like the six-year-olds who made these statements? Often, the choice of words, ideas, images, and phrases we hear are what we might more commonly associate with fourth, fifth, or sixth graders. Sometimes we can't imagine how such sophisticated thoughts and vocabulary can come from children so young!

Can preschool and primary-aged children be gifted? Most school programs suggest that giftedness isn't identifiable before third or fourth grade. Some schools don't begin to address the abilities of highly able children until middle school or junior high. Is it possible that children clearly express talents and abilities in the preschool and early elementary years?

As teachers, we all know that they do. Every September, we look at our new classes of young students and notice characteristics and behaviors that make some children stand out. The fact that we notice these girls and boys is important. What we do about them—and with them—is equally important. If we listen, we hear that their words, questions, observations, and interpretations con-

tinue. Every day, we hear their hunger to know more. And we are impelled to ask, as we do for every student, "What can I do for them?"

In most schools and classrooms, the goal is to provide a program that offers every child the opportunity to experience intellectual challenge and accomplishment as well as delight in learning. Yet most programs typically don't respond to the creative and intellectual needs of gifted children. If we are to provide these children with the same educational opportunities as their classmates of average and lower abilities, we must make special adaptations—in our programs, our activities, our teaching materials, and our perspectives on these children's legitimate special needs.

In this book, we'll share strategies and techniques that will help you identify the high-ability children in your classroom, encourage their talents, and help them to grow. Typically, young gifted students come to us already *knowing* a great deal. Yet, regardless of their advanced knowledge, they enter our classrooms with intellectual and emotional needs that are universal: to be recognized, to be accepted, and to experience the challenge and joy of learning. To meet these children's needs, we need a curriculum that offers developmentally appropriate opportunities for challenge, discovery, mastery of new skills, and sharing of new knowledge.

Young gifted children—even four- and five-year-olds—are hungry to make sense of the world in ways we may not expect from most preschoolers and early elementary students. These children have the desire to exercise and expand their minds intellectually and creatively.

1

In our extensive work with highly able and talented children, we have found that the most effective approaches evolve in an environment that is rich in critical and imaginative thinking, one in which learning is an interactive process. We have also found that these approaches can be successfully implemented within the regular classroom, to the benefit of *all* children, through curriculum practices appropriate to each child's development.

The National Association for the Education of Young Children (NAEYC) describes the important qualities of early childhood education in a series of guidelines. In July 1996, NAEYC adopted its most recent position statement, "Developmentally Appropriate Practice in Early Childhood Programs Serving Children from Birth Through Age 8."* Within the principles and guidelines NAEYC recommends are these components:

- A developmentally appropriate curriculum integrates all areas of a child's development: physical, emotional, social, and cognitive.
- Appropriate curriculum planning is based on teachers' observations and the recording of each child's special interests and developmental progress.
- Curriculum planning emphasizes learning as an interactive process. Teachers prepare the environment for children to learn through active exploration and interaction with adults, other children, and materials.
- Learning activities and materials are real and relevant to the lives of young children.
- Programs provide for a wider range of developmental interests and abilities than the chronological age range of the group alone suggests. Adults are prepared to meet the needs of children who exhibit unusual interests and skills outside the normal developmental range.
- Teachers provide a variety of activities and materials and increase the difficulty, complexity, and challenge of an activity as children are involved with it and develop understanding and skills.

---

* The position statement is published in Sue Bredekamp and Carol Copple, eds., *Developmentally Appropriate Practice in Early Childhood Programs,* rev. ed. (Washington, DC: the National Association for the Education of Young Children, 1997). Write to NAEYC, 1509 16th Street NW, Washington, DC 20036-1426, or call 1-800-424-2460.

- Teachers establish a reciprocal relationship with families that will increase their understanding of the lives of children outside of the classroom. They then can respond more sensitively to parents' concerns and preferences and are able to link families with a range of services for and information about children.
- Teachers bring the culture and language of the home into the culture of the school in order to value each child's background.

In a nutshell, these principles underscore that to *teach* a child, you must *reach* the child. And to reach the gifted children in your charge, you must create experiences that engage the youngest creative and analytical thinkers. Extra worksheets and flash cards won't allow you to do this. What will? We'll tell you in this book, and we'll show you how you can do it successfully in your own classroom.

In arranging the content of *Teaching Young Gifted Children in the Regular Classroom,* we've approached our task in much the same way you approach yours as the school year begins and your program unfolds:

Chapter 1 helps you identify high-ability children in your classroom in an affirming way, making use of the most current knowledge about identifying giftedness and avoiding the pitfalls of stereotypes and politics.

Chapter 2 spotlights the learning environment. We explain how to tailor your classroom setting to entice children to energetically and constructively pursue their interests.

Chapter 3 focuses on curriculum compacting as an essential strategy in responding to high-ability children, who often know much or even most of what is to be presented in the classroom for the entire year. We explain how you can use compacting to expand students' learning opportunities and school success.

Chapter 4 explores creative, integrated approaches to the study of environment, history, and culture. We detail specific strategies that will enhance the discovery process in these subject areas, and describe activities you can use or adapt for your own classroom.

Chapter 5 provides an exciting range of creative strategies for teaching language arts. Drawing on visual art, dramatics, music, photography, film, and video as catalysts, we show how you can generate and sustain the imaginative process in young people, enabling them to produce original and creative work.

Chapter 6 offers a variety of original activities and strategies to help children imaginatively investigate mathematics and science through story making, design, role play, and other explorations.

Chapter 7 examines the use of standardized testing and looks at ways to determine what the young gifted child needs to know, how the child's needs can be documented, and how to advance the child's skills and talents.

Chapter 8 presents the concept of cluster grouping, along with other techniques for enabling children with high ability to find consistent challenge, accomplishment, and growth through group work in the regular classroom.

Chapter 9 shows how you can access parent support to affirm and advance your efforts at meeting the needs of the gifted children in your classroom.

Chapter 10 presents the unique social and emotional needs of young gifted children, offering perspectives that will broaden your understanding of the challenges and difficulties talented students commonly experience. We include a range of useful suggestions that can help you empower children in their struggle to confront and work through some of these challenges.

Chapter 11 investigates the experiences and needs of diverse populations among the gifted, including children from minority cultures, talented girls, students who are "twice exceptional" and those who are highly gifted, and children with high energy.

Every chapter includes "References and Resources"—useful books, periodicals, and other materials related to the chapter topic.

Appendix A lists and describes standardized tests that can be used to identify young gifted children.

Appendix B offers an extensive annotated resource list of additional books and materials for gifted primary-age children, divided into the following subject areas: art, music, dance, and theater; environment and ecology; language arts (including biography and autobiography, fiction and nonfiction, and poetry); mathematics; science; and social studies (including global and multicultural, history and geography).

Appendix C lists sources for gifted education materials.

In addition, a general bibliography provides a wealth of practical references for boosting your background in the many facets of teaching the gifted child.

The ideas we share with you in this book are wholly *doable*: They will work for your students, their parents, and you. As you use them, you will offer the talented and bright young children in your classroom many wonderful opportunities to:

- discover new possibilities for themselves
- delight in fresh challenges and the excitement of learning
- think of school as an exhilarating adventure of intellectual and aesthetic discovery
- thrive in a setting you have created to respond to their individual needs.

In our experience of teaching, counseling, consulting, and talking with thousands of children, parents, and teachers, we have found that early awareness and knowledge of a child's unique abilities will make for a highly motivating educational experience throughout the school year and the child's school career. At the heart of it, we know that all children are looking for a conscious sense of their own value. A purpose and a priority of this book is to affirm children's self-worth. We are certain that the strategies included here will create an environment that will benefit each student. In using them, you can take pride in the knowledge that you're doing what you need to do for *every* child in your classroom: providing an appropriate educational opportunity for growth and success in school and life.

We wish you well!

Joan Franklin Smutny
Sally Yahnke Walker
Elizabeth A. Meckstroth

1

Identifying the Young Gifted Child

It was circle time. The children knew that when their teacher announced it and slowly counted to ten, they were to assemble around the rug. But there was Emily, off in her own world again, submerged in an imaginative and intricate drawing of Columbus landing in the New World. For Emily, transitions weren't just difficult—they were almost impossible. When, at last, she would come to the rug and sit down, she always brought something to play quietly with, rarely giving the teacher her undivided attention. Emily's body was there, but her mind was somewhere else. The teacher often needed to remind Emily to focus on what was taking place in the class.

Maybe, thought the teacher, Emily just expected too much from school. She was a child who seemed to make everything complicated. At work and play alike, Emily tried to direct the other children's performance in elaborate, complex detail until they shrugged their shoulders and walked away. She wanted children to follow all the rules. If she thought something was unfair, she was outraged.

Emily wanted to read as much and as often as she could. She wanted to read chapter books, but there were none in the kindergarten section of the library. Increasingly, she worked and played by herself. The more Emily's teacher tried to involve her with classmates, the more differences surfaced. Emily wasn't unhappy, but she didn't fit in. Toward her teacher, she was both passive and assertive; she would listen quietly, but would absolutely refuse to do her "letter of the week" projects. The teacher was beginning to wonder if Emily would ever be socialized.

This teacher cared deeply about her "problem" student. Anxious about winning the girl's cooperation and helping her gain peer acceptance, she had begun to see Emily's intense determination, creativity, and unusual abilities as barriers to academic and social success rather than as gifts to be nurtured. It's understandable that a teacher might take this view. In the preschool and primary years, most teachers are trained to focus on helping children to acquire social skills and meet "readiness" markers. Yet, in this situation, one thing was clear: Emily's creativity and intellect were not being appreciated or developed in school. To help Emily experience learning *and* fit comfortably into the class, this teacher needed to recognize Emily's giftedness *and* look for ways to accommodate her unique learning needs.

On Being a Pioneer Teacher

In our combined decades of working closely with gifted children, their families, and others who educate and care for them, we have learned that the issue of giftedness is often volatile. Many people have fervent reactions when they think a teacher is favoring one child as intrinsically "better" than another. Much of the problem here lies in perceptions. In the classroom and the home, *each* person develops with some qualities that are similar and others that are unique. The gifted child is not "better" than other children; she is *different* from them.

5

Teachers who want to identify exceptional intelligence and abilities in the lowest grades are pioneers. Usually children are not formally identified as gifted by a school system until the third or fourth grade. For many children, this can be too late.

Why Is Early Identification Important?

Children's brains are highly sensitive and susceptible to new experiences; this is especially true up through about age five. If young children don't receive appropriate recognition and response during this sensitive period, potential skills may deteriorate. By fourth grade, some of the most intelligent children are resentful of waiting for the other kids to catch up. Having learned easy achievement without struggle and persistence, these high-ability students now find little meaning in a school day. Many have fallen into a pattern of low performance. Since they're only required to do general class work that may be far below their ability level, some have come to think of themselves as "the best." At times, they are bored—and "bored" is a low-grade level of "angry." They may be slightly depressed because their anger has turned inward. Or they may act out their anger in the form of behavior problems. The earliest school years are the most essential for finding these children before their eagerness and joy for learning have been conditioned out of them.

Recognizing and rewarding giftedness in young children helps develop their confidence, self-esteem, and enthusiasm for learning. When children are encouraged to use their special abilities for worthwhile results, the outcomes are nearly always positive.

To detect giftedness, we need to notice and accommodate ability, opportunity, and interest. If parents and teachers respond enthusiastically to a child's exceptional abilities and interests, these qualities will be expressed. A young child who is provided with appropriately challenging, stimulating schoolwork can show substantial gains in achievement, motivation, and self-concept.

It is within your power to catch these children before they learn to hide their abilities in order to be accepted by peers, and before they decide that school isn't worth their effort. You have the opportunity to become a pioneer in identifying and cultivating giftedness among the young children you teach.

What Are You Looking For?

Determining what it means to be "gifted" remains a challenge. In general, you're looking for a *type* and *degree* of exceptional ability.

A Type and Degree of Intelligence

In 1972, the U.S. Office of Education defined gifted and talented children as those with outstanding abilities and high performance capabilities in the areas of:

• general intellectual pursuits
• specific academic aptitudes
• creative or productive thinking
• leadership
• visual and performing arts
• psychomotor processing.

More contemporary theories continue to reach beyond cognitive ability to describe giftedness. Yale psychology professor Robert Sternberg's theory defines intelligence by how it is applied in real-life situations—through intelligent behaviors. As indicators of giftedness, Sternberg looks for effective approaches to both identifying and solving problems and for the ability to make the best use of an environment.

Howard Gardner, a psychologist at the Harvard School of Education, extends giftedness into several distinct competencies.* Although all of these *multiple intelligences* exist in each of us, their relative potencies vary.

Linguistic Intelligence: Children who are linguistically gifted are sensitive to word sounds and meanings and to language intricacies and function. They may have unusually acute verbal memories, effusive vocabularies, and a wealth of elaborate stories to tell.

---

* In *Frames of Mind: The Theory of Multiple Intelligence* (New York: Basic Books, 1993), Gardner describes seven intelligences. At a national conference in June of 1995, he identified an eighth intelligence—naturalist. Work on Gardner's model continues, and it is likely that other areas will be identified as well. These descriptions are used with permission of Howard Gardner.

Musical Intelligence: Musical capability includes refined pitch discrimination, easy recognition of musical themes, and sensitivity to rhythm, texture, and timbre. Children with exceptional musical abilities might hum and sing to themselves, express an ardent love for music, and recognize melodies with amazing accuracy.

Logical-Mathematical Intelligence: Children who think logically/mathematically are keenly aware of logical or numerical patterns and able to understand and perform complex math calculations. They might demonstrate their facility for logic in persistent negotiations.

Visual-Spatial Intelligence: Spatial abilities involve seeing, representing, and manipulating lines, objects, and spaces. You will observe children with exceptional spatial acuity playing complex games of chess, creating elaborate LEGO structures, focusing with great intensity on intricate drawings, and eagerly assembling puzzles. These children have graphic memories and can discern subtle visual changes.

Bodily-Kinesthetic Intelligence: A child with bodily-kinesthetic ability demonstrates exquisite whole body or fine motor control. Some children with this propensity are avid sports or dance enthusiasts. Others are so physically inclined that they will almost act a charade when they speak.

Interpersonal Intelligence: Interpersonal intelligence entails empathy for other people—for their words, actions, intentions, and feelings. Young children with interpersonal intelligence are socially adept; their ability to "get inside" other people's minds and emotions seems almost uncanny. Look to these children to organize other students and lead recess games with ease.

Intrapersonal Intelligence: Intrapersonal acumen involves keen insight into oneself. Children with a strong intrapersonal bent can observe themselves and understand their own strengths, needs, and feelings. They may be exceptionally adept at managing their emotions and goals. You see evidence of this intelligence in a child's creative self-expression—exhibited through music, dance, language, crafts, and the like.

Naturalist Intelligence: Some children have a built-in affinity and appreciation for the wonders of nature. Animals are friendly toward these children, who have a deep, knowing relationship with both flora and fauna. Children with strong naturalist intelligence are awed by the beauty of the natural world and find its processes both fascinating and easy to comprehend. These students love to sort and classify things.

———

With many children, particularly those from minority cultures, it's important to be sensitive to the varied emphases and expressions that special abilities can take. Considering Gardner's different intelligences helps you observe all children with a wider lens and more easily recognize exceptional skills and interests.

In Chapter 2, we suggest ways to set up learning centers geared to the eight intelligences. See pages 33–37.

It's exciting and rewarding to be the person who makes a difference to exceptional children and their families. You can make your classroom a safe place that has enough understanding and flexibility for children to exhibit the unusual, idiosyncratic, and even esoteric qualities that make them extraordinary. In doing this, you invite gifted children to identify themselves.

Asynchronous Development

In some ways, gifted children are out of sync with what is developmentally expected behavior for their age. To find these children, you need to look beyond what is usually considered "normal" and into the individual child. Consider this:*

> "Giftedness is *asynchronous development* in which advanced cognitive abilities and heightened intensity combine to create inner experiences and awareness that are qualitatively different from the norm. This asynchrony increases with higher intellectual capacity. The uniqueness of the gifted renders them particularly vulnerable and requires modifications in parenting, teaching and counseling in order for them to develop optimally."

---

* Linda Kreger Silverman. "The Gifted Individual," in *Counseling the Gifted and Talented,* Linda Kreger Silverman, ed. Denver: Love Publishing Co., 1993, p. 3.

Please read the quoted passage again and think about how much it refers to qualities that are immeasurable and emotional. You may find that you need to adjust your expectations for children's mental and chronological ages. The example of Emily (see page 5) shows this need. Rather than try harder to fit Emily into the classroom structure, the teacher might win more enthusiastic cooperation by creating options to expand opportunities that challenge and engage her young student. The fact that Emily is the same chronological age as most of her other classmates doesn't mean that her mind functions at the same level. As a second-grade boy once said, "What does size have to do with what grade you're in? Shouldn't it be how much you know?"

Enigmatic Behavior

Gifted children are an enigma. They differ from each other more than they are alike. For any trait that might describe one gifted child, the opposite will define another. Defining giftedness is like trying to describe a symphony—it encompasses a spectrum of qualities. Children with the same IQ will have different interests, personalities, abilities, and temperaments. Each gifted child is intricate, paradoxical, and complex; the brain that drives him intensifies everything he does. This intensity gives energy to intelligence and abilities, heightening and expanding these capacities even more.

Some components of giftedness present a real challenge to a teacher's traditional training. Astounding precocity can be coupled with gaps in physical, social, and emotional development. There are times when it's just not convenient to accommodate a gifted child's special needs. To meet this challenge, you'll need to keep foremost in your mind the goal of supporting *all* children's growth and learning.

You can engage a gifted student if you get to know the child. In Emily's case, rather than focus on how much and how often Emily doesn't conform, the teacher might get to know Emily and learn about what she loves to do. What is she reading? At what level is she already reading at home? How much does she know about a subject that interests her? What fills her daydreams? Reaching out in this way, the teacher can build a bridge by which Emily can learn and participate through her own heightened interest. Much of

the rest of this chapter provides suggestions for how to get to know a child.

A Passion for the Possible

It can be hard to keep up with a gifted child's series of passions. First it may be dinosaurs, then creative cooking, then slime mold and a fascination with endless propagation experiments—until the child moves on to astronomy. Once, when walking down Chicago's Navy Pier, we saw a young girl's T-shirt that announced, "Another day, another hobby."

"Problem" Behaviors

Young gifted children may show "problem" behaviors that, paradoxically, can indicate giftedness. Parents, too, are likely to overlook exceptional abilities and instead focus on problems of immaturity, socialization, and discipline. Occasionally, gifted children are misdiagnosed as behaviorally disordered. From parents' reports and your own observations, you might consider the following behaviors.

Obstinacy: Acting out and obstinacy can be the result of frustration or anger due to inactivity and restrained progress.

"Showing Off": This might be a way for the child to express who she is and what she knows. Gifted children *do* have advanced knowledge and vocabulary.

Inferior Work: Messy, careless, incomplete, or inferior work can indicate that the task offers no challenge. Gifted children have an aversion to repetition and drill of what they already understand. Inferior work can also result when a child's fine motor development is significantly out of sync with his exceptional cognitive abilities. Children in this situation can become immensely frustrated and may just give up on expressing themselves in writing. Inferior or messy work might also represent repressed anger.

Antisocial Demeanor: Antisocial behavior might suggest that a child is intrinsically an introvert or that her intellectual peers are older children. This child may have difficulty conforming to group tasks if these activities restrain her insatiable curiosity.

Impertinence: "Back talk" and perceived impertinence could indicate divergent thinking or that the student has learned additional information from other sources. Higher-level thinking skills prompt gifted children to analyze and evaluate from surprising viewpoints.

Disruptiveness: Disruptive acts and low impulse control can result when a child doesn't have enough opportunities to appropriately release high energy.

Failure to Follow Directions: Children who are highly creative and inventive like to originate ideas and answers; often these children disregard directions, or balk at them.

Stubbornness: Stubborn, strong-willed behavior can be the outgrowth of many gifted children's intrinsic need for self-control, intense concentration, and persistent, goal-directed ideals.

Emotional Immaturity: Immature emotional responses can reflect intense sensitivity and are often the result of the high expectations many gifted children have for themselves.

Underachievement: Low achievement can be an attempt to gain social acceptance.

Lack of Judgment: Gifted children can make foolish decisions. They haven't lived long enough to learn how some things work in the world. This discernment gap can be part of their asynchronous development.

Getting to Know Your Students

How might you begin to see a child's passion? Giftedness goes beyond the confines of a classroom. To learn what excites a gifted child's curiosity and imagination, you need to look into the child.

Interviews

One of the best ways to learn how to motivate a child is to ask the child about himself, his interests, and his feelings about school. This gives you insights into the child's thinking, aspirations, home situation, and sense of self-determination.

Early in the year, as often as you are able, create time for short interview sessions with each student in your class. Tell students that you want to get to know them and will be spending some "special time" with each of them.

A few days before you begin interviewing students, send home a copy of the "Your Child's Pictures" family letter (page 18). When you schedule a child's interview, ask the child to bring about six photographs or pictures to share with you (these are requested in the family letter). This gives the child a personal stake in the meeting. Usually children have a wonderful time selecting or drawing pictures, and so have an initial positive association with your meeting. They also have some control over the image of themselves that they present to you.

This one-on-one time with you can have an enormous impact on the child and on your teacher-student relationship. The child feels more valued and liked by you. You are likely to see some marvelous ripple effects later in your classroom. Feeling liked by a teacher is one of the most important elements affecting children's school success.

Here are some conversation starters and questions that might help you structure your student interviews:

- What are some things that you do best?
- What are some things that you like to do?
- What are some things that are hard for you to do?
- What do you like best in school? Why?
- What don't you like in school? Why?
- What do you wish you could change to make school better for you?
- What are some things you would like to be and do when you are grown up?
- If you had three wishes that could come true, what would they be?

Portfolios

Another excellent way to identify young gifted students is to collect and examine evidence of giftedness. This is known as creating a portfolio. A portfolio is a collection of products and observations about the child. It reaches beyond the confines of a classroom, integrating what the child is capable of at home and elsewhere.

Portfolios provide *authentic assessment*—evidence of actual witnessed behaviors. Such evidence is valuable in determining instructional plans, especially for children from about kindergarten through fourth grade. Portfolio assessment has many advantages. It:

- validates your observations and hunches about a child
- enables you to talk more decisively about your plans with parents, guardians, caregivers, and support staff
- builds a concrete bridge between you and the parent so that each can see what the other is talking about
- helps you evaluate the child's progress
- guides you to a more child-centered and responsive curriculum
- broadens your ideas and the choices you have to offer all of the children in your class
- justifies what to look for in identifying other students and becomes a learning tool for you
- creates a source of pride and accomplishment for the child.

Another advantage of portfolio assessment is that it gives you a means to find talents that may not be evident when children "perform" in front of other students. This can help you identify advanced or unique abilities in children who are culturally different from the majority of students. A child who feels different from most others in the class might be reluctant to directly reveal unusual abilities that could further emphasize this sense of separateness. However, when children work and play uninhibitedly, their special gifts are likely to become apparent.

The portfolio is a repository of what a child *can* do. Its focus is on strengths, not deficits. Only one rule applies: Nothing negative goes in the portfolio.

Note Strengths

Collect evidence of gifted behaviors. Create a file for each child that includes succinct anecdotal statements of notable strengths. Aim for one entry a week. Yes, this takes time, but it's well worth it. Most teachers find that this process changes for the better the way they perceive their students. Equally important, when you look for and interpret behaviors as exceptional abilities,

you're likely to get a payoff from your students, too. Children will be aware that you are watching for and responding to strengths. A positive reaction from students is a natural outcome.

Because expressions of giftedness vary in children and cultures, you will be looking for and noting evidence that corresponds with some of these indicators of giftedness we have just discussed. Use the "Checklist of My Child's Strengths" (pages 22–23) as a guide, and also consider the categories that follow.

Use of Language: Things to note would include vocabulary range, precision in word usage, and sentence complexity. Example: "Maya asked if she would be 'permitted' to take home her project 'in the foreseeable future.'"

Level of Questioning: Is there more to the child's questions than the usual who, what, where, and why? Do the questions show depth of understanding or an unusual level of complexity? Example: "Luís asks if there is another two-dimensional universe beyond this one."

Problem-Solving Strategies: How does the child attack difficult or novel problems? Does he persist? Does he seem to have a system or strategy for solving the problem? Can the child change his thinking if his strategy is not working? Example: "Bobby found answers when he had manipulatives and visuals to guide his learning. Now I see that he has unusual potential."

Depth of Information: Sometimes a child is a profound expert in an area. This can indicate a high level of curiosity, resourcefulness, and understanding. It also points to an excellent memory. Example: "Grace was able to help me install the new math games on the computer when I was completely stuck."

Breadth of Information: Sometimes a child is interested in everything. A child like this has a variety of interests and also an excellent long-term memory. Example: "I offered a choice of Chutes and Ladders or Connect Four, and Molly asked for Trivial Pursuit."

Creativity: Is the child original in her creations? Can she elaborate on simple details? Are there instances in which you see creative or expressive movement, art, dramatization, or music-making? Are any examples unusual for a child of this age? Example: "Shantelle makes her own products, rather than copying from another child."

Being creative means going against the grain. This can wreak havoc on lesson plans! It can be hard to bring divergent thinkers back to what *you* want them to do.

Focus On or Absorption In a Task: When working on a task or problem, is the child so engrossed that he's unaware of all else that is going on around him? Are there times when the child doesn't hear that it's time to pick up? Does the child resist distractions? Can the child tune others out? Example: "Harry gets so involved with his projects that I sometimes need to sit down next to him and speak directly to him to interrupt his focused concentration."

Profound Interest in Existential and Spiritual Questions: Some children's thoughts and questions are intensely spiritual. They express a deep concern with the existential "Why?" Example: "Clara said, 'It doesn't matter that I was born because Mommy would have had another little girl that she would have loved just as much as me, so why was I born?' "

Self-Evaluation: Does the child appear to have an inner set of standards that he sets for himself? Is the child self-critical or impatient with his ability from time to time? Is he sensitive? Example: "Maruf revised his neighborhood map four times because he couldn't proportion the spaces to accommodate the elaborate details he envisioned."

Preference for Complexity or Novelty: Does the child prefer to work at tasks that are difficult or challenging, rather than on simple ones? Given a choice, would the child choose an unusual or complicated game instead of an easy one? Example: "It's hard for T.J. to find playmates at recess because he comes up with play ideas so complicated that the other children get confused and walk away."

Ability to Synthesize, Interpret, and Imagine: Another way to collect information for your notes is by reading simple, lavishly illustrated stories and asking students questions about the pictures. Use questions that require creative imagination,

such as: "What else could the dog be thinking?" "What might Kai be doing if he lived on the planet Mars?" Listen for and make note of:

- elaborate vocabulary
- use of contextual clues
- logical reasoning to arrive at answers
- integration of factual knowledge
- intense emotional involvement in answers
- vivid imagination.

Observe Sensibility

When creating portfolios, observe *sensibility* as well as sense. Sensibility is a child's capacity to be involved with something. It is a deep internal, emotional response to what other children might not even notice. With gifted children, things matter a lot. Catching a snowflake summons up a keen, intense response. Learning how long it would take to travel to Pluto evokes awe and excitement.

You can focus on sensibility by observing children and asking yourself: How acute are Kavon's feelings when he sees frost patterns on the windows? Is Libby totally immersed in stacking the blocks? Does Brendan talk to the books he organizes? Does Rachel anxiously try to find some food when she sees the guinea pig's dish empty?

At the end of her kindergarten year, five-year-old Katja's portfolio included the following:

- photocopies of her work on math puzzles in workbooks brought from home
- samples of her paper folding in elaborate and inventive three-dimensional shapes
- the teacher's summaries of conversations with classmates demonstrating Katja's efforts to intervene as a peacemaker
- notes on the teacher's observation that Katja often chooses to play by herself with blocks and boxes, creating her own involved world of shapes and scenarios
- Polaroid photograph of her "block world"
- drawings done at the beginning, middle, and end of the year.

It also included the teacher's summary note:

"Katja's fine motor development and social progress are well documented. The math puzzles in the workbooks she brought from home and worked on during her free play time established that her math level is several grades higher than what will be offered in first grade. Katja appears to enjoy working alone, yet she is exceptionally sensitive to other children's needs and feelings. It is likely that Katja is a visual-spatial learner who learns best if concepts are shown to her. She appears to be an exceptionally intelligent, creative child. Because her use of expressive language is about normal for her age, her abilities might not be demonstrated in the regular curriculum."

Child-Created Portfolios

Portfolios that *you* compile are one kind of ongoing assessment. Another valuable window on a student's talents, abilities, and growth is a portfolio created and maintained *by the child*. Child-created portfolios allow you to foster children's passion for learning and gain insights into how children view themselves and their work.

Provide a space, folder, box, or bag for each child to use to collect favorite and special work. Encourage children to label their containers ("Mikiko's 'I Did It!' Collection") and decorate them however they wish, using photos, drawings, or artistic designs.

You may want to make the initial selection for this portfolio. Start with a standard sample of a piece of work that everyone in the class has done, originating in the curriculum and grounded in instruction. This first example gives you a baseline from which to judge children's ability relative to their classmates' growth. From there, invite children to select the work they want to save, using criteria they have established. Guide children who need assistance in determining the criteria: They might select work that is special to them or that they feel represents their best efforts.

When they enter a piece of work in the portfolio, have children explain why they selected this particular item. They can write their explanations on an attached note or dictate them for you or another student to transcribe, as in this example:

"Jason said that he'd included a sheet that had every answer wrong, because that was where he learned the most. This was really hard for him. He explained that he now knew each right answer."

With child-created portfolios, each child has a special space to call his own in the classroom. This communicates to the children that they can make decisions. It lets them see that their work has value. It also encourages them to think critically about what they have done. At the end of the year, you have an exemplar—from the child's point of view—of each child's development.

Dynamic Assessment

In looking for learning potential—eventual ability development—one way to find outstanding qualities is to arrange for a child to demonstrate her learning capabilities. This allows you to measure what a child knows and can do and to offer the next increment of challenge—what the child is ready to do or could do with a little instruction. Steps for this kind of dynamic assessment are:

1. **Test:** Establish competency level.
2. **Train:** Teach just beyond that level.
3. **Retest:** Gauge learning.

These steps are particularly effective for children who may be socially awkward, inhibited, or shy. Exceptional abilities can be harder to detect in children who are introverted or less adept in revealing their thoughts, ideas, and feelings. The strengths of extroverted, socially confident children are more conspicuous; these youngsters get our attention and tell us what they know. Introverted or shy children can be inhibited, slow to warm up, and reticent in their responses. Often, teachers expect less of these children, who may appear to be immature or to have less to offer. But some introverted children only *seem* slower, when in fact they prefer to understand and mentally rehearse activities before experiencing them.

Chapter 7 gives an in-depth discussion of assessing children's ability and development. See pages 121–140.

Enlisting Parents as Colleagues*

As you work to identify gifted children, parents can be of great help. Parents (and other family members) tend to be realistic predictors of their children's abilities and needs. Since about 80 percent of parents of gifted children can identify their children's giftedness by age five or six,** a shortcut to finding young gifted students is to ask the parents.

When Grandmother brought four-year-old Maurice to preschool, she told the teacher that her grandson thought differently from other children his age. Grandmother owned a Laundromat, and Maurice spent countless hours there with her. To occupy himself, he read magazines. He liked to read News-week *and* People; *he liked to learn what was going on in the world. Because time was important at the Laundromat, Maurice had also mastered another important task: making change. Grandmother knew that her son had been very bright, but felt that her grandson was "different."*

This grandmother may not have had the skills to judge the extent of her grandson's precocity. Nonetheless, she recognized that he had abilities unusual for a child of his age. She was able to accurately report his behavior and bring it to the attention of the preschool teacher.

How can you enlist parents' help in identifying children's special talents and abilities? Your goal at this point is to attain insight into children's strengths that might not be apparent in the classroom. To do this, we suggest that you start the school year by requesting three things from parents: pictures, information, and examples of products the child has made at home.

Request Pictures

As close as possible to the first day of school, send home the "Your Child's Pictures" family letter (page 18). You will want to do this before you

---

* Throughout this book, we use the word *parents* to refer to mothers, fathers, guardians, or any other primary caregivers.

** Meckstroth, Elizabeth A. "Guiding the Parents of Gifted Children," in *Counseling Gifted and Talented Children: A Guide for Teachers, Counselors, and Parents*, Roberta M. Milgram, ed. Norwood, NJ: Ablex Publishing, 1991, pp. 95-120.

interview each new student. Use the letter we have provided, adapt it, or write your own request for family pictures.

Request Information

Shortly after requesting pictures, send home the "Information, Please" family letter (page 19) and invite parents to complete "About My Child" and "Checklist of My Child's Strengths" (pages 20–23). If most of the characteristics on the checklist represent their child, you might want to take a closer look.

Request Products

After you have received the written information about children, you may want to follow up with a request for a "personal exhibit" that includes examples of the child's home activities. Ask parents to assemble a collection of items that demonstrate their child's particular interests and abilities. In making your request, you may wish to use or adapt the "Your Child's Personal Exhibit" family letter (page 24).

Even with the family letters, it's likely that some children won't bring pictures or other materials from home. You may want to allow time in class for *all* children to draw pictures of themselves, their families, and their favorite activities. Then every child will have something to share with the teacher and classmates and a foundation for creating a personal exhibit.

A personal exhibit has dimensions to reveal a child's special skills and interests through real evidence that the teacher might not discover in the classroom. It can include photographs, art projects, tape recordings, writings—whatever captures the child's extraordinary interests and abilities. It can be stored or presented in any suitable container—perhaps a shoe box or grocery bag.

A personal exhibit has great additional value if the child can briefly present it to the class. If there isn't time to do this, arrange a time for individual children to show and describe their exhibits to you or to an aide. We suggest that you write a note about the exhibit and add it to the child's portfolio.

Seven-year-old Josh's personal exhibit, which he shared with his second-grade class, included the following:

- a map he used to locate several Civil War battles
- a replica of a Confederate dollar bill
- pictures of military uniforms and weapons.

Josh's teacher wrote this note for his portfolio:

"Josh seemed to enjoy and take great pride in showing his exhibit to the class. I had never seen him so engaged and enthusiastic as he was about his knowledge of the Civil War. We learned that he has participated in reenactments and that he knows weapon types, strategies, and the locations of many battles. He demonstrated a keen sense of technical knowledge and interest as well as logical and sequential knowledge. Perhaps he can relate some of our curriculum to his 'hidden passion.' Josh's exhibit itself was small and simple; he seems to have little patience for creating any representations of his interest or knowledge, but would rather learn more."

Chapter 9 provides more information about communicating and working with parents. See pages 149–164.

What About Testing?

The earlier children's special needs are identified, the better it is for their development. Currently there seems to be an intense focus on finding very young children who have delayed development. Federal programs and money are available to identify any delay or learning difficulty so these children have optimal opportunity for their exceptional learning needs to be met. These young children's scores are considered valid; indeed, entire task forces respond to these test scores.

Formal intelligence testing using an instrument such as one of the *Stanford-Binet Intelligence Scales* or the *Wechsler Preschool and Primary Scale of Intelligence–Revised (WPPSI–R)** provides an objective appraisal of a child's abilities. For a child who is not well assimilated into the mainstream culture, these tests have limited value. They *do*, however, assess a *minimal* level of ability. There

---

* For more information about these and other formal assessment instruments, see Appendix A, pages 196–197.

are many reasons why a child might not demonstrate optimal performance, but the child can't pretend or fake a score such as 133; you know that the child with this score has abilities that are at least this high.

When interpreting test scores, find the ability areas in which the child's performance is most advanced. These point to exceptional ability and potential strengths. This perspective helps to identify gifted children who might be overlooked if only the full-scale IQ test score—which is an average of several scores—is considered.

For young children, physical, social, and cognitive development is rapid and variable. Cognitive and motor skills come suddenly: One moment the skill is not observable, then it miraculously appears! This is just one reason why any assessment you make regarding a child's development needs to be considered as a minimal estimation. We don't know how far a trait can be developed.

You'll find more detailed discussions of assessment and testing considerations in Chapter 7 (pages 121–140) and Appendix A (pages 196–197).

Questions and Answers

"Zach often says something odd, not related to my lesson plan or the class discussion. How can I handle this?"

Gifted children could be described in three words: *more, more,* and *more.* They can be divergent thinkers. They consider information and make intricate, often unusual connections. They need appropriate opportunities to experience intellectual challenge, accomplishment, and satisfaction. You might ask Zach to draw a picture about his idea at home and share it with you or the class the next day. Or arrange to talk with him about his comment later in the day, so he has an opportunity to explain himself.

"I've seen TV programs about gifted children, but I've never had a gifted child in my classroom. How prevalent is giftedness?"

Media hypes the sensational. Prodigies who possess extreme talent and children with astonishingly rare qualities of intelligence make memorable stories. Gifted children can be in every class and school, though most will not be prodigies.

Teachers and administrators have made enormous progress in becoming aware of gifted children and their needs. In 1972, 57.5 percent of school administrators reported that they had *no* gifted children in their schools. By 1994, 35 states mandated the identification of gifted/talented students, 31 mandated required services, and 23 allocated funds to service these students. Still, many thousands of gifted children are unidentified or underserved. Depending on how giftedness is defined, the incidence of gifted children is about five percent of the total population.*

To identify gifted children, we first have to *want* to find them. Then we must know what qualities we're looking for and *deliberately* seek to find them.

"I don't believe in singling out gifted children. Isn't every child gifted?"

Every child is special and unique. However, when we use the term "gifted," we are describing children who, compared to their age mates, have an ability or a depth and breadth of awareness that is far beyond the norm. Although many children may have a particular talent, the designation "gifted" indicates a child who has unusually high abilities in some area and, because of that, has special educational needs. The gifted child experiences your classroom and your program in different ways than the other children in the class do. If we don't identify children's needs, we can't help them use their strengths to become more of what they can be. As teachers, our goal is to provide learning and growth opportunities for every student. To do this, we must identify any gifted children in order to respond appropriately to them.

"One of my students, Eli, is extremely smart—but he still cries in school. How can he be so immature?"

Asynchronous development is a trait of giftedness. For gifted children, physical, cognitive, emotional, and social developmental levels don't evolve at normal rates and don't keep pace with one another. These various aspects of development are out of sync. We can think of gifted children as being several ages simultaneously. These developmental abnormalities can cause confusion for adults who try to formulate reasonable, appropriate expectations for children. They also create

---

* *The 1994 State of the States Gifted and Talented Education Report.* Council of State Directors of Programs for the Gifted, 1994.

inner tension for the children who experience them. It's common for gifted children to have highly sensitive, intense emotions. When gifted children experience a stressful situation, many react with a degree of tension, anxiety, and concern that seems excessive.

When Eli is able, he will stop crying in school. Until then, try not to be impatient. You might help both him and the other children by using the situation as a teachable moment for demonstrating compassion and empathy.

"How can Julia be gifted when I can't even read her handwriting?"

The label "gifted" does not apply to all aspects of the child. Some children may be able to create elaborate models in their minds but not yet have the fine motor control or skill to define these designs on paper. Handwriting then becomes a barricade to the child's expression, and she may react with frustration. If she finds handwriting cumbersome and tedious, Julia may resist laboriously reproducing her thoughts letter by letter. You can help her by giving less emphasis to the mechanics of handwriting and focusing instead on the capabilities she demonstrates verbally or in projects. By assessing her knowledge and accomplishments, you can create a less restrictive environment in which she can reveal her abilities. For example, if you ask her to *write* about her summer vacation, Julia might produce something like this: "Summer was fun. We went places." If, instead, you ask her to *tell* about it, she may describe every detail and nuance of her summertime activities.

"Ricardo's parents think he's gifted. I think he's hyperactive or has attention deficit disorder. What should I do?"

A high energy level—and the need for its release—is sometimes associated with high intelligence. Gifted children have a voracious appetite for stimulation. It's as if they need 2,000 calories of intellectual stimulation a day while most of the other children are satisfied with 1,000. If, in the regular classroom, the environment requires gifted students to wait and wait, most are soon starving for more "brain food."

Before focusing your attention on the possibility of attention deficit disorder (ADD) or hyperactivity, first try to adjust the classroom environment to allow Ricardo more opportunities for intellectual stimulation and challenge. Does he need more to do? Have you asked him what might make his day more calm and satisfying? Lack of enough activity and interest can make adults fidgety, too!

In Chapter 2, we suggest ways to structure the environment to accommodate gifted children's special needs. See "Setting Up Centers for Multiple Intelligences," pages 33–37.

"Sara's abilities are at least two grade levels above her age peers, but in the classroom she shows little creativity or initiative. Why does she just do what is asked and nothing more?"

Very bright children are often unusually socially aware and concerned with peer acceptance. One child in our class read out loud fluently at home but, in school, would move his finger slowly along the lines of type and pause after every word he read. He explained, "This is how we're supposed to read in school."

You might be able to help Sara by connecting her with at least one academic, intellectual peer— if possible, someone in your classroom. This will create a safe place in which Sara might feel more comfortable revealing her abilities.

Conclusion

As a preschool or primary teacher, you are in a position to be a pioneer—a catalyst in discovering and nurturing gifted young children. To do this, you want to infuse your classroom with an atmosphere of wonder and an attitude of acceptance, flexibility, and understanding. Giving a child permission to reveal diverse and exceptional qualities welcomes and honors the whole child. And because gifted children often differ more than they resemble one another, your encounter with each child will be unique.

How do you find gifted children? Look for them. Summon them to show you their uniqueness. Invite the adults in their lives to help you. In the process, you will discover and experience countless hidden assets—in your students and yourself.

References and Resources

Betts, George T., and Maureen Neihart. "Profiles of the Gifted and Talented." *Gifted Child Quarterly*, 32:2 (1988), pp. 248-253. Six profiles of gifted children offer a close look at the feelings, behaviors, and needs of these children. Also included are cues for identifying and nurturing gifted children who fit each profile: *successful, divergent, underground, dropout, double-labeled,* and *autonomous.*

Center for Talented Youth Publications and Resources, ed. *Identifying and Cultivating Talent in Preschool and Elementary School Children*. Baltimore: Johns Hopkins University Press, 1994. A complete course in one brief, concise book. Presents information on testing, programming, and acceleration as well as resources (including educational software) and reading lists. We highly recommend it for both educators and parents.

Clark, Barbara. *Growing Up Gifted: Developing the Potential of Children at Home and at School*, 4th ed. New York: Maxwell Macmillan International, 1992. A classic text to familiarize educators with information and processes for understanding and teaching gifted children.

Gardner, Howard. "Are There Additional Intelligences? The Case for Naturalist, Spiritual, and Existential Intelligences." In *Education, Information, and Transformation*, J. Kane, ed. Englewood Cliffs, NJ: Prentice-Hall, forthcoming. Gardner's paper explores the process of identifying an intelligence and examines evidence of three new intelligences not included in his landmark book, *Frames of Mind.*
———. *Frames of Mind: The Theory of Multiple Intelligence*. 10th ed. New York: Basic Books, 1993. A provocative exploration of intelligence that broadens our conceptions of giftedness.
———. "Reflections on Multiple Intelligences: Myths and Messages." *Phi Beta Kappan*, 77:9 (November 1995), pp. 200-208. Gardner explains uses of his theory and introduces the possibility of an additional intelligence—naturalist.

Kingore, Bertie. *Portfolios: Enriching and Assessing All Students, Identifying the Gifted, Grades K–6*. Des Moines, IA: Leadership Publishers, 1993. Elaborates on purposes, practices, and implementations in creating portfolios for young gifted children.

Lazear, David. *Multiple Intelligence Approaches to Assessment: Solving the Assessment Conundrum.* Tucson, AZ: Zephyr Press, 1994.

———. *Seven Pathways of Learning: Teaching Students and Parents About Multiple Intelligences.* Tucson, AZ: Zephyr Press, 1994. Two books that are components of workshops, complete with handouts. These include lesson plans and activities that allow teachers to observe behaviors representative of the original seven intelligences identified by Howard Gardner.

Lind, Sharon. "Are We Mislabeling Over-Excitable Children?" *Understanding Our Gifted* 5:5A (1993), pp. 1-10. An essential perspective to consider in identifying children who might not match the expected behavior profile. Lind offers many alternative ways to respond to a child's giftedness and to aberrant behaviors.

Meckstroth, Elizabeth A. "Guiding the Parents of Gifted Children." In *Counseling Gifted and Talented Children: A Guide for Teachers, Counselors, and Parents,* Roberta M. Milgram, ed. Norwood, NJ: Ablex Publishing, 1991, pp. 95-120. Specific information on teacher-parent conferences, involving parents in identifying gifted children, helping parents acknowledge and understand giftedness, and organizing and facilitating parent discussion groups.

The 1994 State of the States Gifted and Talented Education Report. Council of State Directors of Programs for the Gifted, 1994. A concise overview of state-by-state information and charts about support, funding, mandates, policies, practices, program populations, and more. At the time of this writing, a new edition of this publication is forthcoming.

Richert, E. Susanne. "Rampant Problems and Promising Practices in Identification." In *Handbook of Gifted Education,* Nicholas Colangelo and Gary A. Davis, eds. Boston: Allyn & Bacon, 1991, pp. 81-96. A provocative perspective on pitfalls in identifying gifted children and sound ideas for programs and identification practices in your school. Richert's article is one of many reasons to have the *Handbook of Gifted Education*—an extensive collection of the writings of many respected experts in the field of gifted education—on your reference shelf.

Silverman, Linda Kreger. "The Gifted Individual." In *Counseling the Gifted and Talented,* Linda Kreger Silverman, ed. Denver: Love Publishing Co., 1993. pp. 3-28. One of many sensitively written chapters depicting the intricate, complex characteristics and needs of gifted children.

Smutny, Joan Franklin, Kathleen Veenker, and Stephen Veenker. *Your Gifted Child: How to Recognize and Develop the Special Talents in Your Child from Birth to Age Seven.* New York: Ballantine Books, 1989. Comprehensive explanations help parents and educators understand the characteristics and needs of young gifted children.

Sternberg, Robert J. *Beyond IQ: A Triarchic Theory of Human Intelligence.* New York: Cambridge University Press, 1985. Information for understanding and appreciating intelligence as demonstrated through intelligent behavior.

U.S. Department of Education, Office of Educational Research and Improvement. *National Excellence: The Case for Developing America's Talent.* Washington, DC, 1993. A conclusive, concise, easy-to-understand document that convincingly reports the imperative educational needs of gifted children.

Webb, James T., Elizabeth A. Meckstroth, and Stephanie S. Tolan. *Guiding the Gifted Child: A Practical Resource for Parents and Teachers,* rev. ed. Scottsdale, AZ: Gifted Psychology Press, forthcoming. Based on information from guided parent discussion groups, this book speaks from people's personal experiences of living with and learning from gifted children. It describes qualities of gifted children in a manner that helps readers become familiar with the ways they can help children develop their best "selves." Includes chapters on motivation, discipline, peer and sibling relations, stress management, and depression. The original edition won the American Psychological Association's Best Book Award.

YOUR CHILD'S PICTURES

Child's Name: _____

Dear Parent/Caregiver:

In the next few days, I will be meeting individually with each child in my class. This meeting will give the children and me a chance to get to know each other.

I plan to meet with your child, _____, on _____ (day and date). On or before that day, could you please send along five or six pictures that are special to your child? These could be photographs or pictures your child has drawn. The pictures might be of your child, your family, friends, a pet, or other things or activities that your child enjoys. Sharing pictures will give your child a chance to tell me about some of the people and experiences that are important to him or her.

Thank you for your help. If you have any questions, please call or stop in to talk. I look forward to working with your child!

Teacher's Signature: _____

Phone: _____

INFORMATION, PLEASE

Child's Name: _____

Dear Parent/Caregiver:

In my effort to get to know every child better, I'm asking all parents to complete the attached forms, "About My Child" and "Checklist of My Child's Strengths," and return them in the envelope (also attached) by _____ (day and date). The information you give will help me to understand and respond to your child's unique emotional, social, and academic needs.

Thank you for your time and help. If you have any questions, please call or stop in to talk.

Teacher's Signature: _____

Phone: _____

ABOUT MY CHILD

Child's Name: _____

My child loves: _____

_____

In her/his free time, my child usually: _____

_____

My child's favorite activities are: _____

_____

_____

_____

My child (can) _____ (cannot) _____ tell time.

My child does math problems such as: _____

_____

_____

My child reads books such as these on his/her own: _____

_____

_____

My child has these special abilities and talents: _____

_____

_____

Specials concerns I have about my child are: _____

_____

_____

ABOUT MY CHILD (CONTINUED)

Use the space below to write some examples of your child's most notable moments during the past year or so. These might be memorable comments or questions, favorite projects or stories your child has made up, activities you or your child have found interesting, or behaviors you have wondered about. If you need additional space, use the back of this sheet.

_____

_____

_____

_____

_____

_____

_____

_____

_____

_____

_____

_____

_____

_____

_____

_____

_____

_____

_____

_____

_____

_____

_____

Parent/Caregiver's Signature: _____

Phone: _____

CHECKLIST OF MY CHILD'S STRENGTHS

Child's Name: _____

Please check any items that *usually* or *often* apply to your child:

_____ Is very aware of physical surroundings.

_____ Asks questions about abstract ideas like love, feelings, relationships, or justice.

_____ Needs less sleep than other children of same age.

_____ Moves around a lot. Is very active—sometimes seems hyperactive.

_____ Talked early.

_____ Has long attention span for activities that interest her/him.

_____ Is extremely concerned, curious about the meaning of life and death.

_____ Reacts intensely to noise, light, taste, smells, or touch.

_____ Craves stimulation and activity. Is rarely content to sit idle.

_____ Is very emotional—cries, angers, excites easily.

_____ Has an excellent memory.

_____ Insists that people be "fair." Complains when things are "unfair."

_____ Is extremely curious—asks "Why?" "How?" "What if?"

_____ Becomes so involved that he/she is not aware of anything else—"lost in own world."

_____ Explains ideas in complex, unusual ways.

_____ Is very interested in cause-effect relationships.

_____ Reasons well. Thinks of creative ways to solve problems.

_____ Is very interested in calendars, clocks, maps, structures.

_____ Has vivid imagination and may have trouble separating real from unreal.

_____ Is extremely creative—uses materials in unusual ways; makes up elaborate stories, excuses; sees many possible answers/solutions; spends free time drawing, painting, writing, sculpting, or singing.

MY CHILD'S STRENGTHS (CONTINUED)

_____ Has spontaneous and/or advanced sense of humor.

_____ Likes to play with words. Uses advanced sentence structure and vocabulary.

_____ Is often singing, moving rhythmically; may tell stories or communicate by singing.

_____ Memorizes songs.

_____ Often prefers playing with older children or being with adults.

_____ Creates complicated play and games.

_____ Gives complex answers to questions.

_____ Becomes extremely frustrated when body can't do what mind wants it to.

_____ Has strong sense of self-control; wants to know reasons for rules.

_____ Is eager to try new things.

_____ Can concentrate on two or three activities at one time.

Describe and check any other strengths that *usually* or *often* apply to your child:

_____ _____

_____ _____

_____ _____

_____ _____

_____ _____

Parent/Caregiver's Signature: _____

Phone: _____

YOUR CHILD'S PERSONAL EXHIBIT

Child's Name: _____

Dear Parent/Caregiver:

As I get to know your child better, I want to do all I can to support your child's development. One way I can do this is by documenting abilities and accomplishments that may not show up at school.

I'm wondering if you have examples of things your child has done or made at home that you'd be willing to share with me for a short period of time. Children will show and explain their "personal exhibits" to me and to the other students. There are many types of items that you could include; please include only those items that your child wants to share. Here are just a few examples:

- a photograph of a completed project, or the project itself
- a cassette recording or video of an exceptional activity or performance
- a poem or story your child has written
- a piece of artwork your child has created
- items that represent a special interest or knowledge.

Please collect the items with your child and bring them to _____ (place) on or before _____ (day and date). Place the items in a simple container such as a grocery bag or shoe box. Complete and remove the form at the bottom of this sheet and tape, staple, or tie it securely to the exhibit.

Thank you for your time and help. If you have any questions, please call or stop in to talk.

Teacher's Signature: _____

Phone: _____

- ✂- cut here -

Child's Name: _____

Teacher: _____ **Room No.** _____

Check those that apply:

_____ You may keep my child's exhibit until the end of the school year.
_____ I prefer to have this exhibit back by _____ (day and date).
_____ I have some questions. Please call me at _____ (phone number).

Parent/Caregiver's Signature: _____

2

Creating the Learning Environment

*onisha bounces into the kindergarten class-
room, bubbling over with excitement and enthusiasm. At home, she has talked for months about
being ready to go to school. She sees school as full of
possibilities—a wonderful place to be. Tonisha wonders why she isn't able to go to school on Saturday
and Sunday. It seems like such a waste of time to
stay home when there is so much to learn and do.*

Most young children love school—or at least
they *want* to love it. From their earliest days, they
see and feel the excitement associated with
school, center stage for discovery and learning.
The evidence is all there: brightly colored alpha-
bets, words and pictures on the wall, abundant
displays of children's art and other work, child-
sized tables and chairs, and activity stations that
shimmer with exciting potential.

Whatever the joys of home and neighborhood, school holds a special promise for every
child. Your challenge as a teacher is to keep that
promise for all children, including the gifted child
who may arrive on the first day of school already
knowing much of the material you plan to cover!

Meeting the Challenge

That simple objective—to make your classroom
one that holds promise for every child—requires
a learning environment that has been consciously
designed not only to open wide the door to advanced pursuits, but also to entice a child to step
through it.

How do you provide that for a four-year-old
child who reads at a fourth-grade level? For a
second-grade junior rocket scientist who can't
seem to get off the launching pad when it comes
to reading? For a class comic who finishes every
activity quickly only to distract the other students
from their efforts?

It may seem easier at times simply to dole out
more activities to the child who cooperates, more
punitive assignments to the one who disrupts.
But experience tells us that such responses aren't
effective—and their cost can be high. A young
gifted child whose intellectual needs are ignored
experiences a loss of hope: for self, for the classroom, and for the future of school as a worthwhile place to be.

This doesn't need to happen. You *can* respond to the gifted child's needs. You are called
on to be sensitive, observant, and flexible. When
you bring those qualities to your program, you
create an exciting learning environment that bal-
ances group and individual activities, rules and
risk-taking, fundamentals and high expectations.
Happily, the effort doesn't require budget-
breaking expenditures of time or money. The two
most important elements for success are at your
fingertips: you and your gifted student.

Think About How It Feels

When we talk about learning environments, we
often think about the part we *see*: activity stations,

materials for thematic units, tables, and chairs. To tailor your learning environment to respond more effectively to your gifted students, you also need to think about how it *feels*.

For a moment, shift your focus away from your program and place it squarely on the gifted child. Consider your classroom environment, examine your normal expectations and responses, and ask yourself: "What will a gifted child's experience of this—and of *me*—be?"

A gifted child may process new information far more quickly than most children. This means the child may become bored as he waits out the time his classmates need to master information and skills.

Young gifted children have talents beyond their years, but patience and diplomacy typically aren't among them. Preferring to chat with you about new ideas or information with little regard for your other obligations, a gifted child may seem (and become) demanding.

Frustrated, some gifted children react by becoming class clowns, challenging authority, or developing other undesirable classroom behaviors. Others may grow quiet and withdrawn as a response to feeling that they don't fit in.

At four and a half, Margo was able to add, subtract, multiply, and divide to find answers for real-life questions. She could calculate on the spot how many doughnuts her preschool teacher needed for a classroom party or how a group of children could be divided into equal teams.

One day, after Margo had finished a math domino activity quickly and correctly, the teacher rewarded her with a sheet of simple addition problems. Margo took the sheet and sat quietly at the table. When the teacher asked her for the completed worksheet, the child burst into tears. "What's wrong, Margo?" asked her teacher in surprise. "I can't do this!" Margo sobbed. Pointing to an addition sign, she cried, "What are those little t's supposed to mean?" Margo had not yet been formally introduced to the mathematical symbol for addition.

Two years later, as a first grader, Margo had a teacher who recognized her advanced analytical abilities and provided her with a "math challenge packet" to work on at home or during free time in class. The packet gathered dust at home while Margo's efforts on much simpler math activities in class appeared uninspired. When her teacher finally asked Margo why she didn't pursue the challenge packet, Margo replied, "I hate math."

In subsequent ability testing, Margo breezed through discussion problems requiring advanced math but stopped halfway through a simpler series of written math calculations, saying she couldn't do them.

For any student, being able to visualize and solve problems is the important task. Margo had that skill. In fact, like some other gifted children, Margo appeared to have an uncanny ability to grasp and solve complex real-life problems. What she lacked was the understanding of how her mental calculations related to the symbols she saw in math books or on worksheets. Once sensitive to this, what might her teacher do?

A few minutes of basic, private instruction with questions and answers may be the lifeline a child like Margo needs. When a child has such a markedly advanced ability to solve complex problems, we sometimes simply assume that she knows the underlying fundamentals. Often, the child has never been shown how to do the work or has not understood its significance. If you have a "Margo" in your class, you may want to start by asking her to write the hardest math problem that she knows how to solve. Explain that the math symbols are a shorthand way of writing the problem. Talk through a real problem and show how it can be expressed and solved with mathematical symbols.

If the child finds the symbols boggling, remind her of the related tasks she is already able to do. Real-life situations and manipulatives can provide a bridge between what the child can do and what she feels she can't accomplish. Remind children that math symbols can be read like letters of the alphabet. You might say: "You know how to read letters and words. Reading numbers and multiplication signs is like reading words."

Parents can be a valuable source of information. What has this child's parent observed? Has the child discussed her feelings about math at home? Does the parent have any insights into the problem?

Help Children Be Successful

Ari was an outwardly bright boy, a cheerful first grader with a huge vocabulary, knowledge of the world, and a sense of humor typical of a boy several years older. However, little of his creativity, wit, or youthful wisdom came through in his classroom assignments. No matter how open-ended the activity, Ari's written work and craft projects were usually no more than perfunctory. Bright but unmotivated, Ari had all the signs of a budding underachiever.

One day, after Ari turned in a superficial story summary, the teacher asked him to take the writing assignment home, complete it, and return a more thoughtful summary of the story the following day. The next day, an excited Ari turned in a three-page, single-spaced typewritten summary and critique of the story and characters. The teacher called his mother to determine how much of the effort was Ari's alone. The answer: all of it. In fact, his mother had insisted that he sign off the home computer at 9:00 P.M. Ari had worked quietly and alone at the keyboard for four hours!

A more focused conversation with Ari's mother proved enlightening. Ari was left-handed and found handwriting a slow and uncomfortable means of expression; so, in class, he kept answers short. For similar reasons, Ari had tended from an early age to avoid craft projects that required the use of scissors. The continued avoidance, unnoticed by previous teachers since preschool, had left Ari feeling inept, certain in his own mind that he was "not very good in art." In fact, Ari felt confident about what he knew, *but lacked confidence in his ability to* do.

As with many bright children, Ari's biggest obstacle was his focus on what he *couldn't* do—on those areas in which he was deficient. Setting up a classroom creatively is the key to helping children like Ari.

Allowing children flexibility in the ways they present what they know and are learning lets them experience success and build upon it. Ari's teacher would be wise to introduce word processing and computer skills in the classroom and allow Ari and other interested children to complete work on the computer as much as possible. Their excitement for learning and documenting that learning will be endless.

It's also important to help children develop needed skills. For the child who needs assistance in developing fine motor control, the teacher can provide opportunities for lacing, stringing bead patterns, writing with wipe-off markers on laminated sentence strips, and using a variety of manipulative materials.

Here again, if you have an "Ari" in your class, communicating with parents can help you get to know the child. Working with parents to overcome misconceptions and obstacles cuts down your time and effort considerably. When your efforts are reinforced at home, the child benefits.

Help Children Work Together Comfortably

Ben was extremely bright. In class, he was always first to raise his hand with the right answer. Socially, however, he was awkward and clumsy. On the playground and in the cafeteria, the other children teased him. Ben's teacher wanted to find ways to help Ben cope, open up in class, and form some peer relationships.

Many gifted children find it difficult to fit in socially. What might Ben's teacher do to help?

He can start by talking privately with Ben. He can explain to Ben that he knows the teasing hurts and can suggest some coping skills. Often, children tease because they feel jealous or inferior. Sometimes, too, they don't know a better way to say "I like you." Understanding why children tease can be a first step towards coping. The teacher should also discuss strategies Ben can use when the teasing occurs—strategies such as ignoring it, laughing along, or telling the children who tease him how it makes him feel.* Ben's teacher can work with Ben to help him learn to be a friend and to value other children's ideas.

The teacher knew that Ben was extremely bright. To help Ben develop relationships with peers and learn to listen as well as express his own ideas, the teacher might try grouping Ben with other children who have similar abilities or shared interests. One way to do this is by using the name card method. Developed by educator Frank T. Lyman, Jr., as a "no-excuses" way to get everyone in class participating, it can also help a child like Ben to build social bonds.

1. Write each student's name on a 3" x 5" card or on a clip-style clothespin.
2. Pair each student with a "discussion buddy." There may be some discrepancies in ability, but try to avoid a huge gap.

---

* Ideas for helping children understand and cope with teasing are adapted from Judy Galbraith, *The Gifted Kids' Survival Guide (For Ages 10 & Under)*. Minneapolis, MN: Free Spirit Publishing Inc., 1984, pp. 49-50. Used with permission.

3. Use THINK PAIR SHARE:
- Ask a question. Give the class 10–20 seconds to THINK about it.
- Have students PAIR up with their discussion buddies.
- Tell them to talk about the question together. So that everyone has a chance to talk, tell them that each person in the pair should have 30 seconds to talk while the other one listens.

4. Using the cards or clothespins, call on students to SHARE. They may share their own response or their buddy's. If they don't have an answer, offer hints or choices. Don't call on anyone to help the student. Instead, tell the child that you will return soon to ask the question again. Don't tell students that a response is correct or incorrect.

5. After responses have been given by several children, ask for volunteers who have something to add that has not already been said. Then call on those with hands raised. Wait until several students have answered before saying that a response is correct.

6. As you finish with a card, place it in the middle of the stack. Shuffle the stack and draw again. If you are using clothespins, place the finished one with the others in a box or bag and shake the container. This gives everyone a fair chance of being called on and lets no one off the hook. This also helps to make sure that no child dominates the talk time.*

Responding to Children's Needs

The examples of Margo, Ari, and Ben point out how important it is that you approach the gifted children in your classroom with *compassion, communication,* and *creativity.*

- *Compassion* lets you put yourself in children's position in the classroom to see how it feels for them.

---

* Suggestions for using the name card method are adapted from "Think-Pair-Share, Thinktrix, Thinklinks, and Weird Facts" by Frank T. Lyman, Jr., in *Enhancing Thinking Through Cooperative Learning,* edited by Neil Davidson and Toni Worsham (Columbia, NY: Teachers College Press, 1992) and from Susan Winebrenner's *Teaching Gifted Kids in the Regular Classroom* (Minneapolis, MN: Free Spirit Publishing Inc., 1992), p. 130. Used with permission of Frank L. Lyman, Jr., Ph.D.

- *Communication* of expectations and perceptions needs to take place among you, the student, and the parent.
- *Creativity*—in lesson content, in the configuration of the classroom and the student groups, and in modes of instruction—allows opportunities for gifted children to blossom.

In the simple structure and naturally creative environment of most early childhood programs, the tools for responding to a gifted child are already in place. The key lies in understanding how to use them to craft an effective response to the special needs of children with high ability. Several things are crucial to consider when using the tools you have at hand to work with gifted children and to create a successful environment for them in your classroom.

A Balance of Structure and Creativity

Young children need some structure and rules to organize their thinking for learning. For the gifted child, it's essential that structure be used not to define learning goals but, like a sturdy ladder, to provide the stability and direction the child needs to reach as high as possible. Creativity provides the spark of intellectual energy needed for the climb.

Individual Learning Styles

It's important to identify the gifted student's learning style and to provide opportunities for the child to work and learn in that mode. There are several ways of looking at learning styles, beginning with an understanding of how the human brain processes information. The brain has two hemispheres and two ways of processing the information it receives. The left hemisphere processes analytically; the right, holistically. We all use both sides of the brain, but some of us may have a built-in preference for one side over the other. *Holistic* learners look at the big picture, while *analytical* learners examine its individual parts. "Traits of Left-Brained and Right-Brained Learners" (page 29) compares the ways analytical and holistic learners process information.

Traits of Left-Brained and Right-Brained Learners

Left-Brained (Analytical)	Right-Brained (Holistic)
Thinks logically, sequentially	Thinks broadly
Looks at the details, pieces of a problem	Looks at the whole problem
Thinks concretely	Thinks abstractly
Plans	Is spontaneous
Is simultaneously rational and emotional	Is creative
Remembers names	Remembers faces
Learns facts, dates, specifics	Dislikes memorizing
Learns in small, logical steps	Learns when presented with the whole
Learns phonics easily	Learns through context
Is systematic, serious	Is playful, enjoys humor

When students are learning, they process information according to which hemisphere they prefer. Neither the "right-brained" nor the "left-brained" child is more or less intelligent or capable. Both children learn equally well when they are taught in ways that allow them to process information in their preferred modality.

An additional consideration is each child's perceptual strength, the *senses* through which the child learns. Drs. Marie Carbo, Rita Dunn, and Kenneth Dunn describe three sensory learning styles: *auditory, visual,* and *tactile-kinesthetic.**

Characteristics of Each Learning Style**

The characteristics of each style differ. By observing a child's preferred style of interaction

with new ideas and materials, you'll be able to determine his preferred style.

Auditory learners think analytically. We often consider a child who is an auditory learner to be a "good" student. Usually her learning needs are readily met in the classroom as she follows directions and moves sequentially from task to task.

Children who learn visually tend to be holistic thinkers. They want the "big picture," not individual pieces. Visual learners *can* learn logically and analytically, but may need to do this by working backward from the bigger picture. These are the students who prefer pictures to words, look for visual clues (photos, charts, and graphs), write or draw about what they are learning, and want to view what the product of their work will look like.

Tactile-kinesthetic learners are holistic thinkers, too, but they need hands-on activities in order to see the whole. These children learn by "doing." They tend to dislike lectures, preferring to develop their own system of organizing information. Many tactile-kinesthetic learners move around while they are thinking. To learn math and symbols, these students use fingers and other manipulatives.

* From Maria Carbo, Rita Dunn, and Kenneth Dunn, *Teaching Students to Read Through Their Individual Learning Styles.* Copyright © 1991 by Allyn & Bacon. Reprinted/adapted by permission.

** Some of the learning style characteristics and the teaching suggestions in the section that follows are adapted from *Teaching Kids with Learning Difficulties in the Regular Classroom* by Susan Winebrenner. Minneapolis, MN: Free Spirit Publishing Inc., 1996, pp. 42-47. Used with permission.

Teaching to the Learning Styles

You can plan activities so that all of your students learn successfully and in their preferred styles. Most classrooms are highly analytical; yours may already include many features that help auditory learners succeed. To meet the needs of your auditory learners, you will want to teach through lectures, reading aloud, and class and small group discussions. Provide recorded stories and music as well. Have conversations with individual children. Use scheduled activities and give step-by-step instructions. In reading, help children to analyze word sounds.

For students who learn visually, include in your instruction pictures, demonstrations, handouts, videos, filmstrips, and transparencies. Provide opportunities for children to write or draw about what they know. Help visual students see the "big picture" by mapping out a story or using graphic organizers. Use color. For children who are visual learners, color is important. Make humor and excitement part of their learning experience.

Keep in mind that tactile-kinesthetic learners need to *touch* and *move*. Help them learn by providing manipulatives, floor games, and task cards. Give these students concrete examples. Using a word processor or dictating to an aide or into a cassette recorder will help children record their ideas. Provide opportunities for both dramatic and physical play. In their reading, your tactile-kinesthetic learners love action, adventure, and excitement; they may fidget while listening to a story.

With awareness, sensitivity, and flexibility, you can teach to every learning style. Later in this chapter we'll suggest ways to approach your students and arrange your classroom to support every child's preferred ways of learning (see "Welcoming Every Child," pages 31–33).

Knowledge Base

Many gifted children easily know, or can quickly absorb, much of the content you plan to cover. It's clear that they need additional resources and encouragement to experience the benefits of learning in a school setting. However, although a gifted child may have an obvious grasp of the "big picture," he may lack a few of the smaller, yet important, "puzzle pieces" that fit together naturally

with age or experience. Use careful observation and curriculum compacting (see Chapter 3, pages 41–56) so that you can design activities that allow him to demonstrate mastery of concepts, gain the necessary knowledge and skills, and then *move on* to an appropriate challenge level.

Intellectual Risk-Taking

Most children find comfort in competence. When competence comes easily, the young gifted child may need special encouragement to venture into unfamiliar territory. Make an activity more challenging by adding an extra measure of creative problem-solving. Watch for signs of any young perfectionists. These are children who:

- are often dissatisfied with their work
- start over and over again (and may destroy work that doesn't measure up to what they feel they "should" do)
- are self-critical
- look for mistakes in others
- tattle
- procrastinate
- are afraid to try new things or take risks.

Teach the value of mistakes and experimentation. Communicate with parents about ways to encourage intellectual risk-taking at home; ask them for insights that might help you more quickly identify areas in which the child needs extra encouragement to experiment with learning.

A Balance of Group and Independent Activities

It's important for the gifted child to learn to work productively with children of all ability levels. It's also vital that the child be able to experience intellectual challenges and the companionship of other children with a similar appetite and aptitude for learning. One of the greatest gifts you can give your young gifted students is the confidence to become activists in their own education—to identify and articulate areas of interest and pursue them independently and productively through available resources.

Katie entered kindergarten as a well-behaved, shy little girl. She was exceptionally compliant and ap-

peared to do everything her teacher asked exactly as she was told to do it. Katie never gave any indication that her ability was far beyond that of her peers. Her reserved demeanor camouflaged her giftedness, leaving it largely unnoticed.

At a parent conference, Katie's mother mentioned that her daughter loved to read at home—in fact, she had read the entire "Little House" series as a four-year-old. Hearing this, the teacher realized that Katie's advanced ability and interests had gone untapped.

What might you do to avoid a similar oversight? How can you recognize, early on, the special abilities and interests of reticent children? You might try a creative strategy such as printing exciting news or information on chart paper and asking if anyone in class knows what it says. This can help you identify those children who are reading.

Once you've identified early and advanced readers, consider allowing them to read with children in a higher grade. Have a reading specialist meet with them on an individual basis, or group and regroup them as necessary to teach missing skills and allow for independent work.

Often, children who have learned to read at an early age have gaps in their learning. It's essential that you fill these gaps and teach the necessary skills a child may have missed. This is not to say, however, that the child should sit through every skill-and-drill lesson. Many gifted children will quickly and easily acquire the basics of printing, spelling, punctuation, using references, and phonics. Assess children's needs; provide opportunities for skills to be learned and mastered within the whole class, in small groups, and independently. Once students master the skills, encourage them to enhance and expand them as they work on more complex projects and activities.

Working with Parents

As the examples of Ari and Katie remind us, parents know and can tell us of unusual abilities that their children may possess. At the beginning of the year, be sure to invite parents to share with you any special observations they have about their child. Chapter 1 includes several family letters and forms to assist you here: "Your Child's Pictures" (page 18), "Information, Please" (page 19), "About My Child" (pages 20–21), and "Checklist of My Child's Strengths" (pages 22–23).

Throughout the school year, continue to foster a dialogue with parents. Formal parent-teacher conferences are only one way to do this; others include phone calls, opportunities for parent participation in your classroom or as assistants on class outings, and student assignments that call for family input. To help parents communicate easily about concerns for their child, send home the "Help Me Help You" family letter (page 40) at the beginning of each month or school term.

Chapter 9 provides more information about communicating and working with parents. See pages 149–164.

Welcoming Every Child

Now, look around your room and think through your program. When the following features are a part of your picture, you've created a child-friendly environment for every child in your classroom—including the gifted ones.

Nine Features of Your Child-Friendly Classroom

1. The classroom invites learning. This helps to frame the curriculum and to let the child know basic expectations. Bright, colorful pictures are posted. Items from nature are displayed. Books with a variety of reading levels are arranged on a ledge or table. At appropriate times, music is playing.

2. You use thematic instruction so the connections among content areas occur easily and naturally.

3. You make available a wide range of materials. This includes those that go beyond the average range of grade-level interests, such as computer programs, three-dimensional puzzles, mazes, and magazines. Bulletin boards and other displays are not only attractive but also rich in content. You might display collections, charts, posters, or cultural artifacts.

4. Your activity centers invite self-initiated, hands-on experimentation. They are well yet simply organized so students can take responsibility for handling and putting away materials. (You'll find suggested materials for classroom centers based on Gardner's eight intelligences beginning on page 33.)

5. Seating arrangements are flexible so you can easily make periodic changes based on different grouping needs. There is space for independent study groups to gather as well as for individual students to work alone.

6. You offer attractive, lesson-related activity options for students who finish work correctly with time left over. These options include a daily balance of large group, small group, and independent activities. For fun, you also post special "super challenge" questions from time to time. (These also help you identify children whose responses reveal advanced reading, math, or other abilities.)

7. In evaluating students, you identify areas of strength, areas that can be improved, and areas in which the student needs more challenge. When a student excels in a particular area or subject, your evaluation includes this question: "What can be done to provide this child with an appropriate opportunity for challenge?" (Chapter 7 gives an in-depth discussion of assessing children's ability and development. See pages 121–140.)

8. You maintain a portfolio of each child's work. The purpose of the portfolio is to document the child's mastery and skill levels. The portfolio, which includes your personal observations, is used as a basis for discussion during parent-teacher conferences. (Chapter 1 includes information about creating and maintaining portfolios. See "Portfolios," pages 9–12, and "Child-Created Portfolios," page 12.)

9. Parents play an integral role in their children's education. You welcome parent communication and invite it regularly and often.

A Balanced Structure

The class structure should allow for a balance between total group instruction on the one hand and small group and individual learning on the other.

Total Group Activities

Total group activities offer a time in which you and your students draw together for discussion, sharing, and learning information. As a whole group, you might do the following daily activities.

Calendar: Look at the day, the month, and the year. Talk about the weather. Discuss important things that happened today or on this day in years past. Note birthdays or special events.

Attendance: When taking attendance, have students answer with their favorite color, a pet's name, a parent's name, a friend's name, or a favorite TV program. Carry attendance-taking further by discussing similarities and differences within your group of students. Are there more boys or girls? How many people's shoes have laces, how many have Velcro fasteners, how many are slip-ons?

Music: Write the words to songs on posterboard that you display while children sing. This helps children begin to identify that reading is simply words written down as if they were spoken or told. Those who are already reading or are becoming readers can sing along with the words.

Brainstorming Activity: Brainstorming stimulates creativity and divergent thinking. Here are some starter ideas:

• yellow (green, purple, red) items found in the grocery store
• ways to show someone you care about them.
• things to do with water (an old tire, a clothespin)
• kinds of hats
• things that are cold (hot, invisible)
• ways to lift a heavy object
• ways we can save energy
• things to do at home instead of watching TV.

Group Sharing Time: Take time regularly for children to share news and information. ("My brother fell and broke his arm." "My cat had kittens.")

Story Time: Select stories related to the content of group discussion. Ask questions that "hook" the children: "Have you ever done that?" "Did you know that?" This invites children to become involved. If the story includes a pattern, have the children join in. Stop the story and ask: "What do you think will happen next?" Reading or story-telling should be enjoyable for you and your students. Make it fun, comfortable, and friendly. Ham it up. Don't be afraid to move, add actions, and change your voice. For a change of pace, have a puppet tell the story. You may want to use soft background music to set the mood. Enjoy what you are reading—your enjoyment is contagious.

You might also build total group activities around a topic or a theme. For example, you might focus on the theme of *patterns* and how they help us to predict. In class activities, you could address the theme in a variety of ways.

You could look at the patterns of the *seasons*, asking children questions: "What do we know about the seasons? What pattern do they follow? What holidays are in certain seasons? Which season is your favorite? Why?" Ask children to brain-storm all of the things that come to mind when they think of winter, spring, summer, and fall. Sings songs related to the seasons or learn the months of the year in a song.

Discuss and track patterns of *weather*. Chart the weather daily. Talk with children about high and low temperatures. Discuss appropriate cloth-ing. Compare the weather in one part of the coun-try and another.

Math is full of patterns. Demonstrate patterns using manipulatives—or the children themselves. Have the children add on to and continue the pat-terns. Discuss *color* patterns: Introduce the color wheel. Learn primary, secondary, and comple-mentary colors. Create patterns with colors. Listen for patterns in *music*. Move to the music. Repeat the movement when the music stops.

Stories have patterns. Pick out the patterns for characters, settings, and plots. In reading, show children that *letters* have patterns too. Talk about how we can predict the way words will sound when we look for letter patterns. Brain-storm *words* that rhyme and show how they can establish a pattern.

Other themes appropriate for young children are change, community, celebrations, and growth. Topics can revolve around food, seasons, holi-days, colors, animals, weather, space, or regions.

By introducing themes, you create complexity beyond what is possible when addressing only a single subject, and you open the door for children to expand their learning and think divergently and

critically. The interdisciplinary connections and extensions among specific subjects lead to com-plexity. For example, the topic of *food* can lead the class into a discussion of food scarcity in different countries and of food for the homeless. You can connect this social studies discussion to science and the study of nutrition. A discussion of *weather patterns* might lead to tornadoes and how they can be predicted. From there, you might ask: "What happens when a tornado touches down? How can you be safe? Why? What if people's homes are hurt by a tornado? What help will the people need?" A focus on *cities* can incorporate literature, history, and economics. Questions you might dis-cuss include: "What's good about living in a city? What are the advantages? What's not so good— what are the disadvantages? What problems do cities have? Who works to solve the problems?" You could use pictures or stories to compare and contrast a modern city and its hundred-year-old counterpart and move to a discussion of inven-tions and of changes in transportation, dress, food, entertainment, family life, and school.

Small Group or Individual Center Time

The activity stations or learning centers in early childhood classrooms are where children spend much of their individual and small group time. To stimulate learning and accommodate each child's preferred intelligence, we recommend that you plan and arrange learning centers that corre-spond to the multiple intelligences identified by Howard Gardner. (These are described on pages 6–7.)

Children may rotate through each center, or they may choose which center they wish to go to, depending on the child, the time available, and the lesson.

Setting Up Centers for Multiple Intelligences

Many early childhood programs already include learning centers; some of these familiar centers can be easily adapted so that concepts, ideas, and information are taught and reinforced in each of the intelligences: linguistic, musical, logical-mathematical, visual-spatial, bodily-kinesthetic, interpersonal, intrapersonal, and naturalist.

Linguistic Center

Verbal learners may be future writers, teachers, librarians, or journalists. The linguistic learner prefers to learn through words, so the materials at this center have to do with reading and language. The linguistic center should be located where it is quiet, away from noise and activity. Have available comfortable floor pillows, chairs, and tables. Materials for this center might include:

- books (a variety: picture, easy-read, and simple chapter books)
- magazines
- encyclopedias
- dictionaries
- storybook character puppets
- stories written by children, displayed on the bulletin board or bound in book form
- paper for writing or drawing stories
- cassette player and books on tape with corresponding printed books
- cassette recorder and blank tapes for recording children's stories
- magnetic letters with board
- overhead projector with letters for children to project on the chalkboard and trace to create words or sentences
- laminated sentence strips and nontoxic wipe-off pens or dry-erase markers
- word searches
- crossword puzzles (simple to complex)
- spelling materials and games
- phonics cards
- pizza wheels with pictures on the outside and a letter in the middle; children clip clothespins on the words that begin like the letter in the center of the wheel
- alphabet games
- games for matching upper- and lowercase letters
- word cards for matching, rhyming, alphabetizing, storytelling
- sentence blocks with articles, nouns, verbs, adjectives, and adverbs; children roll the blocks like dice to form different sentences
- computer software for word processing and story writing.

Musical Center

The child with musical intelligence learns through rhythm and melody—by singing songs, humming, rapping, or tapping a pencil, foot, or finger to a rhythm. Activities for the musical center might include reading stories or poems with music in the background; adapting nursery rhymes or poems into songs; teaching spelling, grammar, or math through rhythm, rap, or song; drawing pictures of images that come to mind while listening to music; holding sing-alongs; and matching instrument pictures to instrument recording. Materials for this center might include:

- piano, keyboard and headset, or MIDI keyboard for linking to the computer
- other musical instruments (guitars, harmonicas, recorders)
- drums
- rhythm instruments, both purchased and homemade (maracas, castanets, spoons, blocks, sandpaper-covered blocks, rice between taped paper plates, bones with a hole in the middle on a wire ring)
- cassette player and a variety of taped music
- cassette recorder and blank tapes for recording children's music
- record player and a variety of records
- instrument picture cards.

Logical-Mathematical Center

The materials in this center deal with mathematical problems, symbols, and logical thinking. Children who are logically or mathematically inclined love to question, explore, and think about things: they may be future mathematicians, accountants, stock brokers, and scientists. Math materials for this center might include:

- felt board with felt objects and numerals
- peg boards with colored pegs
- pattern cards (simple to complex)
- puzzles (simple to complex)
- dice
- number cards for sequencing and matching
- items for matching numbers (symbols) to sets of objects
- math facts cards
- number games, projects, and puzzles
- calculators

- tangrams
- attribute blocks
- beads of various sizes
- LEGOs
- beans, painted on one side so children can create patterns or estimate quantities
- junk to classify (keys, shells, rocks, buttons, bread tags, tickets, letters, tiles, old game tokens, magnets, pictures)
- Venn diagrams, graphic organizers, and matrices
- codes to decipher
- rice table or large container with measuring cups and spoons
- Pentominoes*
- computer software for math games and activities.

Science materials for this center might include:

- simple machines (pulley, inclined plane, simple gears)
- magnifying glass
- microscope
- telescope
- mirrors
- prisms
- magnets
- rain gauge
- thermometers
- objects for experiments (paper clips, rubber bands, buttons)
- objects for viewing (prepared slides, onion paper)
- models of planets, the human body, body parts
- paper and pencil to record/draw data
- computer software for computer-based science activities.

Visual-Spatial Center

Visual-spatial learners may be the artists of the future. They learn through pictures and through visualizing, designing, drawing, or doodling. Materials for this center might include:

- paints, paintbrushes, and easels
- finger paints

- clay
- cookie cutters or sponges to use with paint for making prints
- markers, crayons, colored pencils, and stamps
- paper in various sizes and colors
- scissors
- scraps of ribbon, fabric, and yarn
- glue, paste, and tape
- old catalogs and magazines
- loads of pictures
- photographs
- mazes
- picture puzzles
- artwork displays
- posters
- camera and film
- illustrated books
- maps, charts, and diagrams
- LEGOs
- video player and educational videos related to classroom topics
- computer software (CD-ROMs) showing famous works of art or museum tours.

Bodily-Kinesthetic Center

Children with bodily-kinesthetic ability learn through modeling, through hands-on activities, and by *doing*. They love touching, building, and moving; if required to sit for a long time, they often fidget or twitch. A kinesthetic child may accurately mimic other people's gestures and may be regarded as "dramatic" by other children or adults.

When you observe children playing, you gain a wealth of information about their abilities. It is in this center that young gifted children often demonstrate their capabilities. They may build complex block structures, use advanced vocabulary, and combine materials in imaginative, inventive ways. They may play roles that imitate real life and solve problems by using their imaginations.

Skills that are addressed in play are skills that will be needed for success in school and in life—cognitive skills such as problem-solving, creativity, dealing with abstractions, and acquiring new knowledge; social skills such as interacting, sharing, and showing consideration, tolerance, and self-control.

---

* Available from Creative Publications, 5623 W. 115th Street, Worth, IL 60482. Toll-free phone: 1-800-624-0822.

Basic equipment for this center might include:

- trucks and cars
- equipment and materials for crafts such as sewing, woodworking, mechanics
- large blocks
- cardboard bricks
- dress-up clothes and props for different work, play, ages, and cultures
- a variety of hats
- masks
- kitchen equipment, dishes, pots and pans
- workbench and tools
- dolls representing both genders and a variety of races/ethnic groups
- puppets
- stuffed animals
- manipulatives to sequence
- puzzles.

Beyond the basic equipment, materials that extend and enrich information or themes from the large group discussion give children the opportunity to take information they have learned, explore it, and make connections. At different times, depending on the topic being studied in the class, the kinesthetic center may look like:

- a grocery store with boxes, cans, various containers, a supply of bags, a cash register, and play money
- an undersea world with blue netting, shells, flippers, and goggles
- a campsite with tent, firewood, mess kits, and flashlights
- a restaurant, garage, or community gathering place.

You may also wish to include holiday and seasonal items in this center. A cassette recorder with music that the students can move or dance to is an enjoyable addition, although volume is a consideration in a small, confined room.

Interpersonal Center

The child with interpersonal skills is a "people person" who leads, organizes, mediates, and relates well to other children. The interpersonal center is for group activities. Total group work and general instruction occur here. Activities might include:

- brainstorming
- cooperative tasks
- collaborative problem-solving
- mentoring and apprenticeship
- group games.

Author and consultant Carolyn Chapman suggests five rules for this learning center:*

1. Use six-inch voices (voices that can be heard no more than six inches away).
2. Listen to others in your group.
3. Stay in the group.
4. Look at the speaker.
5. Don't hurt someone else's feelings.

Intrapersonal Center

Because the child with an intrapersonal bent has a strong will and sense of independence, we sometimes regard him as a loner. This child knows himself well; he has a sense of both his strengths and his weaknesses and is capable even at a young age of expressing his feelings. This child is usually quiet and enjoys working alone. For this reason, the intrapersonal area contains desks or carrels for individual work. This area is designated as quiet space for:

- independent assignments
- metacognition ("thinking about thinking")
- journals
- self-paced projects
- problem-solving
- time alone
- reflection
- computer software for word processing.

Naturalist Center

The child with naturalist intelligence loves to sort, classify, order, and categorize. She loves nature—plants, animals, fish, rocks—and the natural order of things. This child enjoys collections of objects from nature as well as those that are

---

* Adapted from Carolyn Chapman, *If the Shoe Fits: How to Develop Multiple Intelligences in the Classroom*. Palatine, IL: IRI SkyLight Publishing, 1993, p. 182.

not in the natural world. Materials for this center might include:

- a variety of rocks
- seeds, pots, and soil for planting
- garden area (potting soil in suit boxes lined with plastic)
- live animals (fish, hamsters, an ant farm)
- a variety of leaves, fossils, and seeds
- pictures of a variety of plants and trees for classifying and comparing
- pictures of a variety of mammals, reptiles, birds, fish, and insects for classifying and comparing
- a variety of plastic creatures; dinosaur models
- paper and pencils for drawing/recording data
- simple database software.

Helping Children Use Learning Centers

Most children will tend to gravitate to certain activity stations and avoid others. To some extent, this is fine: Students need opportunities to choose the centers they will work in. All students, however, need to experience and be exposed to all of the centers and participate at a level appropriate to their ability.

To gain insight into a child's preferred intelligence, ask the child, "What did you do today that you liked?" Note whether the child's response includes writing, singing, counting, drawing, playing, talking, thinking, or observing. Consider, too, what you already know about a child's learning style. In general:

- *Auditory learners* will gravitate toward the linguistic, logical-mathematical, interpersonal, intrapersonal, or naturalist centers.
- *Visual learners* will choose the visual-spatial, logical-mathematical, intrapersonal, or naturalist centers.
- *Tactile-kinesthetic learners* will prefer the bodily-kinesthetic, visual-spatial, musical, or naturalist centers.

Use this information to guide individual children toward both the learning centers and the types of activities that engage them.

Try to provide choices of approximately three or four activities at each center. All of the activities will revolve around the content or theme your class is studying or around students' interests. When you present several options, the child will usually choose the activity that is best suited and developmentally correct for him. Creativity, communication, and balance are the keys. Keep the activities available until the topic is completed or until children appear bored or restless. They will let you know when it's time for a change.

Structured experiences at each of the centers will give you a chance to observe which children have strengths within which areas. Then you'll be able to provide extended activities in each student's area of strength.

One of the main goals of school is to create lifelong learners. This occurs when children are given the chance to take responsibility for their learning and make decisions. You'll be amazed at the decisions children make about what they want to learn and how they wish to learn it.

Planning Lessons Using Multiple Intelligences

When creating lessons using the multiple intelligences, feel free to address any skill, instructional outcome, or theme. Students can have their strongest intelligence addressed while working to develop an area of need. Begin by selecting a topic or theme or outcome. Ask yourself how it can be taught linguistically, musically, mathematically, spatially, bodily, interpersonally, intrapersonally, and naturalistically. Select and plan center-based activities from your ideas. Gather materials and carry out your plan. Modify your lessons as needed. Allow for children to demonstrate mastery and make choices. Document how children learn and what they are able to do.

Questions and Answers

"How can I create this kind of classroom on my limited budget?"

It may not involve purchasing anything new, but rather rethinking and reorganizing what you already have. Inform parents of your plans and needs; invite them to contribute small and large items for your centers.

Be sure to open your doors to the community. Invite the local press to celebrate your accomplishments and to keep the public informed of the wonderful things your class and school are doing.

You might adopt a "sponsor" in the community. Link up with service organizations, such as Kiwanis or Lion's Club, or with local businesses. Let them be aware of your larger needs. Do they have partnership grants available? Could they donate old computers when they purchase new ones? Do they have scrap materials that could be used for art projects? Or people who could donate time and talent?

"I already have five learning centers—isn't that enough? And why should I rearrange them to fit the multiple intelligences?"

It's worth the effort to reconfigure and expand your learning centers. With what we now know about how children learn, gearing whole areas to the different intelligences offers *all* children the best possible opportunity to succeed and excel. Every child deserves the chance to experience new, challenging learning.

"If a bright child is 'at the head of the class' in a subject area, why not let her take it easy and enjoy her success instead of looking for ways to make every moment at school more challenging?"

While children don't need to be challenged *all* of the time, they must be challenged *some* of the time. The question you need to ask yourself is this: "What is the child learning?" *All* students deserve to learn—and no real learning occurs without some struggle. Perseverance is an important skill learned by facing difficulty without giving up. Gifted children can become accustomed to getting the right answer and the top grade with little or no effort. If their work is consistently easy, they learn to equate giftedness with effortlessness. Too many bright children never learn how to study, how to use struggle or failure as a building block rather than a stumbling block. When they eventually encounter hard work (and, sooner or later, they will), bright children who have not been challenged may give up.

"With children of this age, how can I place greater demands on them intellectually when, emotionally, they're still so young?"

Children *are* children, even if they sometimes think like miniature adults. Your purpose is not to push children, but to respond to their needs. Young gifted children need the experience of learning. This can be creative and enjoyable for

them. It's not a matter of *demanding* more from them, but of *inviting* more—of opening more doors to learning opportunities. This is not pushing, but recognizing and responding to the child's intellectual appetite.

"Our two-hour kindergarten program is so busy and full, there's barely enough time for the planned activities. How can a child fit in extra work under these conditions?"

In this situation, you may need to practice selective abandonment. What is essential? What core curriculum *must* you teach? What can you eliminate? Can you assess whether the children already know some of the information so that you can compact the curriculum? (Compacting is discussed in Chapter 3. See pages 41–56.) Instead of spending one month on a topic, one week—or even one day—might suffice. You might also consider designing units thematically, including activities from several subject areas. This holistic way of looking at curriculum can help you be more creative. One more point: Instead of viewing activities as "extra" work, think of them as "instead of" work.

"There's obvious resentment among my first graders toward a highly gifted classmate who finds everything easy. How can I keep the situation from making the others feel bad about themselves?"

Using the multiple intelligences is a wonderful way to alleviate this situation. Gifted or not, all children are good at something! Recognize and build on their strengths. Invite children to share their interests, passions, and areas of expertise. When your students see that their different abilities are valued, their focus is likely to shift away from resentment and toward sharing.

Conclusion

The preschool or early elementary classroom is no place for a one-size-fits-all program. To create an environment that offers a "fit" for young gifted children, you are called upon to be sensitive, creative, and flexible—and to develop a program that fosters the same qualities in your students. In a classroom brimming with opportunities, special care must still be given to ensure that gifted children find challenge and opportunity to develop their potential.

References and Resources

Armstrong, Thomas. *Multiple Intelligences in the Classroom.* Alexandria, VA: ASCD, 1994. Information on exploring your own intelligences and suggestions for bringing Gardner's theory of multiple intelligences into your classroom.

Carbo, Marie, Rita Dunn, and Kenneth Dunn. *Teaching Students to Read Through Their Individual Learning Styles.* Needham Heights, MA: Allyn & Bacon, 1991. A book to help teachers and parents reduce reading failure through early diagnosis of individual characteristics and by matching methods and materials to individual styles and strengths.

Chapman, Carolyn. *If the Shoe Fits: How to Develop Multiple Intelligences in the Classroom.* Palatine, IL: IRI SkyLight Publishing, 1993. Translates the theory of multiple intelligences into practical classroom use and gives understandable information for identifying and developing students' strengths.

Galbraith, Judy. *The Gifted Kids' Survival Guide (For Ages 10 & Under).* Minneapolis, MN: Free Spirit Publishing Inc., 1984. Helps young gifted children understand and cope with the stresses, benefits, and demands of being gifted.

Hands On: Pentominoes. Palo Alto, CA: Creative Publications, 1986. Full of ideas for using Pentominoes. Write to Creative Publications, 5623 W. 115th Street, Worth, IL 60482. Toll-free phone: 1-800-624-0822.

Jackson, Nancy Ewald. "The Gift of Early Reading Ability." *Understanding Our Gifted* 1:2 (1988), pp. 1, 8-10. Precocious reading ability is a complex skill for which specific subskills vary widely. Jackson explains how early development of reading can be encouraged naturally and enjoyably through parent-child activities.

Lazear, David. *Seven Pathways of Learning: Teaching Students and Parents about Multiple Intelligences.* Tucson, AZ: Zephyr Press, 1994. This book, which is concerned with teaching about the original seven intelligences, presents the metacognitive (thinking about thinking) component. It includes helpful ways to expand intelligent behavior in and out of the classroom.
———. *Seven Ways of Knowing: Teaching for Multiple Intelligences.* Palatine, IL: IRI SkyLight Publishing, 1991. The focus of this book is on teaching for the seven intelligences. Its message is that if we want children to maximize their potential, we need to teach specific skills for using each intelligence in developmentally appropriate ways.
———. *Seven Ways of Teaching: The Artistry of Teaching with Multiple Intelligences.* Palatine, IL: IRI SkyLight Publishing, 1991. This book's focus is on teaching with multiple intelligences. It includes a complete lesson plan for each of the original seven intelligences, as well as a model for designing lessons.

Lyman, Frank T. "Think-Pair-Share, Thinktrix, Thinklinks, and Weird Facts." In *Enhancing Thinking Through Cooperative Learning,* Neil Davidson and Toni Worsham, eds. Columbia, NY: Teachers College Press, 1992. Offers techniques to enhance classroom participation.

Moberg, Randy. *TNT Teaching: Over 200 Dynamite Ways to Make Your Classroom Come Alive.* Minneapolis, MN: Free Spirit Publishing Inc., 1994. Describes hundreds of fresh, new ways to present the curriculum, from developing a collection of props and visuals to designing learning "packages" that promote curiosity and anticipation.

Parke, Beverly N., and Phyllis S. Ness. "Curricular Decision-Making for the Education of Young Gifted Children." *Gifted Child Quarterly* 32:1 (1988), pp. 196-199. Describes important curricular considerations for young gifted children: that they have special interests and learning needs, that play is their "work," and that they should have a part in decision-making.

Winebrenner, Susan. *Teaching Gifted Kids in the Regular Classroom.* Minneapolis, MN: Free Spirit Publishing Inc., 1992. Winebrenner discusses what to do with the child who already knows what you are going to teach. She presents specific strategies with step-by-step instructions and reproducible forms.
———. *Teaching Kids with Learning Difficulties in the Regular Classroom.* Minneapolis, MN: Free Spirit Publishing Inc., 1996. Strategies and techniques every teacher can use to motivate struggling students, including those who are gifted.

HELP ME HELP YOU

For Parents

Child's Name: _____

Dear Parent/Caregiver:

If you ever have a question or concern about what's happening for your child at school, I hope you'll feel free to contact me personally. I also invite you to let me know about anything happening at home that might affect your child at school.

You can reach me directly during the school day at _____ (phone number). Or, if you like, complete the brief form at the bottom of this sheet, place it in an envelope, and mail or deliver it to me at the school office: _____ _____ (address).

Thank you for keeping the lines of communication open!

Teacher's Signature: _____

- ✂ - cut here -

To: _____ **Date:** _____

I would like to talk to you about my child, _____. I can be reached during the day at _____ (phone number) or in the evening at _____ (phone number).

Comments: _____
_____
_____
_____

Parent/Caregiver's Signature: _____

3

Compacting the Curriculum and Extending Learning

ichael exudes energy. He bounces into the classroom with eyes sparkling. His hand is always up, his mouth open, his body in constant motion. Michael's knowledge of certain subjects astounds both his classmates and his teacher. When the teacher assigns group work, Michael is consistently the first person finished.

Exciting as it is to have this bright, ebullient child in her class, the teacher often feels overwhelmed as she tries to keep up with him and keep the rest of the class on track. Some days it seems as if Michael completes class assignments before she has even finished explaining them! She finds herself dreading the moment when he will wave his arm and call out, "I'm done—now what can I do?"

Michael's teacher wants to nurture Michael's facility—and his enthusiasm—for learning. She doesn't want to simply keep him busy by giving him additional, similar work, for if the reward for excellence is more of the same material, Michael may begin to play down or even hide what he knows. But, with his abundant curiosity and energy, who knows what he'll do with free time? Will he be on task? What if he disturbs others?

Time and the Gifted Child: A Banking Metaphor

Time is like money: It can be spent wisely or wasted. It seems precious, but its true value lies in what is done with it. Dr. Joseph Renzulli, Director of the National Research Center for the Gifted and Talented, suggests that we allow students to "buy back" time we had planned for them to "spend" in one way and allow them to "spend" it in a different way.

You can take this metaphor further by imagining a "time bank" in your classroom with individual "checking accounts" and "savings accounts" for children. A child's checking account is a given amount of time he needs to learn basic information—time spent in whole group instruction and activities. Some children will need more or less time in their individual checking accounts. The savings account is the time the child has "saved" by documenting that he knows the information. You need to ask yourself:

• How will I know who has some "savings"?
• How will children spend their "savings"?
• How will I organize the curriculum so children's "savings" yield the best "returns"?

How Will You Know Who Has "Savings"?

There are different ways to measure a child's "savings." Work that the student has already done often provides a clue to what she knows, although, with very young children, you won't always have access to past work. The strategies discussed in Chapter 1—interviews, portfolios, and dynamic assessment—can help you identify and evaluate prior knowledge.

As he entered kindergarten, Gerik appeared shy. He was thin and small for his age, the result of an early childhood illness. He volunteered little and carefully assessed every situation before beginning to work. On the surface, Gerik appeared to be behind others in motor and verbal skills. His slight speech impediment left him reluctant to speak.

After the first week of school, the teacher asked Gerik what he was interested in. He responded, "The origins of unicorn mythology." "Can you read?" his teacher asked. "Of course, everyone can," he answered. "No," replied the teacher, "not many kindergartners can read." "That's too bad," said Gerik. "It's how you find out about stuff."

A reading test showed that Gerik was reading and comprehending above the sixth-grade level. It was clear that he didn't need basic instruction and would likely have found the work discouraging, a waste of time. Gerik had a tremendous amount in his reading "savings account."

How Will the Child Spend the "Savings"?

Having confirmed advanced skills and knowledge, you need to consider how best the child can build on them. Observing the child—the learning centers she chooses, what she does there, and how she does it—will assist you in planning and helping her plan ways to spend her "savings." (Chapter 2 discusses setting up learning centers to support multiple intelligences and accommodating children's individual learning styles. See pages 33–37.)

Observe the child's interests and behavior. One good observational indicator is how the student spends free time. What does he do when he has "choice" time? Does he gravitate toward books? Build with blocks? Draw or paint? Socialize?

If a student can read or write, you may wish to ask him to complete the "What I Like" interest survey (pages 51–52). This offers another avenue for identifying learning styles and preferred intelligence modes. Explain that the child should read each entry and circle the ones he likes. On the

second page of the handout, the child should write or draw a picture about something he is especially good at. To use the form with a student who is not yet reading, you or an aide can read the entries aloud and assist as needed in completing the form.

Observe the child's misbehavior. In his book, *Multiple Intelligences in the Classroom,* learning expert Thomas Armstrong suggests observing how a student *misbehaves* as yet another way to discover highly developed intelligences. Does the child talk out of turn (indicating linguistic intelligence)? Does she daydream (visual-spatial or intrapersonal intelligence)? Is she prone to socializing (interpersonal intelligence)? Does she ask "Why?" (logical-mathematical intelligence)? Does she collect and sort things (naturalist intelligence)? Does she fidget or have difficulty sitting still (bodily-kinesthetic intelligence)?

Sasha was in constant motion. When she moved down the hall, she would bounce from one side of the wall to the other. During group time, she simply could not sit still, but moved around the floor touching everyone and everything. Her teacher, Mr. Nguyen, tried keeping her next to him while he taught. Sasha sat more quietly, but later, when her teacher asked her questions about the lesson, she recalled very little.

One day, after teaching a new math concept during which he'd allowed Sasha to move around as much as she wished, Mr. Nguyen quizzed her on the lesson content. Sasha's responses told him that she had heard and recalled nearly all of the lesson. Realizing that Sasha had highly developed bodily-kinesthetic intelligence, he decided to teach math to her, and to some of the other "movers and shakers," using music and movement. The results were revealing: In a matter of a few days, the children had mastered math facts many had struggled with when taught in traditional ways.

As this example illustrates, sometimes we can learn about a child's strengths by looking at what she's telling us in moments of "weakness."

Don't forget the parents! Parents have a wealth of information about their child that they can share with you. When you communicate with parents in a variety of ways—through letters, phone calls, and in-school activities—you stand the best chance of winning cooperation and developing an ongoing dialogue. Chapters 1 and 2 include family letters and forms to assist you in communicating with parents. Chapter 9 provides more information about enlisting parents' support.

How Will You Organize the Curriculum?

Besides making a careful assessment of the child, you need a complete understanding of the content and objectives of your curriculum. What are the children in your class supposed to learn? What skills will they have as they leave you and move on to the next teacher?

With these objectives and your students' needs in mind, you are ready to look at ways to *compact the curriculum* and *extend learning*.

Compacting lets you individualize one or more parts of the curriculum to facilitate and challenge gifted children's learning. When you compact, you compress your basic curriculum into a smaller time frame, thus adding time to the child's "savings account." The idea is to compress the essentials, making sure skills are mastered and concepts understood without belaboring or excessively repeating what the child already knows and can do. You compact only in those areas that represent the student's strengths.

You might begin by looking at assignments you give to reinforce what the child knows. These can include practice worksheets, center time, and group work that focuses on skill development. If the child already knows how to do the work or has the skill mastered, he may not need the skill-and-drill practice many other children in your class require. Ask him to demonstrate that he can do the work by completing just a few of the problems. Use discussion, observation, or testing to confirm that the child has the skill. If he does, he's ready to move on to other activities. Then you'll want to provide *extensions*—opportunities to extend and expand his learning in the area of strength. Extensions are meant to be "instead of" work, rather than more of the same work.

Extending the Curriculum for Children Working in Groups

All children benefit from group activities. For a child who has mastered skills and understandings ahead of her classmates, group work can provide a wealth of opportunities. You might want to try some of the following options and extensions for children working in groups.

Tiered Groups

Instead of having every group do the same activity, vary the assignments and their complexity. This works particularly well in the classroom that has a wide spread in ability. Group children according to the level of mastery they have achieved.

In *reading*, one group might be working on letter recognition, another on combining letters to make new words, and a third on writing stories. A fourth group (or even a single child) can be reading independently.

In *spelling*, one group might be learning their words while a second group is using the words to write sentences. A third group might be creating a word search, and a really advanced child could be using a thesaurus to look for synonyms and then composing sentences or rewriting nursery rhymes with the new words. Be flexible in placing children in skill groups. You can change the makeup of the groups to fit the lesson content and the needs of the children.

You can also form tiered groups based on children's level of *abstract thinking*. In teaching a lesson on money, this might mean that some children count pennies while others learn the value of different coins. Those children who already know this information could set up a play store, decide which coins could purchase chosen items from a catalog, or practice making change. In this way, three or more tasks revolve around the same content, but each is progressively more difficult and complex.

Interest Groups

At times, you may discover that several children have a similar love or interest. When they have mastered the content, you can then allow them to work as a group to pursue that interest. These groups allow for conversation and discussion among members.

Interest groups in reading might focus on a particular author or area of reading, such as fairy tales, bears in literature, or mystery stories. In math, interest groups may work with puzzles, tangrams, Pentominoes, attribute blocks, number squares, and so forth.

The "Tic-Tac-Toe Menu" (page 53) works well as a planning tool. The menu on the handout is a model that you may wish to adapt. The sample menu shown here illustrates how you can use it

with a group of students to extend learning around the topic of bears in literature.

Using the Tic-Tac-Toe Menu with Groups of Students*

1. Create or help groups create a "menu" of possible activities.

2. Select activities that you believe meet the children's interest and ability level and write them in the menu format. Children may provide input.

3. If you wish, leave some blank spaces and invite groups to think of and write down other related activities they would like to pursue.

---

* The sample Tic-Tac-Toe Menu and instructions for using it are adapted from Susan Winebrenner, *Teaching Gifted Kids in the Regular Classroom.* Minneapolis, MN: Free Spirit Publishing Inc., 1992, p. 63. Used with permission.

Sample Tic-Tac-Toe Menu: Bears in Literature

1. Draw a bear story.	2. Act out the story.	3. Tell the story in your own way.
4. Survey other students to find out what they think about the story.	5. Learn a bear rhyme and teach it to the class.	6. Solve a crossword puzzle or complete a dot-to-dot picture of a bear.
7. Listen to another story on tape. Talk about how the stories are alike and different.	8. Build a home for a bear.	9. Tell a new ending for the story.

We choose activities #_____, #_____, #_____, and #_____.

Names: _____   Date: _____

_____

_____

Other Ideas for Extensions Using Tic-Tac-Toe

Here are some additional ideas or options you may want to incorporate in your own tic-tac-toe form:
- sorting, classifying
- sequencing
- counting
- logic puzzles
- board games
- computer games
- working with a clock or stopwatch
- charts, graphs, diagrams
- science materials, equipment
- manipulatives
- calculators
- brain teasers
- mental math calculations
- problem-solving situations
- creating codes or decoding messages
- using money, making change
- Venn diagrams
- mental mapping
- attribute blocks
- tangrams
- Pentominoes
- 20 Questions
- Where's Waldo?
- polls, surveys
- hidden pictures
- mazes
- constructing, building
- kaleidoscopes
- optical illusions
- visualization
- picture library
- picture metaphors
- photography
- color wheels
- using telescope, microscope, binoculars, magnifying glass
- color coding
- keeping a sketch book
- cartoons
- drawing
- doodling
- modeling with clay
- play experiences
- puppets, miniatures, stuffed animals
- simulations
- crafts
- creating collages
- pantomime
- relaxation exercises
- creating letters of the alphabet with the body
- communicating with hand signals
- creative movement
- blocks
- learning through music, rhythm
- using singing to learn facts
- time to learn musical notation or to play an instrument
- cassette tapes, records
- creating melodies
- chanting
- mentorship with older children or adults
- organizing an event
- cooperative learning
- teaching a peer
- team projects
- reading in pairs
- small group discussion
- simulations
- sharing knowledge, experiences with peers
- group brainstorming
- buddy system
- cross-age tutoring
- thinking, explaining from different points of view
- allowing for discussion on a topic
- keeping a log or journal
- writing stories
- creating role plays.

Branching

Branching encourages children to explore content in different disciplines, themes, and intelligence modes. It provides richness and depth. For example, instead of looking at autumn leaves, examine the process of photosynthesis. Note changes that different seasons bring. When teaching about color, introduce primary and secondary colors. Look at the color wheel. Examine cool and warm colors. Discuss shades and hues. Discuss and explore more than the basic colors: With red, introduce ruby, scarlet, cerise, russet, and crimson. With blue, explore navy, aqua, sky, powder, royal, and Wedgwood.

Extending the Curriculum for Children Working Independently

Of course, you can initiate branching with individual instruction as well as groups. Here are some other suggestions to extend learning for children who are working independently.

Point of View

This is an extension that fits easily into any literature study. Upon reviewing a story, you may discover that one or two students already know it well. They can tell you in detail what happens and when. These children don't need to hear or read the story again unless they would like to.

While the class reviews the story, give a child who is already familiar with it the chance to consider it from a different point of view. If Cinderella's stepmother told the story of Cinderella and the prince, how would it be different? If the troll told the story of the "Three Billy Goats Gruff," what would he say? If Little Red Riding Hood lived in the inner city, whom would she visit? What dangers might she face? Who might save her? Whom might she save? If you could rewrite *Alexander and the Terrible, Horrible, No Good, Very Bad Day* as *Alexander and the Super, Wonderful, Terrific, Very Good Day*, what would it be like?

If the child has difficulty writing, have her use a cassette recorder to tape her ideas. Then she can illustrate her story as she plays back her recording.

Resident Expert*

For the primary gifted student who already knows most of the information in a unit of study, independent study aimed at becoming a "resident expert" may be the answer. This student needs the flexibility to explore an area of interest. Given the chance to satisfy his curiosity, he's likely to cover a vast amount of information.

---

* The concept of a "resident expert" and the steps to becoming one are adapted from Susan Winebrenner, *Teaching Gifted Kids in the Regular Classroom*. Minneapolis, MN: Free Spirit Publishing Inc., 1992, pp. 57-61. Used with permission.

Steps to Becoming a Resident Expert

1. Interview or observe the student to determine his areas of strongest intelligence.
2. Help him find a topic to explore. (You may wish to use the "What I Like" form on pages 51–52.) Prompt him to think about where he will find information on the chosen topic. For example, he might read, talk to people, take a "field trip" with a parent, or conduct interviews or experiments. Help him find and collect books and other materials about the topic.
3. Provide a space for the student to keep and use the materials.
4. Encourage him to look through the materials whenever he has free time.
5. Give him a copy of "My Plan to Become an Expert" (page 54) and show him how to write his ideas for the first two sections of the form.
6. Meet with the student as he goes through possibilities and materials.
7. Ask him to select one topic or area of interest.
8. Help him put together the information and plan how he will share it with the rest of the class. As these plans firm up, show him how to write his plan in the third section of the planning form.
9. Schedule meetings with the student to check on his progress.
10. Help him plan and deliver a presentation of the project.

To clearly establish expectations and goals, develop a contract with the child. Your contract will depend on the topic and the degree of independence and understanding he has. Help him determine realistic goals for the project, the product, and the approximate date the product will be complete. A word of caution: If the project takes too long, the child may lose interest. Make the end date somewhat flexible. Check in daily to see how the child is progressing. You'll find sample contracts for older and younger children on page 47.

Tic-Tac-Toe Interest Areas

The "Tic-Tac-Toe Menu" for groups of children (page 53) provides a model for planning and carrying out independent study.

Sample Contract (Older Child)

Name: _Sandy_

I want to learn about: _poisonous snake_
        (topic or subject)

I will need/use these materials and equipment: _books, trip to the zoo, zap-shot camera,_
computer, could conduct interviews, have maps

The product I will make is _model snake (papier-mâché) with map where it lives and story of what it_
does, what it eats, where it lives

I will have the product ready by: _2 weeks_
        (approximate date)

Student's Signature _Sandy Ramirez_   _October 11_
                                                            DATE

Teacher's Signature _Ms. Linse_   _October 11_
                                                            DATE

Parent's Signature _Ray Ramirez_   _October 11_
                                                            DATE

Sample Contract (Younger Child)

Name: _Joe_

I want to learn about: _teeth because I lost one_

I will make this: _model of a tooth_

I will have it ready by: _Friday_

Student's Signature _Joe Milnes_   _October 11_
                                                            DATE

Teacher's Signature _Mr. LaFrenz_   _October 11_
                                                            DATE

Parent's Signature _Elaine Robb_   _October 11_
                                                            DATE

Using the Tic-Tac-Toe Menu with Individual Students*

1. At the bottom of the form, cross out "We" and write "I."
2. Create or help the child create a "menu" of possible activities.
3. Ask the child to select activities from the menu and write his choices on the form.
4. If you wish, leave some blank spaces and invite the child to think of and write down other related activities he would like to pursue.

Trust the Student

Independent study projects can be relatively unstructured. Trust that the child will use the time productively. She is learning that school is a place where she can be passionate—where she has the opportunity to learn a great deal about topics that interest her and to develop her intelligence and creativity.

Documenting Mastery and Planning Extensions

To document the strengths and plan extensions, you will want to keep records. The form on page 55, "Plan for Compacting and Extending the Curriculum," provides a model you may wish to use or adapt.

Parents need to be kept informed about what you are doing in the classroom. One teacher's experience tells a valuable story:

The year she began compacting, it didn't occur to the teacher to tell students' parents what she was doing. One parent noticed that his child had very few papers. When he asked his daughter what she did in school, the child responded, "I play." The rumor mill was activated, and a group of parents went to the administration wanting to know why the teacher wasn't teaching their children the same things!

Once parents know what's happening in the classroom, most are comfortable, even impressed, with what their children are doing and

---

* Adapted from Susan Winebrenner, *Teaching Gifted Kids in the Regular Classroom.* Minneapolis, MN: Free Spirit Publishing Inc., 1992, p. 63. Used with permission.

learning. Before you begin compacting and extending the curriculum, send home a letter explaining what you'll be doing and inviting input from parents. If you wish, use the "I Thought You'd Like to Know" family letter (page 56).

Questions and Answers

"Isn't it better to wait until the child is older to begin compacting?"

When you being compacting and extending the curriculum in preschool or kindergarten, children learn early on how to work independently and manage their time. They become enthusiastic about school, rather than bored and frustrated with doing what they already know.

"Jocelyn doesn't seem able to work independently, and she disturbs the other children. What can I do?"

First, make sure that Jocelyn understands what her options are and that she has all the supplies, materials, and resources she needs. Go over work rules with her, being clear and firm about your expectations. Make certain that she fully understands her task. Also, make it a point to spend time with Jocelyn. Even though she has advanced abilities, she still needs your attention as much as the other children do. If her disruptive behavior continues, contact her parents for additional insight and support.

"I group flexibly by ability. Is it still necessary for me to compact the curriculum?"

Yes! Even within a group of high-ability children, you will find a difference in learning rates and interests. By compacting what each child already knows or can learn easily, you help to meet the child's individual needs.

"What if the child does nothing during 'instead of' time?"

Many children have much of their day "scheduled," both in and out of school. They may have experienced little or no free, unstructured time and don't know how to manage it productively. Offer this child a wide selection of choices. You may need to explain that doing nothing is not an option.

"If I don't cover every page in a textbook, isn't there a danger that the child will miss something?"

The important thing is that the child master the objectives, not simply "go through" a textbook. (In fact, many children who do work through a textbook page by page still don't have mastery of the material.) A textbook is a tool for presenting and reviewing information, one vehicle by which students can learn. If the child has already learned what is in the text, it's inappropriate to use it with that child.

"Won't compacting, extending, and documenting require a lot of extra time?"

Actually, compacting makes *more effective* use of time. Assessing what the child knows, documenting it, and selecting alternative activities is "front-loaded" time. You save time later in fewer papers to correct, fewer discipline problems, and fewer disruptions.

"Should I start with one student or a group?"

In some cases, it may be easier for you to start with one student who you know is really advanced and would benefit from compacting. In others, students may feel more comfortable if they begin with a group so that no one is singled out. Which you choose depends on several factors. What space do you have? How comfortable are you with each option? How many different types of extension activities do you have? Do you have the support of the administration? Is the media center available? Is there an adult there to help? Do you have parent helpers or a classroom paraprofessional?

Conclusion

It's hard to let go and trust that a young child will use his time wisely. Yet looking at the different ways children learn and the ways they demonstrate how they know information provides a wide range of opportunities for extending options for both group and independent study. By providing these opportunities, we open the door for children to be passionate about a subject, to explore it by a variety of avenues, and to present their findings in ways that take them beyond traditional paper-and-pencil tasks.

References and Resources

Armstrong, Thomas. *Multiple Intelligences in the Classroom.* Alexandria, VA: ASCD, 1994. An excellent guide to identifying, nurturing, and supporting individual capabilities of every student.

Daniel, Neil, and June Cox. *Flexible Pacing for Able Learners.* Reston, VA: Council for Exceptional Children, 1988. Explores the different approaches and philosophies of gifted education to assess their value. The research involves large numbers of schools and students with applications to gifted education in general.

Dreyer, Sharon Spredemann. *The Bookfinder: A Guide to Children's Literature about the Needs and Problems of Youth Aged 2–15,* vols. 1–5. Circle Pines, MN: American Guidance Service, 1977–1994. A wonderful resource tool that includes a comprehensive subject index to match children with books they'll want to read. Includes age interest range and synopsis of every book. Later volumes are also available on CD-ROM. Write to AGS, 4201 Woodland Road, Circle Pines, MN 55014-1796. Toll-free phone: 1-800-328-2560.

Hands On: Pentominoes. Palo Alto, CA: Creative Publications, 1986. Full of ideas for using Pentominoes (shapes made with different configurations of five squares) that focus on problem-solving skills, logical thinking, testing of hypotheses, identifying alternative solutions, and recording data. Write to Creative Publications, 5623 W. 115th Street, Worth, IL 60482. Toll-free phone: 1-800-624-0822.

Kaplan, Susan. "The ABC's of Curriculum for Gifted Five-Year-Olds: Alphabet, Blocks, and Chess?" *Journal for the Illinois Council of the Gifted* 11 (1992), pp. 43-44. Enthusiastically discusses several major components of curricula for the gifted child in terms of the child's and the teacher's creativity and preferred approach.

Milios, Rita. *Imagi-size: Activities to Exercise Your Students' Imaginations.* Dayton, OH: Pieces of Learning, 1993. Offers fresh, original activities and exercises to evoke the imaginative responses of children.

Parker, Jeanette Plauche. *Instructional Strategies for Teaching the Gifted.* Boston: Allyn & Bacon, 1989. Designed as a college text for teachers, undergraduates, and graduate students, this book effectively analyzes and evaluates creative, practical strategies that can be put to immediate use in the classroom.

Reis, Sally M., Deborah K. Burns, and Joseph S. Renzulli. *Curriculum Compacting*. Mansfield Center, CT: Creative Learning Press, 1992. Designed to help teachers "compact" or streamline the curriculum through a practical, step-by-step approach. Includes suggestions for pretesting, preparing optional assignments, and record-keeping.

———. "Curriculum Compacting: A Process for Modifying Curriculum for High Ability Students." Storrs, CT: The National Research Center on the Gifted and Talented, 1992. A one-hour training tape and accompanying facilitator and teacher guides.

Renzulli, Joseph S., and Sally Reis. *The Schoolwide Enrichment Model: A Comprehensive Plan for Educational Excellence*. Mansfield Center, CT: Creative Learning Press, 1985. A model for bringing enrichment opportunities to all students.

Rimm, Sylvia. *Underachievement Syndrome: Causes and Cures*. Watertown, WI: Apple Publishing Co., 1986. An expert's interpretation and assessment of the causes of underachievement as related to target populations of teachers, students, and parents.

Samara, John, and Jim Curry, eds. *Developing Units for Primary Students*. Bowling Green, KY: KAGE Publications, 1994. This book's subtitle says it all: "A Guide to Developing Effective Topical, Integrated, and Thematic Units of Study for Primary-Level Students with Sixteen Teacher-Generated Sample Units."

Viorst, Judith. *Alexander and the Terrible, Horrible, No Good, Very Bad Day*. Illustrations by Ray Cruz. New York: Atheneum, 1972. Students will empathize with Alexander and the anger he feels on a day in which everything goes wrong. A modern classic.

WHAT I LIKE

My Name: _____

Circle all of the things you like:

I like to count.

I like to make patterns.

I like colors.

I like to draw.

I like to build things.

I like to invent things.

I like to dance and move.

I like to act out plays.

I like music.

I like to sing.

I like books.

I like to listen to stories.

I like to be with other kids.

I like to help others with their problems.

I like to work alone.

I like to collect things.

I like to sort and arrange things.

WHAT I LIKE (CONTINUED)

Use this page to write or draw a picture
about something you are good at.

Tic-Tac-Toe Menu

1.	2.	3.
4.	5.	6.
7.	8.	9.

We choose activities #_____, #_____, #_____, and #_____.

Names: **Date:**

_____   _____

_____

_____

_____

MY PLAN TO BECOME AN EXPERT

Subject: _____ **Date:** _____

Here's what I want to learn about:

Here's how I will learn:

Here's how I can share this with the class:

Student's Signature _____

DATE

Teacher's Signature _____

DATE

Parent's Signature _____

DATE

PLAN FOR COMPACTING AND EXTENDING THE CURRICULUM

Student's Name: _____

Learning Objective

_____

_____

Level of Mastery

Date demonstrated: _____

How demonstrated: _____

_____

_____

_____

_____

Strengths

Preferred intelligence(s): _____

_____

Preferred learning style(s): _____

_____

Other strengths: _____

_____

_____

Extension Options

_____

_____

_____

_____

I THOUGHT YOU'D LIKE TO KNOW

Child's Name: _____

Dear Parent/Caregiver:

I want to let you know about something exciting we're doing in class.

Because some children already know some of the material we're covering, and some children learn new material more quickly than others, I'm giving kids the chance to do "instead of" activities. If they can show me that they've mastered an idea or a skill that I'm teaching, then they can work on other projects and assignments for a period of time. These "instead of" activities are meant to keep school interesting and challenging for all students.

I know that parents are sometimes concerned if they hear that their children aren't doing the same work as other children in the class. That's why I wanted to let you know about the "instead of" activities. If you have any questions, be sure to stop by or call.

Teacher's Signature: _____

Phone: _____

4

Promoting Creativity, Discovery, and Critical Thinking in the Social Studies Curriculum

"*I'd like to travel—go to China, or maybe to a tropical rain forest, or even to Antarctica where Admiral Byrd was with his penguins. I could watch the penguins with my binoculars and see how they survive the cold, how they catch their food, and where they go to escape from their enemies.*"

Who hasn't heard bright young children speak imaginatively like this—traveling beyond their immediate surroundings to remote places on the earth? Children love to investigate new geographic environments, cultures, and wildlife, all of which give them fresh opportunities for exploration and discovery. Imagination and curiosity emerge in the earliest years of childhood, leading children to a deeper understanding of the world around them. In our classrooms, we can draw on the same creative process our students have used outside of school to keep learning alive for them—to make it interactive, participatory, and stimulating

Creative Learning and Critical Thinking

This chapter offers an approach to academic subjects that can inspire and encourage higher-level thinking in *all* of your students while simultaneously providing incentives and opportunities for your gifted ones. Your goals are to help children:

- use creativity as a channel for critical thinking and research
- explore a range of subjects creatively and make discoveries they might not ordinarily reach
- make connections between their imaginative work and real-world contexts
- become participants in and contributors to a subject, rather than passive spectators or recipients.

We're using creative thinking in a special way here—as a link to intellectual discovery. Activities that call on children's imagination and creativity can do more than "jazz up" the curriculum. You can use creativity *as a means to promote critical thinking and discovery*. Creative thinking stimulates children's curiosity to discover the world in ways that other methods don't.

In addition, creative thinking enables young children to make personal contributions to whatever subjects they undertake. This is an important dimension of learning, especially for talented students. If we expect the gifted to contribute to the world in meaningful ways, we need to nurture their creative potential and confidence that they can make a difference. The classroom is the ideal place for this process to begin.

Creative Processes for Classroom Use

E. Paul Torrance, a pioneer in the study of creative thinking, describes four basic components of creative thinking that we use as a guide for teaching young children: *fluency, flexibility, originality,* and *elaboration.** To this list we have added *evaluation*—an element we feel brings an important dimension to creative work. The "Taxonomy of Creative Thinking" on page 59 gives examples of how you might use these five components in your classroom.

Fluency: In creative expression, fluency is the ability to produce many ideas with ease. We encourage fluency when we ask students to respond to problems or assignments by producing an abundance of ideas.

Flexibility: Flexible thinkers view problems or assignments from different angles—often ones that are unconventional or untried—and are inclined toward the beat of a very different drummer. We encourage flexibility when we invite students to think of alternative ideas and solutions.

Originality: Original thinking is highly unique and innovative. Students often use fluency and flexibility in the early stages of their work; to foster originality, we encourage them to discover ideas and concepts uniquely their own.

Elaboration: With elaboration, students add details to make their ideas more useful and practical. More than a mere extension of creative work, elaboration often requires students to use fluency, flexibility, and originality to develop concepts beyond the idea stage.

Evaluation: Evaluation is an ongoing process of analysis, investigation, experimentation, and synthesis. Students exercise judgment, reassess their ideas, and consider ways to adjust, refine, or further develop them. As they evaluate their work, they analyze the different parts of their

---

* E. Paul Torrance. *The Search for Satori and Creativity.* Buffalo, NY: Creative Education Foundation, 1979. Used with permission of E. Paul Torrance.

idea, see what does and doesn't work, consider new adjustments, and then reintegrate these new or changed parts into the whole.

———

As you can see, these five components often overlap. It's never easy to contain creativity within artificially imposed parameters. Nevertheless, you can still emphasize different mental processes at different points in your work with your class. We recommend that you use whatever ideas most readily apply to your students and to the subject area. As new possibilities emerge, both your students *and* you will be rewarded.

A Map of Creative Activities

Within your social studies curriculum, you can develop lessons and activities so *all* students can participate, learn creatively, and learn at their own level. All you need to do is include more advanced activities and opportunities that appeal to high-ability children while guiding the rest of the class in the more fundamental processes of creative work. In the end, you will inspire *all* of your children to shift into more advanced thinking as they engage in the projects that interest them.

As you read this chapter and consider how to use these ideas and suggestions in your classroom, we recommend that you:

1. Start a process as soon as the class has mastered enough of the basic facts to begin a more creative exploration of the subject.
2. Treat these suggestions as creative projects within a general subject area, such as the environment, that enable the children to work at a higher level of thinking.
3. Read through the detailed description of the process to gain a basic grasp of how it works, but without feeling pressured to duplicate it exactly.
4. Consider the different activities within the sequences and extract segments that seem most responsive to the academic needs and abilities of the children in your classroom.
5. Feel free to take the ideas offered here and adapt them to subject areas other than those we have used as examples.

In other words, use these ideas as a guide to your own activities, and feel free to improvise!

Taxonomy of Creative Thinking

Category	Focus	Process	Example	Outcome
Fluency	Generate many ideas	Free association; brainstorming	Children name different ways animals can help people	An abundance of ideas for creative work
Flexibility	Think of alternatives to the conventional	Imagining; integrating subjects	Children imagine some other unusual ways animals *could* help people	Alternative, divergent ideas; limitations overcome
Originality	Conceive innovations unique to context	Reviewing alternatives; imagining; combining	Children use their ideas to create a unique solution for a species (wild or tame) that is in need	Highly novel, unique ideas
Elaboration	Extend new ideas; provide details for application	Testing; analyzing; synthesizing	Children expand on their idea, explore whether/ how it might work	Ideas tailored to fit new contexts
Evaluation	Assess performance; examine gaps; exercise judgment	Analyzing; comparing; experimenting; fine-tuning	Children compare their idea with actual current practices; they analyze strengths and weaknesses, anticipate problems, make adjustments	New perspectives on idea and application

Adapted from E. Paul Torrance, *The Search for Satori and Creativity.* Buffalo, NY: Creative Education Foundation, 1979. Used with permission of E. Paul Torrance.

Fluency: Imagining Environmental Solutions

David was fidgeting in his seat. His second-grade class was studying one of his favorite subjects—animals! Under the general theme of extinction,

students were learning about the different species that had disappeared from earth, including dinosaurs. But after the first thrill, David had grown tired of merely identifying the animals and doing simple vocabulary and reading exercises on the subject of extinction and its causes. He stopped raising

his hand and began doodling on his paper. Once en-
thusiastic, he had become apathetic—retreating to
his own thoughts, scribbling distractedly.

David—and other children, too—would probably benefit from a more creative approach to the
subject. Although identifying and fact-finding interested him initially, he eventually became bored
when the class remained on that level. By incorporating the process of fluency, David's teacher
could invite him to delve into the study of disap-
pearing animal species more broadly and deeply.

In *fluency,* you ask children to generate as
many ideas as possible, even outrageous ones.
The focus at this point is on quantity, not quality.
Gifted children like David enjoy the shift from
gathering already established facts to generating
their own ideas. The more you encourage your
students and acknowledge the ideas they offer
(recording each one on the board), the more
eager they will be to take greater risks and use
their own imaginations.

1. Set the Stage

Ask the children to choose an endangered animal
species *they* would like to explore in class. Be
sure to have plenty of resources available for
them to use once they make their selection.* For
example, let's say a child or group of children
chooses the African elephant as the focus for a
more general study of extinction. To help students acquaint themselves with the particular environment and challenges of the African elephant,
you could choose any number of media, such as:

- a short video for children that will give them a
  direct impression of the animal and its circumstances
- fictional stories, poems, and pictures—anything
  that provides images, impressions, and facts
  about elephants
- animal posters that include factual information
  on the back
- resources available on computer via software,
  CD-ROM, or the Internet
- nonfiction resource books.

---

* You'll find some resources related to the activities discussed
in this chapter in the "References and Resources" section beginning on page 75, in Appendix B beginning on page 198, and
in Appendix C beginning on page 211.

For older children or gifted children who are
reading more, also make available articles from
newspapers or environmental magazines outlining
the problems of African elephant herds in a way
that isn't too graphic or defeatist.

Give the children time to respond to these
stimuli through discussion, drawing, or writing.
Ask questions such as these:

- What are your animal's needs? What is its habitat? Its food? Its shelter?
- What are the greatest threats to your species?
- What kinds of threats are these? Are they environmental (examples: pollution or loss of habitat)? Are they predatory (examples: being
  hunted, fished, or trapped for food or other
  human needs or wants)?

These questions can turn the children toward
identifying both the *sources* of the animals' problems and the *types* of threats to survival faced by
the species.

2. Generate Solutions

The children can now generate their own solutions—ideas for saving their animal species. You
could start them off by saying something like this:
"Now that you've explored the problem a little,
imagine that you have all the power, money, and
people in the world to help this animal. Anything
at all is possible to you. What would you do?"

Sentence Completion

To help children organize their thoughts, you
could give them sentences to complete. Sample
sentences on the subject of endangered animals
are shown on page 61. With younger students,
you can simply state the sentence starters and
ask children to complete them. For students who
are more skilled in reading and writing, you may
want to provide a handout or write the sentence
starters on the board.

To stimulate fluency, be open to both proba-
ble solutions and improbable ones (example:
"transport the remaining elephant population to
another planet until the animals are better pro-
tected here on earth").

Sample Sentences to Complete: Endangered Species

Name: _____

Species: _____

The threat to this species is: ❏ environmental
                                        ❏ predatory

The species is endangered because: _____
_____
_____
_____

It's important to save this species because: _____
_____
_____
_____

If I could do anything in the world to help this animal, I would: ___
_____
_____
_____

If I could say anything I wanted to the people who are threatening this species, here's what I would say:
_____
_____
_____
_____

If I wanted to make people care more about this animal, here's what I would do:
_____
_____
_____
_____

Imagination Exercises

Children who aren't used to fluency activities may need encouragement. Try an imagination exercise. Ask them to pretend they are a member of the species they have chosen; identifying with thespecies will help children grasp its needs and problems. For example, say to the students: "You are a wolf." Then offer one or more of the following activities:

Describe the animal's life. Say: "Tell us about your *habitat*. Where do you live? How do you feel about your home? Tell us about your animal community. What is your *pack* like? What do you love about being a wolf? How do you protect your young? How do you look after each other? How do you work together to find food?"

Draw a picture. Invite children to draw a picture or make a mural of their adopted animal family and its home.

Write about it. Suggest that children write a description of their life as a wolf. Encourage them to turn their writing into an illustrated booklet.

Write a letter. Say to the children: "Write a letter to humans and tell them how you feel about what they are doing to your species. Is it hard for you to find food? Is your air or water unsafe? How is your family being hurt? Tell the humans what you would like them to do to save your species."

Hold an "animal rally." Suggest that children hold a meeting of the members of their species. Ask them: "How will you let the other animals know about your meeting? What will the speakers say? What music will you have? Who will be in the audience? Other animals? Humans?" Encourage children to plan aspects of their rally such as its purpose, agenda, and program.

———

Encourage children to let their imaginations run free. To get the most out of this exercise, they must pretend that they have no limitations and no lack of resources. Anything is possible! You can give a few examples to prod their thinking, such as starting a mass media campaign to discourage people from buying anything with ivory or using satellites to guard the remaining whale population.

3. Make the Link to Critical Thinking

At any point in this process, you can always improvise other activities you feel will solidify children's ideas, inspire new ones, or prompt a deeper inquiry into the issues involved. Your gifted children will probably be ready for a more critical inquiry earlier than other students. For those ready to make this leap, you can easily provide small projects similar to the following:

Make posters. The purpose is to generate publicity to make the public aware of the problem.

Create poems, songs, or skits. Performing these works offers another way for children to teach other people about the plight of an animal species.

Use the earth's perspective. Say: "Pretend you are the earth. Write a letter to humans defending the endangered animal. As Mother Earth, explain how much you want to keep your waters clean and all your creatures living in harmony with each other."

Organize a group mural. Children can organize, plan, and create a mural that highlights the beauty and uniqueness of the species.

Write to the newspaper. Suggest that children write an article, editorial, or letter to the editor to submit to the local newspaper. The article can feature the plight of the endangered animal and suggest steps for its protection.

Create a cartoon. To start children thinking about novel ways to depict human actions, you might give an example of a strategy, such as reversing human and animal roles. The cartoon could depict humans as endangered by animals that are taking over human habitats and food sources.

———

Throughout this process, your goal is to inspire as many creative responses as possible, thereby stimulating deeper inquiry or research. Keep asking questions: "How else could you save the habitat? How else could you protect the species against overhunting? How else could you meet the needs of your species and at the same time not deprive humans of what they need? What other approaches would you use to stop humans from harming the animals?"

With a long list of solutions in front of them, students have a wealth of catalysts for a more critical analysis and investigation. For example, once they decide that elephants need a new, safer place to live, they will automatically want to know more about the animals' natural habitat in Africa. This in turn will prompt them to research something in response to an interest *they* have, rather than to simply perform a task demanded by the teacher. They become more invested in their own ideas and, therefore, in their own learning.

When creativity through fluency is used as a link to critical thinking, there are several benefits. The children learn to tackle the problem from a standpoint of *possibility*. Beyond what already exists, they see what alternative solutions *might be*. The solutions, even the outlandish ones, give children an investment in the research they undertake. Because they have already imagined ways to tackle the issue, they will want to discover how workable their ideas are, what adjustments they may need to make, and what plans they may have to undertake to see their ideas through. Perhaps most important, they will learn the value of invention. Tell them not to toss out ideas that may appear unreasonable at first—there may be components that could work in an unexpected way. Many inventions and innovations appear unreasonable and unrealistic at first.

All young children, including the gifted, need to feel confidence in their ideas. When they launch into the study of a subject without engaging in any creative work, they miss the opportunity to make a personal contribution to the discovery process.

Flexibility: Alternative Histories

Eight-year-old Kendra didn't like history lessons. They reminded her of the news her father always listened to before dinner. She had to be quiet then, too. Sometimes she would listen with interest, but mostly she just went off by herself to read or draw. One of Kendra's favorite games was to take a book she loved and create different endings, add more characters, or invent new conflicts and events. But, in her experience, this secret fun had no place in school—especially not in history studies!

For a gifted child like Kendra, learning basic historical facts isn't challenging enough to hold her interest. The conventional approach to learning history can feel inhibiting to a child with imagination. The tasks of memorizing distant dates, putting events in sequence, and studying remote characters are too one-dimensional. Incorporating flexibility into the teaching of history invites children into different, more interesting dimensions.

In the process of *flexibility,* you ask children to diverge from an established sequence, fact, norm, formula, or phenomenon in order to explore alternatives and gain new perspectives. Applied to history, flexibility means exploring the "what ifs?" of the past. It asks the child: "What if you were there in that village in that time? What would *you* see that others might not? What would *you* experience? Who would *you* be? What does the past have to do with your life in the present? How are historical figures similar to you and your friends?"

A flexibility process departs from the deterministic view of history as a series of events that just "happened." People make history. When you put your students into a past and let them imagine how they lived, what they did, and what they aspired to, you help them see history as it moves forward in time—as a process that is alive and relevant.

1. Set the Stage

To begin studying a historical period, first select an engaging and informative book—either non-fiction or historical fiction—that will ground the children in the basic facts and also interest them in the story.

As an example, let's suppose the children are studying the Pilgrims. *The Pilgrims of Plimoth,* by Marcia Sewall, is a good source for this period. Read the book aloud to the class and use it as a springboard for creating a conceptual base for the subject, building vocabulary, and generating discussion and questions. Show pictures or sketches of Plymouth that will give the class visual images of the land, the architecture and design of the town, the style of dress, and some of the main historical figures.

Next, read the story of the *Mayflower* to the children. Talk to them about the motivations that led the people to attempt such a perilous journey.

After covering some basic ground on the Pilgrim story, you can move on to more creative activities. Have a collection of books, pictures, sketches, maps, and other materials available for children to use as they explore the subject imaginatively. Begin by posing a few questions. Ask students to imagine they lived 300 years ago and took a ship across the ocean for many weeks to come to a new land they didn't know. Then ask them:

- How did you feel about taking such a trip?
- What did you experience on that long trip across the ocean?
- What hardships did you face? How did you deal with them?
- Who else was on the ship with you? How did you get along?
- What did you do for fun? Did you play? How?
- What were your hopes as you waited to reach shore?
- Why did you make the trip?
- What did you take with you? Why? What did you leave behind? Why?

- What did you eat on the ship? What did you wear? Where did you sleep?
- When you landed, how did you go about making a home?
- Were you surprised to find other people already living in the New World? How did these people feel about your coming?
- What is a "pilgrim?"

Children will enjoy learning about the Pilgrim experience much more if they do it within the context of imagining themselves living in Plymouth—the first generation of white settlers. Have them choose roles for themselves in the village—servant, carpenter, weaver, soldier, farmer—and think of the kinds of families and friends they would have. It might be fun to assume the roles of real characters, since records of many actual historical figures survive today. By knowing some of the basic facts of life in Plymouth and having a cast of characters, students should be able to imagine and produce a variety of stories about the Pilgrim experience— stories that reflect the alternative historical world they are attempting to create.

To avoid a one-sided treatment, also expose the children to Wampanoag life and culture. Marcia Sewall's *People of the Breaking Day* offers a vivid portrait of these indigenous people—their customs, beliefs, and way of life. Some students may want to explore their experience and imagine what they thought of these foreign people from across the sea. Children could draw a Wampanoag village scene or a picture depicting their responses to the newcomers. Guide them with critical questioning:

- What do your people eat? Do they farm? Hunt? Fish? Trade?
- How do you dress? How do you make clothes?
- What is your home like? How did you build it?
- What do you do for fun?
- What do you think of the Pilgrim people? Are they strange to you? In what ways?
- What are some of your experiences with the Pilgrims?

Very young children with limited reading or writing skills could draw or paint pictures of a scene they have imagined. For children who need ideas, you might suggest a scene about Massasoit,

a famous chief who made a peace treaty with Governor John Carver. Or you might divide the class into Pilgrim and Wampanoag groups and ask each group what they saw and felt when they met the other.

2. Imagine

The focus of the flexibility process is different from that of fluency. The persistent question in flexibility activities is: "What else might have been?" You and your students will approach the past as a territory full of unknowns—a place where they can gain new insights. By putting themselves back in time, they begin to discover what's important to *them* as participants in this unique period of history.

Identifying with the Pilgrims or native peoples gives children perspective they wouldn't acquire by reading a book or listening to the teacher. Exercising their imagination allows them to find some common ground with people of times past—ideals that many people still value centuries later, such as freedom from political and religious domination.

Children can empathize with the fears and concerns the Wampanoag felt about losing their world to foreigners. They can understand how a mother might worry about her children's uncertain future with the Pilgrims, or how a father might fear losing the land on which his ancestors lived and worked.

In this way, children see that history isn't dead and gone, but correlates with the present in unique ways. And there are *many* histories for students to discover—stories of the past that they can imagine happening in a particular place and time long ago.

When you tell children that you're sending them back in time, explain that in the 1600s, North America was mostly wilderness. Be sure they understand the unique circumstances the Pilgrims faced in this early period—the lack of modern conveniences and the differences in dress, transportation, communication, and manners. The Wampanoag also had their own unique way of life, means of food production, style and construction of housing, dress, and other customs. Some of your students can "go back in time" to one of these environments and look at life from their perspective. Children might also explore how the Wampanoag people helped the

Pilgrims produce food and maintain peace with other native populations, or how interacting with the newcomers changed Wampanoag customs.

Try to locate sources (pictures, anecdotes, stories, and videos) that are authentic or based on authentic history. Children can use these resources to create their own narratives of life in Plymouth and surrounding territories. They will enjoy collecting vivid impressions of the environment of the 1600s—the homes, furniture, clothing, tools, ships, buildings, and landscapes of the town. Have diagrams of Plymouth and scenes of Wampanoag life available. These will feed their imaginations and provide personal contexts for creating stories that diverge from the stereotypical versions of the Pilgrim experience.

What kinds of stories? A child's story. A mother's story. The story of Susannah White—later Susannah Winslow—who gave birth to a child on the *Mayflower*, survived the hardships of the first winter, and lived to 85, a rare age at a time when so many women died young. The story of a Samoset's first meeting with the Pilgrims, or of the first treaty concluded between the Pilgrims and Native Americans. The tale of the first Thanksgiving. The story of the first governor, John Carver, or of the second governor, William Bradford. The story of a new settler Bradford expelled because he played games in the streets on Christmas Day, or of another who was caught in a deer trap. The tale of John Billington, who was lost among the Indians, or his brother Frances, who almost blew up the *Mayflower*. The story of impulsive Myles Standish, the leader of the Pilgrims' little "army."

Here are some questions to get students started thinking:

- What did you and your family hope to find in the New World when you came?
- Did you find it?
- What are the people in Plymouth like? What do they do?
- How do you learn? What do you learn?
- Do you have friends?
- Are you glad you came?
- What do you wear? What do you eat?
- Where do you travel? How do you get there?
- What chores or jobs do you have to do?
- What do you like better about your new home than your old one?
- What do you miss about England (or Holland)?

- What do you find difficult in your new home?
- What kind of world are your family and other families trying to create in this new land?
- How do you relate to the Native Americans?

3. Make the Link to Critical Thinking

Critical thinking plays a role in this process right away. You can either write the children's answers on the board, or ask them to write them down. Break students into groups and ask them to work on the questions together, using what they have already learned as well as the resource materials you have provided. Here are a few other activities you might incorporate:

Create visual depictions. Ask children who are not yet reading historical materials to think of one main response for whatever question they have. They could then create a visual image that represents their idea—a painting, collage, cartoon, or model. Later, invite them to share their work as a catalyst for class discussion.

Draw maps. Mapping provides a more complex visual-artistic and tactile-kinesthetic project. Tell children: "You live in a Pilgrim village. Some relatives are coming from England. You want them to find your home when they reach your town. Draw a map of the village. Include as many details as you can: the meeting house, fort, paths, streams, harbor, and main street."

Tell stories. Have students imagine that each of them is a reporter sent back in time to interview people about what's been happening in Plymouth. Ask them to think about what questions they might ask.

You might also suggest: "You're a storyteller, and you want to describe your Thanksgiving feast for future history students. Tell us how it started in your village. Who came to the feast? What foods did you eat? What games did you play? How long did the celebration last?"

Or present another storytelling opportunity: "You're a Native American from the Wampanoag tribe. Describe how you helped the first settlers grow their first crop of corn and find other food to eat. Describe the Thanksgiving feast in which you and your family participated."

Some children might prefer to create fictional stories around the characters they have imagined in their Pilgrim village.

Write letters. If children can read and write, have them write letters to friends back in England or Holland, describing their new surroundings and how they differ from those on the other side of the Atlantic.

Create biographies. Have the students create short biographies of themselves and their families. The biographies can be written or oral.

Children can accompany these with drawings of their homes and families, maps or sketches of their town, examples of their tools, or recipes.

To help children craft biographies, you may wish to prepare a handout similar to the sample below. The children would complete the sentences from the perspective of a real Pilgrim they know about or invent a fictional one.

Sample Sentences to Complete: My Life as a Pilgrim

Name: _____

I am a Pilgrim living in Plymouth. My name is: _____

In the town of Plymouth, I am a: _____
_____
_____

I live with these people: _____
_____
_____

My jobs at home and in the village are: _____
_____
_____

I left my old country to come here because:
_____
_____

What I like best about my new home is: _____
_____
_____

What I don't like about my new home is: _____
_____
_____

What I hope for our future is: _____
_____
_____

Talk to the Children

As you supervise the children's work, you'll find many opportunities to talk with them about their "histories." Keep reminding them that they are not living in the United States of America, but in a world that is not yet a country. Plymouth Colony sits on the edge of a huge territory of wilderness that has many Native American tribes and many plant and animal populations.

Provide Opportunities for Sharing

Provide opportunities for the children to share their work. Hang their pictures and biographies on the wall, and guide the students around the room to see each other's work.

Walk around the room with children and talk about the representations. As you discuss the various pieces of work, there will be many opportunities for you to refer to historical events and conditions. As you do, ask questions such as: "Could this event have happened to this family in the 1600s? Would the Pilgrims have had a telephone back then? Or did that come later? How did people send messages to each other?"

Encourage Editing and Refining

Whether the histories take the form of visual art, maps, dramas, or written works, give children a chance to refine, polish, and edit. This is an on-going process of exploration, not an exhibit of final products. As you share the children's work, think about the possibility of creating an entire village out of their stories, pictures, maps, and diagrams. You may already have enough to comprise a simulation of Plymouth. Using additional factual information, you and the class could create a large map, diagram, or scale model of the town. The children could then place their "family" homes at various locations, and you could decide jointly where the meeting house, fort, and other community buildings should be.

Connect the Past to the Present

As a conclusion to this process, you might also ask the children to write letters to people in our present time. These letters could tell families, members of the school community, public officials, and others what part of the Pilgrim experience is important for people of today to know. What would the children like today's history teachers to teach about that long-ago time? What do they feel is most important for parents to

know? What aspect of life in Plymouth could be applied to improving or changing today's world?

The children could write or dictate these letters; you could transcribe as necessary and attach the letters to students' work. This gives the students a chance to distill in their minds what *they* found unique and special about the Pilgrim experience and how that experience contributed to the world in which we live today.

Originality: Creating Culture

Pilar had a dream of traveling to faraway places. Her family had moved to the United States from Argentina before she was born, and Pilar had never been to her parents' birthplace. Traveling to South America would be far too expensive, so she had to be content with pictures and stories that her parents told her—and, of course, with her imagination, which was considerable. Pilar loved airplanes. She would often watch them as they passed overhead, imagining many different destinations and concocting wild and interesting adventures for herself in each place.

When her first-grade class began studying other cultures and places, Pilar was delighted. Students were exploring basic concepts of culture by looking into their own families' cultural roots, interviewing family members, reporting the findings to the class, and drawing pictures of the worlds described by their parents and other relatives. Sharing the differences in language and customs was fun. Pilar wanted to talk about so many questions! "Why do different kinds of people sometimes misunderstand each other? Why are some other families so different from mine? What are their lives like? Will other people like me and accept me?"

Pilar was an original thinker who needed to know the "why" of things. Identifying and classifying customs, languages, and cultural practices would never feed her inquiring mind. The child who has to know "why" all the time is a child already on a higher level of thinking, more interested in what makes things the way they are than in what size, shape, or quality those things have. Pilar's tendency to imagine adventures in faraway places also revealed a desire to invent worlds of her own—worlds based on what she knew, but still uniquely hers.

Students like Pilar will thrive within the framework of originality. Like the other two processes we've explored, originality has a distinct emphasis or focus. Fluency produces a large quantity of ideas; flexibility seeks alternatives to the commonplace. *Originality* is a little different. Children may draw on the other two processes, yet they are creating something uniquely their own—something that not only stands apart from established inventions but also *exceeds* the status of an alternative or digression. An original idea may or may not use any known thing as a reference point. It may temporarily use something already established as a way of exploring a range of alternatives, but eventually it will assume a distinct shape of its own.

1. Set the Stage

Nothing delights most young gifted children more than discovering that they can create something completely unique. The study of culture offers many opportunities for this to happen.

Let's say that, as in Pilar's class, you approach the whole subject of human cultures by involving the children in researching their family backgrounds.* This kind of inquiry is very beneficial for young children. While learning about their own cultural heritage, they can also contribute to the class's pool of knowledge about human cultures in general. The students become producers as well as recipients of knowledge. For children in the younger grades who may not be reading much, this is an ideal approach to a very basic kind of research. You could ask children to interview family members and collect answers to the following questions:

- Where was your mother or father born? What about your grandparents? Where were your great-grandparents born?
- Who in your family first came to the United States?
- When did they come? How did they get here?
- Why did they come here?
- What hardships did they face?
- What language did they speak? Do they still speak it? Do you know some words you could teach us?

---

* Be sensitive to the needs and feelings of children who are adopted, are in the care of foster parents, or live in stepfamilies or blended families. They may want to research their family backgrounds, or they may not. Offer alternatives for those who don't.

- What foods do people in your family eat that others in our class might never have tasted?
- What are some of your family's customs or traditions? Do you celebrate special holidays? Eat special foods? Sing or dance to traditional music? Light candles? Tell stories? Wear special clothes?
- Is there special artwork—like paintings, pots, dolls, or baskets—made by people who come from the same place your family came from?
- If you're from another country, how do you feel about the way we live here? What do you like? What don't you like? What do you miss about where you used to live?

First, write the questions on the board and go over each one. Make sure the children understand them. We also recommend sending some questions home; if you wish, use the "Your Child's Cultural Heritage" family letter (page 78). Also ask the children to bring in pictures or other artifacts that represent the country or culture they come from.

2. Explore and Share Personal Backgrounds

Get an extra-large map to hang on a bulletin board or the wall. Write out the children's names and ask them to tack them to the country or area of their origin. (If their roots involve several places, which is often the case, ask them to pick the most dominant ones or the ones they know most about). Then follow through with other activities:

Draw maps. Have children draw a map of their country or geographic area (in pencil first), filling in landmarks such as towns or community gathering places, lakes, forests, and oceans that surround it. Some children may feel that their areas of origin are less identifiable. Assure them that they may identify a general area. For example, they might mark out a geographic area such as the Arapaho lands on the Great Plains, which cover parts of Kansas, Nebraska, and Colorado. The purpose of the activity is to expose the children to the richness and diversity of their own cultural heritage.

Tell stories. Next to their maps, children could write stories describing their family's background: how people were related, the town or area in which they lived, what work their ancestors did, how and why life changed for the family.

This assignment can be as simple or complicated as you like. You can ask children who are just learning to read and write to tell their stories using a few very simple sentences. Encourage others, especially those of higher ability, to describe their family's life vividly, as in a storybook. Children who don't yet write can create a drawing that tells their story, with an arrow pointing to the place on the map where they lived. They could also dictate captions for you, a parent volunteer, or another student to write.

Share customs. Ask the children to write about the language, dress, and some of the customs of their family. Again, offer the option of drawing, painting, collage, or dictation.

Share artifacts. Assure the children that this is *their own* story of their family's culture, and that they can add all sorts of things to make it more vivid, including family pictures, images and articles from magazines, poems that reflect their heritage, and small objects, tools, or mementos that could be posted near this representation.

————

Each product or presentation can be unique—different in size, style, medium, etc. The children should feel free to draw upon their creative strengths. Those who are more confident in the visual arts, for example, may feature visual images more than written ones. While there may be certain required elements, students should be allowed to integrate them in their own way so they can take possession of the process.

3. Make the Link to Critical Thinking

Once the children have completed their work, display the maps and other representations around the room so the class can see them. Encourage students to walk around and look at the different countries and cultures represented. Invite children—especially those who haven't written on their maps—to talk about their work. This will give them an opportunity to elaborate on whatever they wrote or depicted, describing customs and cultural practices in more detail to the class.

Compare Cultures

After a systematic tour around the room, ask the children to select two cultures *not* from their own heritage. With many basic facts about different

cultures now at their fingertips, they can begin a more critical inquiry. Give each child two copies of "Me in a Different Culture" (page 79). Ask them to put the name of a selected culture on each sheet.

Next, ask them to pretend that they are from one of the cultures. As they look at the language, customs, and dress of the people, the children should imagine that these are *their* language, customs, and style of dress. Have them write down two things (more for older children) about each culture and its people that they find most interesting. Tell them to be as specific as possible. For less apt writers, elicit one or two simple words; these will be enough to spark productive discussion when students share their ideas with the class.

You could also integrate into class discussion the children's impressions of other cultures. What have they noticed in particular about one or more of these other cultures? Do some of the customs or practices seem unusual? Why or why not? What similarities are there among cultures? This helps children understand that our own culture influences the way we view other cultures, and that each of us may seem "strange" to someone else. Children from cultural minorities will quickly grasp this and will appreciate the opportunity to share their experiences.

Make the Familiar Strange

A natural extension of the process just described is to ask children to think of a custom or behavior common to them that might look very foreign to someone from another part of the world. Have them select a simple behavior that seems perfectly ordinary, such as eating hamburgers and French fries at a fast-food restaurant, jogging, or celebrating Independence Day.

Introduce the activity by saying something like this: "Many things we've described about other cultures seem strange to us because we're not used to them. These things are very ordinary to the people who do them. Now I want you to imagine that you *don't* live here in our country. Instead, you're a visitor from some faraway place that has very different customs. For example, pretend that, in the place where you live, there are no restaurants like McDonald's or Burger King. Or imagine that where you come from it's considered very rude to eat food in public. How would you describe to your friends at home what you see happening in our country?" The children could choose from many other subjects—clothing, entertainment, or whatever inspires them. You and the class can have fun improvising with this.

You could also treat this as a homework assignment in an ongoing exploration of culture in your classroom. Have the children go home and observe life around them, recording their observations—perhaps on a simple form such as the "Custom Observation Form" (page 80).

Children might consider some of the rules, spoken and unspoken, connected with mealtime. Or they could observe what people in their home do to entertain themselves or to relax. As they visit public places with their families—museums, train stations, restaurants, banks, libraries, clinics, shopping malls—they can notice how people behave in these different environs.

In class, ask the children to share some of their observations. How do people behave in a given situation? Examples could include:

- being quiet in a library
- standing in line at a bank
- waiting until everyone sits down before starting to eat
- walking quietly around a museum
- pushing to get on the train
- raising hands to speak in a classroom
- screaming and jumping up and down at a ball game
- sitting silently at a concert or singing and clapping along
- "oohing" and "aahing" while watching fireworks on the Fourth of July or the Chinese New Year
- decorating a tree at Christmas
- lighting candles at Hanukkah or Kwanzaa
- eating matzo at Passover or coloring eggs at Easter
- fasting during Ramadan.

Ask children to choose one thing to observe and to imagine that they've never seen that particular place or behavior before. They should just watch what happens and try to make sense of it. The idea is to make the familiar strange. The children should have fun with this. Encourage them to be creative in their descriptions. Ask them to describe the behavior as if they were explaining it to friends from another place. They could also accompany their descriptions with pictures or magazine cut-outs or photos. They might start by

saying: "I'm standing inside a tall building where people are doing _____. I'm not sure what this means, but it looks like _____."

Through this wonderful process of originality, you'll be giving the children direct experience in constructing the reality of another culture based on their *own* fictional culture's standards, customs, and values. Gifted children in particular will enjoy this mind-bending process. They will love sharing the scenarios of what they found "foreign" and the kinds of conclusions they made based on what they saw. At the same time, you'll be encouraging the whole class to think critically and creatively about culture. The students will recognize that behaviors and customs that have meaning for people within one culture may mean something very different to people who are not part of that culture. By assuming the position of someone outside their own cultural world and trying to interpret what seems strange or unusual to them, they will begin to see the connections between culture and meaning.

Create a Fictional Culture

To extend this to a more complex level, high-ability students who show an interest could take on a project of imagining an entirely fictional culture. There are a number of benefits to this type of project:

1. It gives gifted children an opportunity to draw on their conceptual understanding of how cultures invent a unique system of commonly held values, communication styles, and customs.
2. It challenges creative, artistic children to think and work in a way they love as they invent all sorts of unusual worlds and decide how the societies within these worlds will organize their lives.
3. It places children on the inside of their fictional worlds as "cultural experts" who can make sense of practices and customs that seem inexplicable to others.
4. It gives children the opportunity to envision culture in a way that addresses current world issues—for example, by inventing a society that deeply values the environment, or one that is opposed to war.
5. It can foster an increased appreciation of cultural differences as children think more logically and sympathetically about cultures different from their own.

You could start the process by encouraging children to think about what they value in their own and other cultures. Here are some possible questions:

- What kind of cultural world would you create if you had the power to do so?
- What would you name it?
- What behaviors would be common in this culture?
- What would be the celebrations and special holidays connected to historical events, anniversaries, and beliefs?
- What would the language sound like?
- What would the people wear?
- What kind of geographical environment would the people of this culture live in?
- What would the homes and other buildings look like?
- What would the transportation system be like? How would people get around?
- What kinds of jobs or work would the people do?
- What would their food look like? How would it be prepared?
- What would be the history of this culture?

Drawing on cultural information from a variety of resources (TV programs, movies, software programs, online computer services, videos, books, or personal experience), the children will relish the opportunity to invent their own worlds.

If this process seems complicated or unmanageable, or if you would like to give a whole class of older children an opportunity to create a fictional culture, you might consider having the class work together to create a single culture. Divide the children into groups and assign each one a particular domain such as clothing, foods, political organization, architecture, history, or environment. To be successful, you'll need to spend some whole-class time setting a few parameters, then follow through by moving from group to group, keeping track of what children are creating for their areas. If the group working on clothes invents attire at odds with the kind of environment another group has devised, you'll need to give them time to negotiate this discrepancy. Have plenty of books, pictures, and videos available for the children as their ideas evolve.

You can adapt this process for younger (preschool and kindergarten) children. Focusing on simple things such as clothing, language, food, and fundamental customs and celebrations, the children can first explore differences among real cultures. Maureen Cech's *Globalchild: Multicultural Resources for Young Children* is a wonderful resource for beginning this process. Or introduce fairy tales from other cultures—stories similar to those students might already know, such Shirley Cimo's *The Egyptian Cinderella*, Martin Rafe's *The Rough-Face Girl* (a Native American Cinderella story), and Ed Young's *Lon Po Po* (a Red Riding Hood story from China). Through these sources, young children can begin to conceptualize what "culture" is.

In devising their own fictional culture, preschool and kindergarten students could begin with the environment. Ask the students to choose a climate and geographical setting for their culture. This will lead to discussions of the clothing people make; the food they gather, grow, hunt, and prepare; and possibly the kinds of ceremonies and traditions they develop. Young gifted students can also consider the technology their imaginary culture has developed in response to environmental factors.

As with older children, have younger students create cooperatively. Organize their work around some key questions:

- What do your homes look like?
- How do the children learn?
- What are some of your celebrations?

Students can draw or dramatize a history of the people, explaining how certain customs evolved. They can paint or draw pictures of this world and create models of villages.

Although you may feel reluctant to spend too much time on a fictional culture, building a world that makes sense unto itself—that has a history, an environment, and a way of responding to challenges and celebrating special events—teaches the class a great deal about the inner workings of culture. Gifted children especially will appreciate the complexity of culture and enjoy its planning.

There are a number of related activities you could consider as well:

- Create laws of behavior for this new world—laws you would value if you lived in it.
- Create a new kind of architecture for buildings in this culture.

- Write some patriotic songs.
- Design a flag.
- Design a map of the country or area and its surroundings that shows cultural landmarks.
- Devise a transportation system.
- Write or create murals depicting the culture's history.
- Design clothing.
- Develop recipes.
- Create the beginnings of a language.

After this sort of in-depth learning experience, the students will be less inclined to make superficial assessments of other cultures. Despite the apparent strangeness of certain practices, they will begin to look for inner cultural consistencies—the links that connect a people's way of thinking and doing things into some understandable pattern.

Elaboration and Evaluation: Translating Creativity

Elaboration and *evaluation* don't necessarily occur separately from the processes of fluency, flexibility, or originality. Rather, they extend out from these processes, translating novel ideas into practice. We'll consider elaboration and evaluation together because they usually complement each other. To employ these processes in your classroom, you'll need either a problem-solving context (in which students are attempting to grapple with an issue in a new way) or a creative context (in which the product or idea works as a unique invention within the framework of certain requirements or standards, as in the case of a fictional culture).

It's not unusual for gifted students to have a difficult time pursuing their idea to the point of elaboration and evaluation. When an idea has taken them as far as they want to go, they may be impatient to move on to something new. Persisting with their idea may seem dull in comparison to the more exciting processes of discovery and innovation they experienced in creating it. Yet evaluating their work to see what adjustments might be necessary, or what further developments might make it more useful, can present new and exciting challenges. As a teacher, the main points for you to remember are that gifted children tend to be harsh judges of

their own work, and that they need help elaborating and evaluating. What follows are some useful practices to help *all* of your students develop their ideas and evaluate their work in constructive ways.

1. Set the Stage

Even very young children—preschoolers and kindergartners—can benefit from these processes. Let's say, for example, that the children have just created their own fictional cultures. You can then walk the class around the room to examine and analyze the different projects. Original insights often emerge from this process, enabling students to elaborate in unexpected ways on what they have created. Young gifted students will enjoy this process, because it inspires critical and creative thinking.

Start by introducing elaboration and evaluation as phases of discovery. Gifted children will lose interest if they think that this process means aborting or severely altering their ideas to "fit into" an external standard of what is reasonable and possible.

Whether the child is trying to devise a new language or test a hypothesis on an idea for a new kind of car, you can use the same simple principles. Try introducing the idea like this: "Now I want you to try this out to see if it works. To do this, you need to be a true inventor. Don't give up on your idea if it doesn't work right away or if it seems impossible. Many inventors have felt just like that. To make this work, you need to stick to your idea, but be open-minded enough to make changes where you think you need them. Don't be too hard on yourself. If Edison had judged himself too harshly, we might still be reading by candlelight today!"

Point out that even failed experiments have contributed valuable knowledge that has paved the way for other significant discoveries. The history of flight is an example. You could choose several examples of real inventors and pioneers to set an encouraging tone for your children's work. The process of putting their ideas in practice should be fun, leading to new ideas they might not have otherwise considered. To a large degree, a child's ability to see the elaboration and evaluation processes as satisfying and rewarding requires your efforts in patiently establishing such a mind-set.

2. Use Questions to Guide Students

Like fluency and flexibility, elaboration and evaluation are creative processes. You don't want to assign specific steps for children to take in order to make their ideas work; doing so is likely to cause students to quickly lose their own investment in their idea and in some of its most innovative features.

We've found that the best approach is to present students with a series of leading questions. The questions should prompt critical and creative responses—students' own. You'll need to select and adjust the questions depending on the age and ability of the children as well as the project they have chosen. Are they seeking a solution to the extinction of a species? Attempting to create an original alternative piece of historical writing? Designing a new concept in transportation? Also bear in mind that elaboration and evaluation don't happen quickly with all children, but may need to span several days or even weeks.

To Begin

To put this process in context, let's say you have children who are developing a campaign to stop the poaching of elephants for ivory. Some children have composed songs, written poems or short articles for a newspaper, or created cartoons, slogans, small sculptures, or paintings. Others have devised plans to transport endangered animals to a new site in another country. Still others have created ads to increase elephant awareness among consumers and to dissuade them from purchasing the ivory. At this point, you might say to the students:

- Look at your idea (or product). Think about what you would like it to do. What might you still need to do to make it work?
- Tell us all you know about the role or setting you have planned for your idea. What problem does your idea solve? What sort of place will be good for your creation?
- What might still be missing from your idea to make it work in the place you've chosen?

These questions help children begin thinking of natural extensions to their ideas. This can occur on different levels. Very young children who have invented a new environment for endangered elephants can build models or draw

sketches, adding details as they think through the questions. Older students who have written fictional accounts of their experiences in Plymouth or in a Wampanoag village can test their stories against the historical facts, developing and refining them from the new insights gained. You may not want to provide a lot of structured feedback at this point. Gifted students often prefer to elaborate on their ideas *before* receiving responses from you or other students.

To Continue

After students have worked for a while, they'll be ready to share their ideas. To ensure that the class gives productive criticism, set two ground rules:

1. Offer helpful ideas. Tell students that negative remarks aren't helpful. Make it clear that you won't allow them. Ask the children to focus only on what they think would make the idea work better—not on what they think is wrong with it.

2. Don't judge or criticize. Don't accept or allow value judgments like "This is stupid" or "That won't work." If children foresee certain problems with an idea, ask them to state what they think might not work. They should do this without criticizing the idea itself.

Guide your students through this stage of the process with comments and questions such as these:

- What changes are necessary?
- How could you make the changes? Write down or brainstorm all the ways you can think of.
- Are there parts of your idea that don't work? Which parts? Can you keep these parts by changing the way you would apply your idea?
- If you have to change part of your idea, can you create something new in its place?
- There are gaps between what you have made and what is still needed. You can use your imagination to fill these gaps. Keep asking yourself, "Is there another way I can approach this?"
- Stay focused. Ask yourself, "What do I want my idea to do? What do I want it to accomplish?"

Encourage children to respond to the suggestions. This will stimulate critical and creative thinking, and will help the students see new possibilities for their work.

To Finish

After the children have spent some time experimenting, they can bring closure to their work. As you guide the class through the elaboration and evaluation process, you'll find that some students benefit most by collaborating, others by working independently. Be flexible and allow children to complete their ideas in the way they feel most comfortable. Here are some questions you might pose:

• What things do you need to have or do in order to complete your idea?
• Who might be able to help you? Are there questions you might have for your teacher? For another student or group of students?
• Generally speaking, what do you need to reach your goal? Time? Materials? Space? A way to convince other people?
• Does your project require a team, or just you? If you need a team, what kind of workers do you need? How many? What do you need this team of helpers to do for you?

This is a good exercise, because it keeps the children's thoughts focused on their own vision and ideal for their work, which is very important at this point in the process. Children—especially gifted ones—are often highly sensitive about their work, extremely critical of it, and quick to abandon all or part of it if they think it will fail. You need to support your students' efforts by helping them to stay focused on what is important *to them*. This will keep them from becoming distracted or overly concerned about how "good" their project looks on the surface or about what other people think of it.

3. Create Opportunities for Sharing

Once the children complete their work to their satisfaction, they should have a chance to share it with the rest of the class. It's a good idea to discuss the sharing of ideas beforehand and coach the class on positive ways to respond to others' efforts.

When students share their work, it's an extremely powerful and effective teaching and learning process for all—including you! From the children's perspective, it's practically revolutionary for them to be in a position where *they* are the experts, leading the class through their own discoveries and ideas. This alone often transforms the dynamics of the class. We've found that most young students are quiet, respectful, and willing to ask probing questions when their classmates make presentations. For gifted children who often fear what others will say or think about their work, it can be extremely beneficial to find that people respond well to their ideas *and* that people can be a valuable resource for their work.

Sharing isn't about deciding whether a child's creation is good or bad, right or wrong. It's about continuing the discovery process—acknowledging and praising the accomplishment, helping the child investigate where else to go or what else to do to carry the idea further.

Exploring children's work together as a class provides many opportunities for you to support creative learning, using their work as a catalyst for higher-level thinking. This kind of class environment will teach all of your children that learning is a discovery process, that everyone has a role to play in this process, and that each of them has a unique contribution to make to the world around them.

Questions and Answers

"Wouldn't some gifted children prefer to work alone rather than share their work?"

The stereotype of gifted children as contented loners, capable and happy to work completely on their own, is a potentially damaging one. We should not regard isolation as an unavoidable aspect of giftedness. Even the brightest, most talented children need others just as much as anyone else does. Frequently they feel pressured to figure out everything on their own, and often they think that asking for help represents a failing on their part. Yet they want and need to ask for help and to get some honest feedback. These children need support—not just from the teacher, but also from their classmates.

It's a sad thing to see an older gifted child struggling on a project alone, afraid even to ask for assistance or to consult peers for fear of rejection or ridicule. Often, these fears are unjustified, based on a lack of experience in sharing with others. This is one of the reasons we believe in early intervention. Gifted children need to learn that, although some people may disagree with their ideas or find them offbeat, others will welcome fresh approaches and may have constructive criticisms to help improve them. They need to learn this as early in life as possible. If we don't teach them this vital lesson, how can we blame them later when they become uncommitted or underachieving, content with using only a fraction of their true talents?

This is why it's important that gifted students in the preschool and primary grades have opportunities to share their work in a relaxed, informal, and cooperative atmosphere. All through this chapter, we've emphasized the importance of encouraging students to strike out in new directions, to test new ground, to challenge the assumption that there is a right or wrong answer for everything. At the point of application and evaluation, it's vital that you maintain this same attitude and encourage it in your students.

"Are these processes and activities applicable only to environmental studies, history, and culture?"

No. As you'll see in Chapters 5 and 6, many of the basic principles from which these activities evolve also apply to other subject areas—language, visual, and performing arts, and math and science as well. By the time you finish reading Chapter 6, you'll see that although the activities may differ to some extent, many of the processes translate easily from one subject to another. They also provide effective means for integrating subjects.

"What can I do if some students excel in these imaginative activities while others find them difficult or uninteresting?"

Rather than anticipate that children won't be interested, remember that in a diverse student body, many children have difficulties adjusting to instructional methods. Some children may not know that there are ways to approach learning that draw on their interests and abilities. Or they may think they don't have abilities worth applying. Creative children may be sitting in your classroom right now, barely using their talents! Some children who have never shown a spark of interest in your class may suddenly come alive.

Although your students will move at different speeds and in different directions, you can inspire all of the children in your classroom. Give them enough preparation time *before* the activities begin, then share and display student work at regular intervals.

Conclusion

Nothing excites young children more than discovery! The first lessons they learn are a function of this fundamental process and provide a powerful and natural incentive to explore. The entire world of the young child is creative—undivided and uncompartmentalized. Each new discovery leads to further inquiry and research, which in turn lead to more discovery.

The principle underlying many of the processes in this chapter is the simple act of *pretending*—of placing children in roles or giving them opportunities to invent stories and situations around the facts they are learning. This is a familiar process to young children. And it's this critical act of invention that enables young students—particularly gifted ones—to make unique discoveries that transform them into enthusiastic learners.

References and Resources

Barth, Edna. *Turkeys, Pilgrims, and Indian Corn: The Story of the Thanksgiving Symbols.* New York: Clarion Books, 1975. A thorough treatment of all the legends and symbols of the American harvest celebration, this book is a good reference for studying the early colonial experience and how the first Thanksgiving evolved.

Baylor, Byrd. *I'm in Charge of Celebrations.* Illustrated by Peter Parnall. New York: Aladdin Paperbacks, 1995. Set in the desert, this is the story of a young girl who creates her own celebrations, based on the unique moments and experiences of her daily life. An excellent source for classes on culture.

Bowden, Marcia. *Nature for the Very Young: A Handbook of Indoor and Outdoor Activities.* Illustrated by Marilyn Rishel. New York: John Wiley & Sons, 1989. A lively collection of activities that educate and delight young children, using nature exploration as a catalyst. Designed for home or school.

Bruchac, Joseph. *Between Earth and Sky: Legends of Native American Sacred Places.* Illustrated by Thomas Locker. New York: Harcourt Brace & Co., 1996.

Bruchac draws on his Abenaki heritage to relay an enchanting lesson between uncle and nephew, emphasizing respect for and protection of our world. Locker's accompanying illustrations are wonderful.

Burningham, John. *Hey! Get Off Our Train.* New York: Crown Publishers, 1989. This book by a British author-illustrator received a Parents' Choice Award in 1990. Describes how a young boy climbs aboard a toy train to go on a trip around the world where he encounters, one by one, endangered animals who want to climb on to escape destruction. A charming, surprising ending!

Cech, Maureen. *Globalchild: Multicultural Resources for Young Children.* New York: Addison-Wesley Publishing Co., 1991. Uses a seasonal format (harvest, new year, spring) to introduce a wide range of cultural traditions in music, art, games, food, and other areas and to emphasize the commonalties all people share.

Cimo, Shirley. *The Egyptian Cinderella.* Illustrated by Ruth Heller. New York: HarperCollins, 1989. Beautifully told and illustrated, this is the Cinderella story, re-created and set in the world of ancient Egypt.

Cook, Carole, and Jody Carlisle. *Challenges for Children: Creative Activities for Gifted and Talented Primary Students.* Illustrated by Dave Dillon. West Nyack, NY: The Center for Applied Research in Education, Inc., 1985. Designed for K–3 teachers, this volume offers a unique and vast collection of activities in social studies, language arts, math, and science as well as in specialized areas such as library skills, creative arts, and independent learning. You can select activities to support the curriculum, a specific skill, or a particular content area in meeting the individual needs of talented young children in the classroom.

Craig, Janet. *Wonders of the Rain Forest.* Illustrated by S.D. Schindler. Mahwah, NJ: Troll Associates, 1990. A very helpful introduction to the intricate ecological system of the rain forest. Well written and vividly illustrated.

Eby, Judy W., and Joan F. Smutny. *A Thoughtful Overview of Gifted Education.* White Plains, NY: Longman, 1990. Includes two chapters for teacher and parents that provide a clear conceptual background for understanding creativity and the needs of young gifted children.

Field, Nancy, and Corliss Karasov. *Discovering Wolves: A Nature Activity Book.* Illustrated by Cary Hunkel. Middleton, WI: Dog-Eared Publications, 1991. An adventurous journey into the world of wolves and an outstanding contribution to environmental awareness for young children. Offers 18 fun, thought-provoking activities that encourage critical thinking on the subject of the wolf. Produced in cooperation with the Timber Wolf Alliance.

Fogarty, Robin, and Kay Opeka. *Start Them Thinking: A Handbook of Classroom Strategies for the Early Years.* Palatine, IL: The IRI Group, 1988. Includes a wide range of activities for K–3 children that develop skills in critical and creative thinking, problem-solving, and decision-making. The activities are easy to integrate into the existing curriculum.

Harness, Cheryl. *Three Young Pilgrims.* New York: Aladdin Paperbacks, 1992. This book draws young readers into the everyday life of the Allerton family as they cope with the challenges of being among the first settlers at Plymouth. Includes Harness's vivid illustrations and many useful facts.

Hayes, Joe. *Watch Out for Clever Women!/¡Cuidado con las Mujeres Astutas!* Illustrated by Vicki Trego Hill. El Paso, TX: Cinco Puntos Press, 1994. An entertaining collection of Latin folk tales in English and Spanish, featuring amazingly clever women who repeatedly manage to save the day. Hayes is a recognized raconteur from the American Southwest.

Kindersley, Barnabas, and Anabel Kindersley. *Children Just Like Me: A Unique Celebration of Children Around the World.* New York: DK Publishing/United Children's Fund, 1995. Explores cultural commonalities and differences—as well as the unique challenges and advantages—of children from all over the world. Young students will enjoy the book's perspective of children speaking to other children.

Levine, Ellen. *If Your Name Was Changed at Ellis Island.* Illustrated by Wayne Parmenter. New York: Scholastic, 1993. An engaging question-and-answer book for young readers about Ellis Island and the immigrants who came through there. Full of illustrations and personal accounts.
———. *If You Traveled West in a Covered Wagon.* New York: Scholastic, 1986. Another very useful and informative question-and-answer book for young readers. Traces the life and experiences of a pioneer traveling to Oregon in the 1840s.

Martin, Rafe. *The Boy Who Lived with the Seals.* Illustrated by David Shannon. New York: G.P. Putnam's Sons, 1993. A poignant retelling, enhanced by luminous paintings, of a classic Chinook Indian legend about a boy who disappears one day while playing by the river.
———. *The Rough-Face Girl.* Illustrated by David Shannon. New York: G.P. Putnam's Sons, 1992. This haunting and richly illustrated version of the Cinderella story comes from Algonquin Indian sources.

McDermott, Gerald. *Arrow to the Sun: A Pueblo Indian Tale.* New York: Puffin Books, 1977. Through very original and colorful illustrations, the author relates an inspiring Pueblo tale of a child's meeting with his father—the sun.

McGovern, Ann. *If You Grew Up with Abraham Lincoln.* Illustrated by George Ulrich. New York: Scholastic, 1992. A very imaginative—and historically accurate—book that invites children into everyday life in the frontiers of Kentucky and Indiana, the prairie town of New Salem, Illinois, and the city of Springfield.

Milios, Rita. *Imagi-size: Activities to Exercise Your Students' Imagination.* Dayton, OH: Pieces of Learning, 1993. A rich collection of activities for first—fourth graders and a wonderful source for visual learners who enjoy using their imaginations to solve problems. Integrate the activities into existing lessons or use them as readiness activities for other content.

Miller, Frances A. *Eliza Lucas Pinckney.* Castro Valley, CA: Quercus, 1987. A short biography from American history, this is a good story-time book about the early colonists of South Carolina.

Milord, Susan. *Hands Around the World.* Charlotte, VT: Williamson Publishing, 1992. Designed to expand cultural awareness and global respect, this volume is packed full of activities and information about cultures and races around the world. Includes an appendix listing organizations of interest and suppliers of multicultural materials.

Musgrove, Margaret. *Ashanti to Zulu: African Traditions.* Illustrated by Leo and Diane Dillon. New York: Dial Books for Young Readers, 1976. An ABC book that depicts 26 of Africa's ethnic groups and communicates that vast continent's rich cultural heritage. Beautifully written; colorfully and elegantly illustrated.

Sewall, Marcia. *People of the Breaking Day.* New York: Atheneum, 1990. Masterfully re-creates the world of the Wampanoag people, who lived in southeastern Massachusetts when the Pilgrims landed. A wonderful companion book to *The Pilgrims of Plimoth.*
———. *The Pilgrims of Plimoth.* New York: Atheneum, 1986. Using the Pilgrims' style of speech, the author has vividly re-created the voyage to the New World and the daily life in the early, foundational years of Plymouth Colony.

Sisk, Dorothy. *Creative Teaching of the Gifted.* New York: McGraw-Hill, 1987. A useful resource for teachers and parents that offers a conceptual understanding of how to meet the creative needs of talented children. Includes a range of helpful ideas and examples.

Smutny, Joan Franklin, Kathleen Veenker, and Stephen Veenker. *Your Gifted Child: How to Recognize and Develop the Special Talents in Your Child from Birth to Age Seven.* New York: Ballantine Books, 1989. Focusing on the needs of gifted children from birth to age seven, this book offers creative ideas and practical advice on how to best support talent development in the very young.

Stanish, Bob. *Sunflowering: Thinking, Feeling, and Doing Activities for Creative Expression.* Illustrated by Nancee Volpe. Carthage, IL: Good Apple, 1977. Using "analogy strategies" to develop creative expression, flexibility of thought, and sensitivity in young children, these activities emphasize the use of feelings, metaphors, and imagination to discover and use information in original ways. Includes suggestions for variations and extensions.

Terrell, Sandy. *Roberto's Rainforest.* El Cajon, CA: Interaction Publishers, 1995. This innovative and activity-filled book is a scientific "canoe trip" that allows young naturalists to explore a tropical rain forest in South America.

Torrance, E. Paul. *The Search for Satori and Creativity.* Buffalo, NY: Creative Education Foundation, 1979. A groundbreaking work on the creative process, including a recognition of the Japanese understanding of *satori*—a concept Torrance applies to discovery and invention in the classroom.

Treffinger, Donald J. *Encouraging Creative Learning for the Gifted and Talented: A Handbook of Methods and Techniques.* Los Angeles: National/State Leadership Training Institute on the Gifted and Talented, 1980. A comprehensive study of critical and creative problem-solving by a major creativity researcher, this book offers many useful ideas and strategies to promote original and higher-level thinking in talented students.

Waters, Kate. *Sarah Morton's Day: A Day in the Life of a Pilgrim Girl.* Photographs by Russ Kendall. New York: Scholastic, 1989. With detailed photographs from Plymouth Plantation, this story of the daily life and duties of a young girl makes the historical period far more accessible and interesting to primary-age students.

Weller, Frances Ward. *I Wonder If I'll See a Whale.* Illustrations by Ted Lewin. New York: Philomel Books, 1991. An engaging book about a young girl's seafaring trip to find a whale. Young readers encounter the great but gentle "monster" of the sea and learn much about its daily living habits.

Young, Ed. *Lon Po Po.* New York: Philomel Books, 1989. A fairy tale told in exquisite detail, this is a dramatic rendition of the Little Red Riding Hood story, set in China.

YOUR CHILD'S CULTURAL HERITAGE

Child's Name: _____

Dear Parent/Caregiver:

In school, we're discussing the children's cultural heritage. Your child will want to know many things about his/her ancestors. Here are some questions your child might want to talk about:

- Where was I born? Where were my parents born?
- Where did my ancestors come from? Why did they come here? How did they get here?
- What hardships did they face?
- What language did they speak? Can you teach me any words?
- What customs do we have in our family now that came from our ancestors?
- What can I tell my class about my family heritage? What can I show them to help them learn more about it?

Your child may also want to bring something from his/her cultural heritage to school: a picture, a decoration, or another memento. We promise to take good care of any items and return them on _____ (day and date).

We want to be respectful of each family's customs, beliefs, and culture. Please call me if you have any questions. Thank you for your help.

Teacher's Signature: _____

Phone: _____

ME IN A DIFFERENT CULTURE

My Name: _____

Culture: _____

What would it be like to be part of this culture?
Write or draw your ideas.

CUSTOM OBSERVATION FORM

For Students

My Name: _____

Observe some customs at home or somewhere in your community.
Write or draw about what you observe.

Where I was: _____

What I observed:

5

Promoting Imagination in the Language Arts Curriculum

Beth slumped down in her chair. "We're supposed to write a story by tomorrow, but I can't think of anything. All I know is I don't want to start with 'Once upon a time.'" Sam leaned over and said, "I have an idea of how you can start. Mrs. Rodriguez says you can use pictures in magazines and imagine walking into them. Or just look at a picture and try to imagine what happened there or what's about to happen. I'm going to look at my mom's Audubon *magazine—it always has great animal pictures."*

Juri was reading a new book, Hist Whist and Other Poems for Children, *by e.e. cummings. Without looking up, he said quietly, "Do you know where I get ideas? I read poems, and every poem I read has so many ideas in it—sometimes even one line says as much as a whole story. I like to look at poems. They help me think of things to write about."*

Creative Learning as a Link to Imaginative Thinking

You've just listened in on several gifted second graders during a language arts class. This chapter will explore some of their suggestions in an attempt to answer this question: How do we inspire young children to express themselves creatively?

Our goals are to:

- present creative strategies that stimulate students' imaginations in language arts—poetry, fiction, and biography
- show how integrating the visual, theatrical, and language arts with children's multiple talents serves as a catalyst for children's writing
- guide you in developing creative projects that meet the needs of children at different levels of ability and experience.

While Chapter 4 focused on using creative processes as a link to intellectual discovery, this chapter focuses on creativity as a link to *imaginative* discovery—the world of creative ideas within children.

Integrating the arts, a strategy frequently used in this chapter, is a powerful catalyst for creative work, and one that involves the whole child in the process. It gives children multisensory experiences—images and ideas they can see, hear, feel, and embody, rather than just observe. At many different stages of the creative process, we encourage the mixing of media to achieve this multidimensional experience for children.

Take, for example, a multimedia activity we have conducted with our students, using as a catalyst the Disney film classic, *Fantasia.* The children watch and listen to the segment based on Stravinsky's *The Rite of Spring* that depicts the origins of the universe and follows the progress of the Earth from a molten mass of gases through the passing of the dinosaurs.*

To begin, students focus on the music—the rhythms, melodies, and instruments. They think and talk about how the music makes them feel.

They imagine *themselves* there at the beginning of the earth with the dinosaurs. They write, draw, or paint about how they feel there. We ask the children: "How did you feel watching the beginning of the earth? What was it like to see the dinosaurs? To move around them? To feel their heavy breath? To sense their giant shapes?"

The children move to the music, reenacting the beginning of the earth, embodying the movements of the dinosaurs or of the earth or its elements. After watching the segment, they listen to it again with their eyes closed. Then they either write or draw some of the qualities and images that have come to them.

Each artistic medium adds another layer or dimension to creative work. For gifted children, who respond sensitively to the mixture of visual images and musical sounds, films like *Fantasia* are powerful incentives for creative work. But you don't have to confine yourself to theatrical films or videos. Visual images in paintings and photographs, combined with music audiocassettes, offer textures and colors for environments or characters, helping children formulate creative ideas for self-expression. Georgia O'Keeffe's painting, *Music—Pink and Blue I,* resulted from this kind of multimedia experience. As she explains:**

"I never took one of [teacher] Bement's classes at Columbia University, but one day walking down the hall I heard music from his classroom. Being curious I opened the door and went in. A low-toned record was being played and the students were asked to make a drawing from what they heard. So I sat down and made a drawing, too. Then he played a very different kind of record—a sort of high soprano piece—for another quick

drawing. This gave me an idea that I was very interested to follow later—the idea that music could be translated into something for the eye."

Children don't need to wait until they reach college to benefit from a creative multimedia activity. We've combined art prints and laminated posters of black-and-white nature photographs by Ansel Adams with a variety of music—classical recordings, movie soundtracks, and popular tunes. This enables children to feel and sense a creative work as a live, full-bodied reality. While feeling their way through these different creative media, your students can experiment with writing, drawing, movement, and drama. This process exposes children to a broad range of stimuli and helps them form very specific images and textures for their ideas.

Integrating the Creative Processes to Stimulate Imaginative Thinking

Chapter 4 presented five components of creativity that are essential for nurturing imaginative thinking: fluency, flexibility, originality, elaboration, and evaluation. However, while in the last chapter we focused on these processes separately, here we will integrate them under four general umbrellas: *creative response, creative divergence, creative exploration,* and *creative composition.* Each process emphasizes one particular medium (such as story, painting, music, poetry, or drama) but also combines this with other media to provide a multidimensional catalyst for students' creative responses. The processes are somewhat progressive, but not exclusively so. As the teacher, you can easily pick and choose from among these activities without having to conduct any of them in sequence. The "Taxonomy of Imaginative Thinking" on page 83 gives examples of how you might use these processes in your classroom.

As with the "Taxonomy of Creative Thinking" in Chapter 4, use this more as a general guide than as a formula or recipe. Although the different stages advance in complexity and involvement, we suggest that you select ideas and activities from any of the sequences according to the needs, strengths, and interests of your students. The purpose of this chapter is to help you nurture creative development in *all* of your students,

---

* You'll find some resources related to the activities discussed in this chapter in the "References and Resources" section beginning on page 96, in Appendix B beginning on page 198, and in Appendix C beginning on page 211.
** Georgia O'Keeffe. *Georgia O'Keeffe.* New York: The Viking Press, 1976, p. 14.

Taxonomy of Imaginative Thinking				
Category	*Focus*	*Process*	*Example*	*Outcome*
Creative response	Free response to catalysts	Exposure to art, music, film, theater, photos, and interpretation	Children listen to or read a fairy tale	Awareness and expression of creative ideas
Creative divergence	Variation of an existing creation	Changes made to stories, myths, and art to create new pieces, embellishments	Children create an alternative ending or add another ending to the existing one	Adaptations of existing works
Creative exploration	Discovery of many dimensions to an idea; intuitive insights	Development of an idea in depth through structured imaginative activities	Children consider aspects of the tale in new ways; they experiment with meaning, delve into plot to re-imagine what might happen	Interpretive expression (theatrical productions)
Creative composition	Unusual, novel invention	Creation of unique images and perspectives	Based on the fairy tale, children create a dramatization to illustrate it, compose a poem, write a new story, dramatize new story	Original composition (poems, stories, theater, songs, and art)

enabling you to meet the needs and interests of gifted children as well as those of others.

There are two fundamental needs that young children have in creative work: *catalysts* and *guidance*. Your students need a repertoire of images with which they can improvise and then go on to craft their own inventions. A multimedia approach fulfills this basic need. You should also provide specific steps and sequences that structure and support the students' work. All children, including those who are gifted, need teachers who provide workable contexts and reachable goals. These contexts and goals help children formulate unique ideas and then develop them into poems, stories, theater, or whatever else they choose to create. Without that structure of support, many creative ideas fall by the wayside because the children feel uncertain about how to proceed with them. When there's no one standing by to provide constructive criticism and encouragement, even highly creative children may abandon a promising idea.

We have included here a philosophy for teaching art written by Marji Purcell Gates, an itinerant art teacher. We feel that you can apply its basic principles to all creative teaching.*

* Marji Purcell Gates, Art Teacher, Palatine, IL. Used with permission of Marji Purcell Gates.

Taxonomy of Teaching
(The Job of a Traveling Teacher)

Take a deep breath.
Dramatic entrance; intriguing tools.
Unfurl exemplary creative expression.
Examine its power.
Teach technique.
Tell true stories.
Engage imagination.
Bestow possibilities.
Protect incubation and reflection.
Respect evidence of flow.
Reward striving.
Steady each stumble.
Encourage, nourish, reinforce.
(Learn to whisper, "Yes.")
Bestow more possibilities.
Return to earth.
Clear debris.
Step back.
Promise more.
Tiptoe out.

A Map of Imaginative Activities

As you use ideas from this chapter, we recommend that you:

1. Choose the process you feel will be most accessible to the whole class (and most relevant to the curriculum) to try first; encourage your gifted students to go further with it. One of the advantages to creative processes is that they can easily be adjusted to the talent and experience levels of individual students.

2. Improvise in unique ways with the activities outlined here. This might include combining processes you feel would work together well in your curriculum.

3. Use as many media as you can. Children benefit enormously from the integration of art, video, music, literature, magazines, dramatics, and creative movement.

4. Incorporate these activities into lessons on entirely different subjects. For example, you might have children create stories out of a historical event or write poems on an environmental issue.

Creative Response: Interpretive Expression

A group of children were examining a landscape their teacher had brought in for a language arts class and discussing what they might do in response to it. José fingered his paper and said, "I can't decide whether I want to write about the kinds of animals that live by the river in this picture or make up a story about an eagle who fishes there every day." Tessa said, "I'd rather draw another picture showing what you can't see in this painting—the train that zooms by the river a little farther down—and then write an adventure story." "Not me," said Angie. "I would write about this place from the river's point of view. I would explain how the river came here and tell about all the animals that use it—the muskrat and beaver who swim and build homes near it, the fish who swim through it, the people who fish near it, and the birds who fly above it."

1. Catalysts

José, Tessa, and Angie reveal several different ways young students can make a *creative response* to visual images. To demonstrate how to involve children in creative interpretation—responding to the images they see in unique or unusual ways—we use the *Sky Tree Portfolio* by Thomas Locker and Candace Christiansen as a catalyst.* This portfolio includes 14 paintings of the same tree, made into posters. On the backs are quotations, questions, answers, and scientific information for the children to discuss or ponder.

One poster, for example, is a painting called "The Autumn Tree." This tree is brilliant orange and rust, set against a background of deep blue sky, a cloud, and several busy squirrels scurrying around the trunk. The quote on the back is: "Autumn came. The leaves of the tree turned to gold, orange, and red. Squirrels hurried to store acorns and nuts." The poster then asks children if they ever wondered why the leaves change colors. In the answer, the poster states that chlorophyll—which creates the green color and has helped the tree to create food all summer long—recedes, and red and yellow pigments become more visible. At the bottom of the poster, the

---

* If you don't have the *Sky Tree Portfolio*, you can improvise with your own visual images and add any kinds of questions, quotes, and pieces of useful information you think will most inspire your children.

scientific section explains the process in more detail—how chlorophyll breaks down as the days become shorter, thus enabling the carotene pigments of the leaves to dominate and change the color to red and yellow. This catalyst gives children a broad range of creative choices in responding to the tree.

2. Questions

With encouragement, all the children in the classroom can respond by writing a story, by describing the tree in novel ways, or, if they are inexperienced writers, by creating paintings, drawings, or illustrations of their own. You can help them by asking questions such as these:

- What do you see in the poster?
- What are the colors?
- Does the tree change through the 14 posters? How?
- How can you tell that the tree has gone through the four seasons—winter, spring, summer, fall?
- The tree is on a hill. Could there be any animals or anything else alive on or behind the hill?
- If you were the tree in the picture, how would you feel about the change of seasons? What would you like about autumn? About winter? What wouldn't you like?
- If you were the tree, what stories might you have to tell about the world around you?
- If you were a scientist looking at the tree, what would you notice? Would you notice something different if you were an artist painting, or a photographer taking a picture?
- How does the artist show that the sky and the tree are related to each other?
- How does the artist use light to show differences in seasons?
- How does the artist show "hot"? "Cold"? How does he express "wind"? "Stillness"?
- What sounds do you hear in the painting? Any birds? Is there anyone or anything else that might be making noise around the tree?
- Do you think a tree moves? How would you move like a tree?
- How would you describe the tree in the painting you love best? What words would you use if you wanted to describe it to someone who couldn't see it?

These questions represent different ways you can approach visual images with your students. Feel free to adapt this kind of questioning to your own materials and the children in your class. Keep asking the students for their own perspectives on the different trees: the tree as a part of nature, as a person, as a story. Every student should be able to respond in some way after this exposure to visual images, the questions about them, and follow-up discussions. When children give you words or phrases that describe their experience of the tree, write them on the board. Eventually you'll accumulate a lot of descriptions, and the class can use these to aid or inspire their own drawings or compositions.

3. Responses

Children will naturally respond in different ways. Invite children of different abilities, preferred intelligences, and learning styles to respond in ways that inspire them to be their most creative.

Artistic Responses: Nonwriters or inexperienced writers and the artistically inclined may choose to respond visually through drawing, painting, or collage. These children may also want to focus more on the artistic quality of the painting: How does the artist manage to produce the effects of wind, light, atmosphere—even feeling? Or a child may wish to paint a part of the landscape he imagines exists *beyond* the poster or picture. Your discussion will have already brought oral language into the creative process, but since the emphasis here is on imaginative and interpretive response, you don't need to confine it to language.

Scientific Responses: Children who want to use scientific information in their stories or descriptions will find the *Sky Tree Portfolio* an immediate stimulus for learning more about trees. Many calendars and other sources of nature prints also include science facts on the back. Gifted science buffs in your class could pursue the following questions:

- What makes the leaves turn colors?
- What are clouds?
- How does a tree hold all the heavy snow?
- Where does maple syrup come from?

Children could draw diagrams that illustrate how clouds form or what causes the leaves to change color, write brief descriptions or captions, and write or tell a story from a cloud's or leaf's perspective.*

Kinesthetic Responses: The questions noted earlier also draw on kinesthetic and auditory sensibilities. Students can imagine themselves to be trees. How would it feel to be perched at the top of the hill? To endure all the seasons? To sense the world around them—the constantly shifting movements and the stillness of the dawn? Questions like these will appeal to kinesthetic learners, who may be inclined to perform a scene or embody the tree through dance or creative movement set to music.

4. Expanding the Experience

To expand the experience of visual images, add sound. Bring various audiocassettes of both music and environmental sounds so students can improvise with visual imagery. For example, Vivaldi's *The Four Seasons* combines nicely with other artistic representations of seasonal change. If you add music or sound to the tree image, children will experience yet another dimension—absorbing atmospheres, subtle meanings, and a variety of story lines. Some students will imagine themselves to be the tree, others the wind or cloud, still others the people who live at the bottom of the hill. You could divide the class into children who will be trees and those who will be other elements—wind, snow, clouds. With the music and image present, the children can improvise. The students playing trees can grow, bend with the wind, sag under the weight of the snow; those who play the wind, snow, moonlight, and other elements can weave around the "trees."

You can extend this further with other activities—more writing and painting. Creative movement and drama always inspire imaginative thinking in children who feel comfortable in this kinesthetic mode. Those who don't can still imagine themselves in particular roles without actually moving to demonstrate or interpret the process.

---

* Chapter 6 includes more explicit ideas on using the *Sky Tree Portfolio* for science exploration. See pages 109–112.

Creative Divergence: Alternative Fairy Tales

Lakesha was brimming over with excitement. Her class was doing something new—making fairy tales into stories of their own. "I'd like to do 'The Three Little Pigs,'" she said. "Maybe I'd make the pigs big instead of little, or maybe I would make the wolf nice so that one smart pig could talk him out of hurting them."

"Not me," replied Hai-Ping. "I want to do Cinderella. I'd make Cinderella run away from her mean stepmother and stepsisters into the woods. I'd pretend that she found a dog in the woods, a dog without a home like herself. And I'd pretend that it was the prince's dog who was lost and that she helped him find his way home and that's how she met the prince. Then the fairy godmother would come to help Cinderella get a nice dress for the ball because she did this good thing for the prince's dog. When Cinderella got to the ball, the prince would say, 'I know who you are—you're the one who found my dog.' And they'd fall in love and get married."

"But what about the slipper?" asked Nate, who was listening to Hai-Ping's story. "I like the slipper part." "Well," said Lakesha, who had momentarily forgotten her pigs and become thoroughly absorbed in Hai-Ping's story, "you could pretend that Cinderella had boots on when she was in the woods. Maybe when she took the dog to the prince's house she got scared and ran away and left her boot behind. So when she came to the ball, he had all the ladies try the boot on and then Cinderella said, 'Hey, that's my boot!' And it was."

These children are using *creative divergence* to invent stories of their own. Once started, possibilities and options expand, and the children begin creating alternatives to stories they know well. One of the most enjoyable ways to do this, especially for primary-age children, is to use fairy tales or myths. However, because many young children love these stories as they are, assure students that you will not be replacing the originals. All you will ask is for them to think of *other* Little Red Riding Hoods, Cinderellas, and Three Bears besides the ones they already know.

1. Catalysts

There are many delightful examples of "fractured" fairy tales you could use. Three that we recommend are:

- *Pondlarker* by Fred Gwynne (a creative alternative to the frog prince story)
- *The True Story of the Three Little Pigs! by A. Wolf* (as told to Jon Scieszka)
- *Little Red Riding Hood: A Newfangled Prairie Tale* by Lisa Campbell Ernst.

All three present completely new versions of the stories and, in so doing, alter the tales in interesting ways. The wolf in Scieszka's tale is not so big or so bad. The grandmother in Ernst's "prairie tale" is not the feeble little creature we find in the traditional Red Riding Hood story. And the frog in *Pondlarker* decides, after a long search for the princess of his dreams, that he'd rather return to live in his happy little pond than mess around with finicky princesses who hurl insults at frogs!

2. Questions

Reading such books with the children will suggest all sorts of possibilities for diverging from well-known tales. It may help if you also read the traditional versions, so that both renditions will be fresh in their minds. After reading the stories aloud, ask probing questions. Here are some for Ernst's *Little Red Riding Hood*:

- What's unusual about this story?
- Who is different in this story? Red Riding Hood? The wolf? The grandmother? How are they different?
- What parts of this story don't exist in the other one?
- What events occur in both versions? How are these events alike? How are they different?
- Does the new version make you feel different? How?
- What do you think the writer is trying to say in the new story?
- Do you like the new version as much as the older one?

3. Responses

This line of questioning will help children identify where changes occurred and also give them ideas about where further changes are possible. Next, see what the students can do to make the story different. Finally, invite them to share their stories. This sharing will help young storytellers see how they can alter the characters or plot to transform one story into a different one.

This process accomplishes two goals simultaneously. First, it's a wonderful way to teach children about the basic elements of a good story (character, plot, conflicts, and solutions). Second, it gives the children opportunities to exercise their own story-making powers.

Create a class story. Before giving students the assignment of creating their own version of a fairy tale, you may need to create one—in abbreviated form—with the whole class. Gifted children will most likely not require this preparation; you can excuse them from sitting through this process by asking them to start on their own alternative fairy tales right away. For the rest of the class, we would advise an activity where everyone *together* experiments with one tale.

Change characters. Begin by explaining that children can change the characters *or* the plot and affect the story. In looking at *The Three Little Pigs,* the main characters are the pigs and the Big Bad Wolf. Ask the class to change the descriptions of those characters. For example, the pigs could be big and mean, the wolf simpering and frail.

Once the children have changed the characters, ask, "How would this change the story? How would the wolf approach the pigs' houses? How would the pigs respond to the wolf?" As the children respond, write their answers on the board.

When you get to the end of the story, ask children to write or draw their own ending, keeping it private. Afterwards, they can share their responses and the class will see how many different responses are possible, even when they all have similar characters and plot. Through this activity, students will understand how the simple process of changing characters will give them an alternative story.

Change the plot. Another approach is to focus on plot first. An example is Hai-Ping's story of Cinderella: No dramatic changes in characters emerge, but the plot takes a turn when Cinderella runs away from the home of her stepmother and stepsisters.

Children can choose to preserve the essence of the story in terms of characters, atmosphere, and meaning, but arrive there in a different way—with a contemporary perspective, or through a different cultural lens. An example of this is *The Rough-Face Girl* by Rafe Martin, a story based on Algonquin sources that has a plot similar to that of the Cinderella fairy tale. Other examples include Shirley Cimo's *The Egyptian Cinderella* and Ed Young's *Lon Po Po*, a Chinese version of *Little Red Riding Hood*. Bring in a few of these stories so children can see other ways of creating their own alternative tales. Children from minority cultures will especially enjoy this.

Create conflict. Some of the choices children make may take the conflict out of the story. If, for example, they have the pigs and wolf become friends, then there will no longer be any suspense in the tale. This will not be a problem as long as the children find something else to take its place. In the example on page 86, Nate still wanted Hai-Ping to include the slipper part of the Cinderella story. Nate was probably missing the suspense created around the slipper—the possibility that the prince might not find Cinderella and that she might continue to serve her mean stepmother and stepsisters.

To get at this idea of conflict, talk to the children about what excites them in the original fairy tales. What keeps them listening? Ask questions such as:

• What made you feel excited when you heard/read about Cinderella?
• What's your favorite part of the story? Why?
• While you listen to the story, what are you hoping will happen to Cinderella?

As they begin to think of ideas for their own fairy tales, ask the children to create a feeling of excitement similar to what they experienced when they heard the original versions—something that will make their readers keep asking, "What happens next?" It's a good idea to work through an example together. You could present a scenario where the three pigs and the wolf are friends. Then you could have the class create a new problem or conflict and describe the characters' resulting adventures. This would make a new story—another version just as exciting and adventurous as the traditional one.

Then move to having children create new fairy tales individually or in small groups. Nonwriters can dictate their stories or draw illustrations of some of their favorite scenes.

Share stories. Once the children finish their stories, they can begin to share them with each other. This should be fun and will spark humor in the class. The stories don't have to be long, elaborate creations. The process is designed simply to give children experience manipulating one idea in order to make an entirely different creative concept—something professional writers often do. Students will realize, "Wow! I made this story out of that one, and they are very different stories!" Not only is this an imaginative process, but it builds the children's confidence in their own ability to invent one story out of another.

4. Expanding the Experience

In order to convert this experience into a multimedia one, you can involve the children in both art and drama activities as extensions to their stories. Give them plenty of choice in determining what other dimensions they would like to add. You may find all sorts of hidden talents in your students as you go through this process with them. Musical children may like to compose something—a song or other short musical number—or even create a dance that evokes images from the story. Others may prefer the visual arts—sketching out illustrations or creating a painting or mural, a distillation of their story through a specific set of images. The theatrically inclined may prefer to dramatize their stories using either a narrator and mime or chamber theater techniques (these are described in "Creative Exploration: Chamber Theater and Playwriting," beginning on page 89).

You'll need to supervise these group extensions somewhat. Be sure that the children work well together and don't distract the rest of the class. Suggest alternatives: For skits, the children could narrate their own stories, leaving the dialogue to actors, or one child could read his story with several others miming the action. Other children in the class can then discuss how the story changed from the original and what they liked about it. The goal is to have a variety of new stories and different media for their expression: dramatizations, illustrations, written narratives, paintings, shoe box dioramas of key scenes, songs, or whatever else the children may wish to create.

Creative Exploration: Chamber Theater and Playwriting

Tanya and Will are chatting about their current favorite books. "I really like Charlotte's Web," *says Tanya. "It's the best story. I wish I could never be finished with it." Will replies, "I think there's a movie of it. You could see the whole story again." Chloe, the class actor, jumps in with another suggestion. "Why don't you make your own play of* Charlotte's Web?" *Tanya groans, "Kids can't just make a real play—and who could memorize a whole book?" But Chloe persists: "It's not a big deal if you do it like they did that play at the community center. It's called chamber theater and somebody's the narrator, and other kids are the actors, and they just choose scenes they like and read their parts on stage. It's really fun and it's really easy!"*

Chamber theater, sometimes called reader's theater, is a very effective way to instill in young children a deeper understanding of the elements of story—character development, plot, and fictional environments. By embodying segments of a full-length book, as Chloe proposes—selecting passages to narrate and perform for an audience—children acquire insights about the creative machinery of literature that they might not gain otherwise. You could also ask the children to break up into groups, and choose smaller books or stories to translate into dramatic form for the rest of the class. This process of creative exploration is an excellent foundation for the students' own story inventions—developing full-bodied characters and believable plots, conflicts, and resolutions.

1. Catalysts

Try a chamber theater version of a book or collection of stories. One child can take all the narration lines. (There's no need to include the "said" parts.) Each of the other children can take a character. The narrator can probably take the role of leader. Gifted children who are quite young—even first graders—will be ready to take the narrator's part. With younger children, you can do this yourself the first time.

After you divide the class into groups, have each group choose a different book or, if the class wants to tackle a longer work, different sections of one book. Either way, have the students familiarize themselves with the book, discuss it, and share ideas.

A word to the wise: The first time you try this, don't get too ambitious and choose too much to perform. Perhaps a shorter book would be best until you and the children become experienced in the medium.

2. Questions

The first phase of this process is to identify the main elements of the story or book. To facilitate this, ask the children some fundamental questions to focus their thoughts, such as:

- What is this story about?
- Who are the main characters?
- Where does it take place and when?
- What are the problems that the main characters face? How do they solve these problems?
- What are some of the most exciting parts? Why are they so exciting?

Choose a child in each group to record answers to the questions. If the whole class is doing one book, you can write their responses on the board for reference.

3. Responses

Through your questions, you're encouraging your students to think analytically about the book and thereby heighten their own awareness of the key elements that hold the story together. This in turn will help them choose passages to enact in chamber theater.

Choose critical passages. Based on the questions, help students choose the chapters or passages that seem most critical to the book or story. For a book like *Charlotte's Web,* this probably includes the first few chapters (introducing the major characters and problem), middle chapters that are critical to the story development, and finally the chapters that solve the problem, particularly the last three or four. Have the children select the sentences and dialogue and descriptive statements in each chapter for the stage performance. Reassure children that no one has to memorize lines. Explain that they will do one of two things:

- plan a dramatization in which actors read lines or use their own words to reenact the scenes, or

• write narration for scenes that the actors will enact as the narrator reads them.

As the children work through the book or story, keep them focused on the important or critical moments in the development of the plot. They could begin by listing the memorable scenes—those that most interested them as readers or listeners. After the group has compiled the list, have them put it in chronological order and review it. Tell students to look at each scene and ask themselves:

• Is this an exciting scene? Why?
• Is this scene necessary to understand the plot?
• How important is it?
• How could we act it out? If we don't do that, is there a way we can retell the scene using mime and narration?
• What will we gain by keeping this scene?
• What will we lose if we don't use this scene?

Somebody in each group should keep a record of the selections the children wish to perform. Circulate among the different groups and mediate disagreements where they arise. Put a limit on the number of scenes allowed for each group. Otherwise, the process will quickly become complicated and unmanageable.

Choose roles. Each group can choose one child to be the narrator, and then the students can choose the characters they would most like to dramatize, read, or mime. The unique circumstances of your classroom (time constraints, number of children, students' needs and interests) will require you to be adaptable in determining children's roles. If more than one child wants to play a particular role, you can either audition students for the role or have them take turns. If you have more students than roles, consider distributing the role of narrator to several good readers. Another possibility is to expand the enactments by having children briefly mime parts of the plot that will *not* be dramatized, with narrators summarizing what happens in the intervals between dramatized selections. This solves two problems at once—what to do with children who don't yet have parts, and how to inform the audience about what has occurred between scenes. Some children may also wish to provide the sound effects or work on props.

Become the characters. Chamber theater production encourages students to take ownership of a story in depth. They are impelled to do far more than merely read or write a brief summary. A kinesthetic learning process is at work here. In order to embody the story vividly, students have to become thoroughly familiar with the characters whose lines they deliver. Ask questions to get at:

• specific characteristics ("Where do you sleep? What do you eat? How do you move around?")
• the emotions that drive the character ("What are you worried about? What do you want more than anything? Why do you want that? If you could be whatever you wanted, what would you be?")
• the character's history ("How long have you been a spider? What do you do every day? What do you enjoy about being a spider?")
• how the character feels about the other characters and what they do ("What do you think about this new pig who has moved in?").

As they probe the characters, children begin to make the story *their* story. By internalizing the story in this way, they gain an inside knowledge. Their discovery becomes a dynamic process rather than a finished product.

Stage it simply. Encourage the children to keep their staging clear and uncomplicated and to use simple props, costumes, and sound effects. Circulate among the different groups as they work, offering suggestions on staging and the selection of lines as well as on summaries that operate as transitions from scene to scene or chapter to chapter.

Place the narrator to the side of the dramatic action. Also, groups who plan to use any props, costumes, or sound effects should assign someone to keep a list of any items required for the production. Remind the class that the main purpose of props, costumes, and sound is to *suggest* an environment, to *evoke* (give the feeling or sense of) an atmosphere that will inspire the imagination of both performers and audience.

Keep the performance relaxed. When the class reaches the performance stage, be as informal and relaxed as you can, and encourage the children to do the same. This process is not intended to lead to a flawless theater event, but to expand students' experience and understanding of the great art of story-making.

Be positive as the children perform. If a child makes a mistake, minimize it and offer encouragement. Before the performances begin, explain to children that the dramatic process is a way to give stories a new life, not to criticize! After each performance, ask the performing group what new things they discussed about the story. Then ask the rest of the class for their comments and questions.

4. Expanding the Experience

When children attempt to develop their own stories in this way, the chamber theater experience will generate untold benefits. Your students will create more developed characters—and plots that evolve organically from those characters. With performance experience, the children will develop a habit of examining issues of motivation in characters and how this relates to the creation of conflict and suspense in a good story.

To build an effective bridge from this kind of theatrical work to creative writing, try this activity:

Create a new setting. With the props and costumes used for their production, have the groups create a setting for a different imaginary scene. You could say: "Using your table and a couple of chairs, make a *setting*—a place—for another imaginary scene. Think about the people who will be in this setting. Is it a room in someone's home? A desk in someone's classroom? A cab on a semitrailer truck? Seats in a theater? Who uses this space? What does that character look like? How old is he? What is she doing? What is happening here?"

Depending on the time you have available, you could give children a day to think about this and plan any other props or items in the classroom they want use (or others they wish to bring from home). Give the children time to set up their environment. Ask them to keep it simple, but to use very specific objects that fit the kind of characters they imagine in the space. To help them expand their imaginative thinking, ask questions about the space and the characters who occupy it—their history, their feelings, what is happening in their lives. Use the props to spark ideas, too. You might ask: "Where did the lady buy that shawl? What does the boy do with his kite?"

Generate ideas. After children have had time for their ideas to begin taking real shape, ask a question such as this: "What has *just happened* in this space?" Children can either write their ideas or discuss them openly in class. Assure students that there is not one "right" answer. The point of this process is for them to see how many different ideas can come from a single visual image. This should be as fun as it is productive. The children will feed off of each other's ideas and delight in seeing how many different interpretations are available from one simple setting.

Write stories. By the end of the process, each child will have a number of scenarios or potential story starters. Explain that in sharing ideas about the characters and what they are doing in these fictional settings, children have created the beginnings of stories—stories *they* can develop. All the elements are there: a specific setting, characters, and the beginning of a plot. These are the elements they have just explored in the chamber theater process. Now, they can translate this understanding into a writing process. Let children know, however, that they should feel free to make changes if they want a different sort of story starter. For example, they might want to add or remove characters or tell more about "what has just happened."

Students may choose to work alone or in a group. This depends a great deal on their needs and experience. Gifted children often like to work alone; others may need the support of their peers in developing ideas. All of your students will enjoy entering a new world of settings and challenges for their creative work.

If you find the idea of creating a setting too complicated or time-consuming, students can get story starters from many other sources: paintings, photographs, magazines, newspapers, comic strips, history books, even poems. You can practice with your students. Show them paintings, images, or simple news articles and ask them to take what they see and imagine a beginning of a story. You could also make up some of your own story starters based on the curriculum you are currently working on and the interests of the children. All you need are some interesting characters, a specific setting, and at least the beginning of some dramatic action. Then turn the children loose!

Creative Composition: Free-Verse Poetry

Mrs. Gromicek's second graders were studying biographies of great inventors and pioneers. They had already read together and explored and discussed the lives of pioneers in various fields, what made these people unique, and how each one dealt with obstacles. Now Mrs. Gromicek was giving the children an opportunity to use this information to create an original product or idea. She asked the class for ideas. Rafael suggested, "I want to write a poem. But I want it to tell a story like a picture—not with lots of facts or dates." Alyson sighed, "But I don't like finding rhyming words. I can think of the story, but I could never find all the words to rhyme." Tim, who also loved poetry, piped up, "You don't have to rhyme, you know. A lot of poems don't rhyme at all, and they're great." Alyson mused, "So I could write a poem about Amelia Earhart flying around the world in an airplane, and I wouldn't have to worry about rhymes?" The answer, of course, was yes!

Creative composition uses many of the other processes already described in this chapter. It *responds* to many stimuli and reinterprets their varied images and textures. It *diverges* from and improvises with products already made, embellishing and altering them. It also *explores* the inner depths of a painting, a book, or a story to locate other meanings than the more apparent ones. Creative composition draws upon all these processes and then invents something unique—something more than a variation, a version, an interpretation, or a response.

1. Catalysts

You can design a creative composition process within any general topic you happen to be working on. In the scenario we use here, the children focus on the life stories of famous pioneers and inventors as catalysts for composing free-verse poems.

Free-verse poetry is an ideal medium for enabling children to develop original compositions. Gifted children especially enjoy the process of creating vivid images in poetic form. Poetry, like painting, combines feelings, textures, and ideas to create unique, multidimensional visions of human experience. Poetry has the power to help children distill their deepest perceptions and thoughts; it also acts as a springboard to other creative work. Children can use their poems as

"seeds" for other inventions—for paintings, songs, stories, and dramatizations.

Expose children to poetry. Teaching free-verse poetry is a simple process, especially in the primary grades.

When Alyson expressed a keen interest in writing a poem on Amelia Earhart, Mrs. Gromicek distributed some free-verse poems as examples. She read one or two brief ones to the class and then led a discussion on how poets compose lines of different (and often uneven) lengths, vary the rhythms, and use no rhymes (although there may be similar sounds within the lines). Mrs. Gromicek also read a few poems written by children she'd taught in previous years. One of the poems was a response to a Monet painting, and she showed the class the painting as she read the poem aloud to them.

Create a joint poem. Working as a group to create a poem gives children the benefit of hearing a variety of ways they can use language to express ideas.

Mrs. Gromicek picked up a poster on Amelia Earhart and asked the students what they saw in this picture of a woman standing by her airplane, preparing for her solo flight around the world. She asked for one sentence describing the feeling, the atmosphere, the color, the excitement, or whatever else struck the children. One child began tentatively. Mrs. Gromicek wrote down the sentence and then remarked, "There is the beginning of our free-verse poem. Now can I have another? What else do you see? What do you imagine you might hear or feel if you were hiding in the back of that plane?"

Emboldened by the first child's offering, more children responded. Soon, practically everyone in the group interested in Amelia Earhart had contributed a phrase. Then Mrs. Gromicek asked for a title for the new poem. Some discussion ensued before the children decided on "Flight to the Skies."

2. Questions

As with all the processes we have explored, asking questions helps children find and structure their ideas. Like Mrs. Gromicek, you could use a series of questions to set some general, but loose, guidelines for children's own representations. As they respond and explore, be sure to have available plenty of books, magazines, biographies, autobiographies, historical fiction, pictures, posters, poems, and stories that offer a rich variety of images and perspectives for the children's compositions. (Several are suggested in "References and Resources," beginning on page 96.) Returning to the example of great people, you might ask questions such as these:

- Who is the person you want to be? Why?
- What was her contribution to the world?
- What qualities about her do you most admire? Was she brave? Determined? Adventurous?
- What challenges and obstacles did she overcome?
- Would you like to have known this person? Why or why not?
- What do admire most about this person? Why?
- What facts about this person's life do you find most important?
- If you were to think of this person in colors, what colors would they be?
- If you were to think of this person as music, what would it sound like?
- What pictures, stories, or paintings help you find what was special and important about this person?

3. Responses

After the children have written their poems, ask them to share their work. If they seem reluctant at first, you can read a few poems first and talk about the different images and feelings the poems evoke. Since there is no pressure for a rhyme scheme at the ends of lines, most students will feel free to manipulate the form in the way they want and will probably enjoy sharing their work.

In Mrs. Gromicek's class, one student decided to write a free-verse poem describing what was in the picture. Another child wanted to talk to Amelia Earhart as she stood by her airplane and write a poem that resembled an interview for a newspaper. Another preferred to be the plane itself and to talk about his life and the feats he will perform for this famous lady who flies so daringly in the sky.

Following are a few examples of free-verse poems written by primary-age children in "Worlds of Wisdom and Wonder," a program for gifted children.* The poems illustrate how talented young children can write from unique perspectives, creating images that are vivid and even rare:

Mona Lisa
Jessica, Grade 1

Maybe her smile
means she's sitting there
smiling and thinking,
or maybe just daydreaming,
or just thinking.
She's dressed up like
she who's going to temple.
Mysterious smiles,
mysterious looks, but
Da Vinci must have fallen
in love with Mona Lisa
and painted
a picture of her.

Lighthouse by the Ocean
Maria, Grade 2

I am a lighthouse
by a beautiful lake with
flowers floating on it.
The water is swooshing and swaying,
waves, you can hear,
and seashells, when you pick them up
to your ear,
you hear the ocean inside.
There are mountains of rocks
that you can climb on,
and flowers bloom above.
People fish and go on boats
above the water,
and sometimes seagulls
fly above.
It is very quiet.

Here Is There
Craig, Grade 2

When here is there,
Then there is here.
When they come together
There is here and so is here
Then something is taken from the past,
But if here is there and so is there
Then something is taken from our time.

* The "Worlds of Wisdom and Wonder" program is conducted through The Center for Gifted at National-Louis University, Evanston, Illinois. These poems were written by students in creative writing classes taught by Joan Franklin Smutny and are reprinted here with the permission of the children and their families.

The Winter Trees
Alex, Grade 3

As the wind fluttered across the open land
the trees bent down as if they were soldiers
Once, as the wind passed,
snow began to touch earth
After several months,
the snow melted
and warmness came
The kids came
and played
Some kids climbed on the tree
while others played on the ground
Then all the leaves
fell to the ground
Snow fell
to the earth
A new season had begun

Response to *Music—Pink and Blue I*
(a painting by Georgia O'Keeffe)
Eric, Grade 3

music is a wonderful song
notes soaring, rests roaring
a painting is the one we are pouring
to make our notes and rests and stops
we can find it in our hearts
a painting, a note ready to sound
a tune, the colors and skies and chicken pot pies
a rhythm, the painting's beat,
 is always a special treat
get ready, now we make a staff
that is a painting, a musical painting

Giants
Marissa, Grade 3

These giants roam the earth
In numbers very few.
They seem as if to touch the sky.
Hunted by man for their
precious ivory tusks.
All wrinkled and gray,
A breathtaking sight.

4. Expanding the Experience

When you use creative composition in this way, you'll find *all* your children eager—and able—to compose in vivid and evocative language. If you

wish to extend your students' work to other media, encourage them to use their free-verse compositions as catalysts. The class can do a multimedia project around the poems—including stories, drawings, diagrams, maps, cartoons, songs, and dramatizations. Encourage children to choose whatever media they enjoy using and they feel best enhances their poems. You might ask: "What would be the best way to build on the feeling in your poem? What will help you share the mood of your poem? How can you show that heavy air? How can you make us feel that cold, fresh rain? Can you do it with a painting? A cartoon? A story? Another poem? A song? A skit?"

When creating these new media, children don't need to confine themselves to merely *representing* the poem. They can also *complement* it in interesting ways. For example, take the poem "Mona Lisa" by Jessica, a first grader (page 93). Jessica could decide to write a story on what Mona Lisa is daydreaming about.

Sharing Creativity with Others

Children love to share the work they have done, especially creative productions. It validates their worth as originators and makes them feel that they have something unique and valuable to contribute. You can be creative yourself in orchestrating a variety of opportunities for your students to share their work:

- Ask the children for their ideas on how they would like to share their projects.
- Display on your bulletin boards pictures, poems, stories, and other works created by your students. If you have magnetic chalkboards, you can display their work quickly using strong magnets.
- Invite younger or older children into the class to see your students' creations.
- Have each group present their work to the rest of the class or to another class at your grade level.
- Create opportunities for the performers in your class to present their chamber theater pieces, songs, dances, poems, and stories for the school.
- Invite parents to come in and see the children's work.

- Start a newsletter in your class where students can regularly report on their creative accomplishments. Distribute the newsletter to the rest of the school, as well as to parents.
- Present students' work at a Grandparents' Day event, or take the completed creations "on the road" to a hospital or senior center.
- Make a video of the children's work. Show the video at an open house or another appropriate schoolwide event. If your students have pen pals, make copies that they can send in the mail.

If your school or district has a Web site, you might also share examples of students' creative work online for the whole world to see.

Questions and Answers

"I don't have much experience in the arts. Can I still teach using these processes?"

Yes! You are not training a child to become an author, a painter, or a performing artist. Rather, you are using the arts to offer a wonderful way for children to freely explore their creative potential. The point of creative work is not the product, but the process of making thought more flexible. Start on a scale that feels manageable for you, and encourage your students to have fun!

"How can I set tangible goals for projects that seem so open-ended?"

It depends on how you are using these activities. Most teachers will want to integrate them into the existing curriculum. If you do this, your goals are already established. If you don't, you can set tangible goals that still provide freedom for children to improvise.

For example, you may want the children to identify and understand the different elements of a story (characters, plot, setting, theme, and so forth). After introducing these elements and discussing them (perhaps within the context of a story or movie), you could allow your students to explore them creatively by inventing alternative fairy tales, mini-dramatizations, or visual representations. Or you may wish to have students analyze the stages of a story: the beginning (often a descriptive paragraph), the introduction to the main characters, the conflict, the climax, and the ending.

With students who choose to work more independently, you may wish to create a contract that will help them commit to their goals.

"What's the best way to manage situations in which children want to work in groups?"

We recommend grouping children according to their strengths—the talents they share. When your students start on creative projects, you may want initially to have them group themselves randomly. As the projects get underway, you will probably discover other, more useful ways of grouping the children based on mutual interests and motivations that become apparent. Gifted children accomplish the most on this basis. (You will find additional information about grouping children in Chapter 8, "Cluster Grouping to Help All Children Learn Cooperatively.")

"Does this kind of teaching in language arts also support skills such as critical reading, writing composition, and vocabulary building?"

Absolutely! In fact, these creative processes can accomplish more in the area of basic skills and advanced thinking than many more conventional approaches to language arts. The use of theater, painting, music, story invention, and creative movement encourages children to explore the world of words imaginatively. In the process, they also acquire vocabulary and reading skills.

Conclusion

Involving young children in the creative arts can be beneficial to students at all points on the academic spectrum. Those who struggle with reading and writing will begin to discover that reading is not merely acquisitive, but creative; that writing is not just a skill to learn, but a way to think. Gifted children will love the freedom to stretch beyond traditional skill learning to activities that invite imaginative thought and expression.

An emphasis on creativity is valuable in all areas of study. Language arts in particular lends itself to this kind of focus. Students who seem lukewarm toward language arts will find new life in the subject when they realize *they* have something to bring to it. You have a valuable opportunity to turn your young students' focus away from what they *must absorb* to the unique strengths and abilities they *can apply* to the work at hand. All of your students can expand their talents if they take this plunge into a new adventure now, when they are young.

You can help each child find the courage to do so. You can give children the confidence to believe that what they have to offer is valuable and worthy of sharing with the world. All students—including those who are gifted, those who have learning differences, and those who struggle with the discrepancy between their ideas and their writing or reading skills—need this. Through the processes and activities we have shared in this chapter, students can experience breakthroughs in creativity and self-esteem.

Children need the opportunity to use language imaginatively—through reading, listening, discussing, writing, acting, and speaking—and to share the products of their creative efforts. Beyond this, gifted children need to know the purpose of their talents. Sharing is a first step to discovering what they have to give and the purpose of the giving.

References and Resources

Adams, Ansel. *1997 Calendar.* Boston: Little, Brown & Co., 1996. Little, Brown & Co. publishes a calendar of Ansel Adams prints yearly. Representing a variety of natural environments and seasons, the photographic prints are useful catalysts for creative activities in the classroom. We suggest laminating them for repeated use.

Beethoven Lives Upstairs. Produced and directed by David Devine, 1992. Based on historical fact, this video captures the unique relationship that develops between a great composer and a young boy. Features more than 25 excerpts of Beethoven's greatest works. Available at most libraries and video stores. For help in finding videos to purchase, call Video Finders, 1-800-343-4727, or PBS Video, 1-800-344-3337.

Bledsoe, Lucy Jane. *Amelia Earhart.* Illustrated by James Balkovek. Belmont, CA: Simon & Schuster, 1989. This well-told story of Amelia Earhart's life includes a great deal of background information for classroom use.
———. *Phillis Wheatley: First in Poetry.* Illustrated by James Balkovek. Belmont, CA: Simon & Schuster, 1989. An inspiring odyssey of Phillis Wheatley's rise from slavery to her life as a poet.

Blizzard, Gladys S. *Come Look with Me: Enjoying Art with Children.* Charlottesville, VA: Thomasson-Grant, 1990. Using 12 works of art that feature children, the author poses questions that invite young students to probe the world behind the paintings. A wonderful book for introducing imaginative and critical thinking.

Bryant, Margaret A., Marjorie Keiper, and Anne Petit. *Month by Month with Children's Literature.* Tucson, AZ: Zephyr Press, 1995. Offers a dynamic curriculum for teaching to all literacy levels and includes a year's worth of literature-based language units effectively integrated into content areas. Specific and comprehensive, this book offers many creative activities for the primary level.

Carter, Polly, May McNeer, Doris Faber, and Harold Faber. *Exploring Biographies.* New York: Scholastic, 1992. Simply told biographies of Nellie Bly, Albert Einstein, and George Washington Carver are informative, useful aids for a class on great pioneers.

Christensen, James. *The Art of James Christensen: A Journey of the Imagination.* Retold by Renwick St. James. Shelton, CT: The Greenwich Workshop, 1994. The extraordinary fantasy art of James Christensen mingles with myths, legends, and fables to create a rich source for teachers and parents to use when inspiring creative expression in themselves and their children. The text of the artist's imaginative "journey" lends enchantment and inspiration to this special book.

Cimo, Shirley. *The Egyptian Cinderella.* Illustrated by Ruth Heller. New York: HarperCollins, 1989. Beautifully told and illustrated, this is the Cinderella story re-created and set in the world of ancient Egypt.

Cook, Carole, and Jody Carlisle. *Challenges for Children: Creative Activities for Gifted and Talented Primary Students.* Illustrated by Dave Dillon. West Nyack, NY: The Center for Applied Research in Education, Inc., 1985. Designed for K–3 teachers, this volume offers a unique and vast collection of activities in social studies, language arts, math, and science as well as in specialized areas such as library skills, creative arts, and independent learning. You can select activities to support the curriculum, a specific skill, or a particular content area in meeting the individual needs of talented young children in the classroom.

cummings, e.e. *Hist Whist and Other Poems for Children.* Illustrated by David Calsada. New York: Liveright Publishing, 1983. A wonderful collection of poems to stimulate creative responses in young children.

Ernst, Lisa Campbell. *Little Red Riding Hood: A Newfangled Prairie Tale.* New York: Simon & Schuster Books for Young Readers, 1995. A clever retelling of the Red Riding Hood fairy tale with some notable differences from the traditional version. Includes engaging illustrations by the author.

Fantasia. Produced by Walt Disney, 1940. Now available on video, this film is a modern classic. Includes an array of program music performed by the Philadelphia Orchestra under the direction of Leopold Stokowski. Available at most libraries and video stores. For help in finding videos to purchase, call Video Finders, 1-800-343-4727, or PBS Video, 1-800-344-3337.

Farjeon, Eleanor, and Herbert Farjeon. *Heroes and Heroines*. London: J.M. Dent & Sons, Ltd., 1987. A delightful collection of poems that cleverly portray the lives of heroes and heroines (beginning with Alexander the Great) through rollicking rhymes and ironic, witty portraits.

Fisher, Leonard Everett. *Marie Curie*. New York: Macmillan, 1994. Through spare but evocative prose and striking black-and-white illustrations, the author-artist re-creates the remarkable life of Marie Curie.

Fogarty, Robin, and Kay Opeka. *Start Them Thinking: A Handbook of Classroom Strategies for the Early Years*. Palatine, IL: The IRI Group, 1988. Includes a wide range of activities for K–3 children that develop skills in critical and creative thinking, problem solving, and decision making. The activities are easy to integrate into the existing curriculum.

Graham, Terry. *Let Loose on Mother Goose: Activities to Teach Math, Science, Art, Music, Life Skills, and Language Development*. Nashville, TN: Incentive Publications, 1982. Transforms the popular and well-known Mother Goose rhymes into a source for integrated learning with activities that you can easily incorporate into your curriculum. Students will love using the enjoyable and familiar rhymes for their work in class.

Gwynne, Fred. *Pondlarker*. New York: Simon & Schuster Books for Young Readers, 1990. A witty alternative to the traditional frog prince story, this tale offers a surprise ending to Pondlarker's quest for that magical princess he hopes will turn him into a handsome prince.

Heller, Ruth. *Behind the Mask: A Book about Prepositions*. New York: Grossett & Dunlap, 1995. The author uses clever, rhyming text and bold illustrations to take young readers on a tour through the world of prepositions and how they function.
———. *Color*. New York: The Putnam & Grossett Group, 1995. Through playful verse and vibrant illustrations, this book introduces young students to some of the most basic and scientific principles of color.

Leimbach, Judy, and Sharon Eckert. *Primary Book Reporter: Independent Reading for Young Learners*. Illustrated by Elisa Ahlin. San Luis Obispo, CA: Dandy Lion Publications, 1996. Designed for use in kindergarten through second grade, this resource provides useful activity sheets that offer meaningful, imaginative experiences for young students who are already reading.

Levy, Nathan, and Janet Levy. *There Are Those*. Illustrated by Joan Edwards. Hightstown, NJ: N.L. Associates, 1982. This mind-bending book uses a poetic essay and a series of intriguing visual images to introduce and explore the art of perception. A creative book for parents and teachers alike.

Livingston, Myra Cohn. *I Never Told and Other Poems*. New York: Margaret K. McElderry Books, 1992. The author helps young readers to cherish these poems, recognize many of their own experiences and feelings, and explore new ways of thinking.

Locker, Thomas, and Candace Christiansen. *Sky Tree Portfolio*. Stuyvesant, NY: Sky Tree Press, 1995. An exciting and original resource for creative activities related to the visual and language arts. Each of the fourteen 16″ x 20″ full-color posters invites the interest and response of students of all ability levels, scientific interests, and aesthetic sensibilities. Adapted from the book by Locker and Christiansen, *Sky Tree* (New York: HarperCollins, 1995). To order the portfolio, write to: The Center for Gifted, National-Louis University, Evanston, IL 60201-1796, or call (847) 251-2661.

Marshall, Rita. *I Hate to Read!* Illustrated by Etienne Delessert. Mankato, MN: Creative Editions, 1993. Designed to entice the most reluctant reader, this book offers children a wacky adventure in which a little boy discovers that words in a book can take on lives of their own.

Martin, Rafe. *The Rough-Face Girl*. Illustrated by David Shannon. New York: G.P. Putnam, 1992. This hauntingly beautiful equivalent of the Cinderella story is from Algonquin Native American lore.

Milios, Rita. *Imagi-size: Activities to Exercise Your Students' Imagination*. Dayton, OH: Pieces of Learning, 1993. A rich collection of activities for first through fourth graders and a wonderful source for visual learners who enjoy using their imaginations to solve problems. Integrate the activities into existing lessons or use them as readiness activities for other content.

Monet: *Legacy of Light*. Produced by WGBH Educational Foundation and the Museum of Fine Arts, Boston, 1989. This video provides an intimate portrait of the life and works of Claude Monet through his magnificent Impressionist paintings and through excerpts from journals and personal interviews. To order, call 1-800-826-FILM (1-800-826-3456).

O'Keeffe, Georgia. *Georgia O'Keeffe*. New York: The Viking Press, 1976. Includes a discussion of the stimulus behind the painting *Music—Pink and Blue I* (1919, oil on canvas).

Perry, Sarah. *If . . .* Venice, CA: Children's Library Press, 1995. The author-artist presents extraordinary wonders (cats that can fly, mountains that appear like sleeping dogs) and helps young children perceive the inconceivable and imagine the unimaginable. A useful source for young writers and artists.

Polette, Nancy. *The Best Ever Writing Models from Children's Literature.* Illustrated by Paul Dillon. O'Fallon, MO: Book Lures, 1989. Introduces young writers to the world of words through a range of activities including alliteration, limericks, metaphors, personification, similes, character sketches, poetry, and much more.

Schenk de Regniers, Beatrice, Eva Moore, Mary Michaels White, and Jan Carr. *Sing a Song of Popcorn: Every Child's Book of Poems.* New York: Scholastic, 1988. Drawn from the work of renowned poets, 128 selections come even more alive with exquisite illustrations by nine Caldecott Medal-winning artists including Marcia Brown, Trina Schart Hyman, Arnold Lobel, and Maurice Sendak.

Scieszka, Jon. *The True Story of the Three Little Pigs!* By A. Wolf. Illustrated by Lane Smith. New York: Viking Penguin, 1989. This is a whimsical version of the three little pigs story, told from a unique perspective—that of the Big Bad Wolf, who claims he is neither big nor bad but was "framed" by irresponsible reporters.

Shange, Ntozake. *I Live in Music.* Illustrated by Romare Bearden. New York: Welcome Enterprises, 1994. A poem that embodies the syncopated style of the music she loves, this piece by Shange—evocatively illustrated by Bearden's paintings—is a moving tribute to the power and magic of music.

Silverstein, Shel. *Falling Up.* New York: HarperCollins, 1996. The latest book of whimsical poems and drawings by one of America's best-loved children's authors.

Smutny, Joan Franklin. "Enhancing Linguistic Gifts of the Young." *Understanding Our Gifted* 8:4 (1996), pp. 1, 12-15. This is a conceptual framework for and introduction to language arts and the young gifted child. The author challenges the limited expectations conventionally held about the potential of primary students and demonstrates how to nurture in these young ones a love for reading and writing—even poetry.
———, Kathleen Veenker, and Stephen Veenker. *Your Gifted Child: How to Recognize and Develop the Special Talents in Your Child from Birth to Age Seven.* New York: Ballantine Books, 1989. Focusing on the needs of gifted children from birth to age seven, this book offers creative ideas and practical advice on how to best support talent development in the very young.

Solga, Kim. *Draw!* Cincinnati, OH: North Light Books, 1991. For parents or teachers, this is a creative and uncomplicated book, offering ten unique drawing projects as well as numerous variations that will stimulate the imagination of children ages six to 11.
———. *Paint!* Cincinnati, OH: North Light Books, 1991. Crystal colors, dots of color, and face painting are some of many activities offered in this book to help young children uncover their unique creative talents.

Speed, Toby. *One Leaf Fell.* Illustrated by Minerva McIntyre. New York: Stewart, Tabori & Chang, 1993. An imaginative approach to studying the seasons, this is a charming tale of the experiences of one leaf that begins its long journey falling from a tree in autumn.

Stanish, Bob. *Sunflowering: Thinking, Feeling, and Doing Activities for Creative Expression.* Illustrated by Nancee Volpe. Carthage, IL: Good Apple, 1977. Using "analogy strategies" to develop creative expression, flexibility of thought, and sensitivity in young children, these activities emphasize the use of feelings, metaphors, and imagination to discover and use information in original ways. Includes suggestions for variations and extensions.

Sullivan, Charles, comp. *Imaginary Gardens: American Poetry and Art for Young People.* New York: Harry N. Abrams, 1989. This book has no adult-imposed categories, no chapter divisions: open it to any page and begin reading. Young readers can make their own discoveries and select their favorite poems.

Telling Stories in Art Images: Teacher Manual. Chicago, The Art Institute of Chicago, 1996. Intended for classroom use before and after visits to a museum, this manual is a gold mine of ideas for integrating children's exposure to art with activities in drawing, painting, writing, and performance. To order, call (312) 443-3600.

Thomas, Joyce Carol. *Brown Honey in Broomwheat Tea.* Illustrated by Floyd Cooper. New York: HarperCollins, 1993. Through a series of tender and moving poems, the author invites us to share in the love, traditions, and heritage of a young African-American girl and her family.

Torrance, E. Paul. *Creativity: Just Wanting to Know.* Pretoria, South Africa: Benedic Books, 1994. The value of this particular volume is that the author, a well-known pioneer in researching and teaching creativity, has compiled his articles and papers from 1958 through 1994. A very useful text for any teacher of creativity. To order a copy, write or call: Creative Education Foundation, Torrance Center for Creative Studies, University of Georgia, 323 Aderhold Hall, Athens, GA 30602-7146; (706) 542-5104.

Vivaldi, Antonio. *The Four Seasons.* A stimulating musical catalyst for children's creative thinking and writing. It's also one of the most-recorded of all musical works, so you'll find a wide variety of recordings in your local library or music store.

What Do You See? The Art Institute of Chicago, 1993. This video is an excellent resource for teachers on how to generate critical and creative thinking through art. Includes recorded sessions of children discussing various works of art with program host Philip Yenawine. To order, call The Art Institute of Chicago's Department of Museum Education at (312) 443-3600.

White, E.B. *Charlotte's Web*. Illustrated by Garth Williams. New York: Harper, 1952. Charming classic about the friendship between a barnyard spider and a pig who becomes famous.

Young, Ed. *Lon Po Po*. New York: Philomel Books, 1989. This dramatic rendition of the Red Riding Hood story, set in China, is an imaginative resource for any primary language arts class.

6

Promoting Discovery and Higher-Level Thinking in Math and Science

Simone was bending over the table she was sharing with four other second graders. They were adding two-column numbers, using a method of regrouping. Simone had finished her assignment and decided to help her friend, Jenna, who didn't understand place value. Simone, a gifted child, told Jenna a story. "Think of it this way," she said, drawing a large house on a piece of paper. "Pretend a family moves into this house and they have three kids. There are five people in this house. Then the man comes home one day and brings four more kids. Now they have nine people in the house. The woman starts wondering how she's going to find beds for all these kids. She tells her husband, 'No more kids!' But a year later, one more child is born to them. Now ten people live in that house. The wife says, 'This house can't hold more than nine people! We need a bigger house.'

"So the husband builds an enormous house to the left of the smaller one," Simone said, drawing another house. "It's divided up so any family with ten people can fit into it. Then the whole family moves one house to the left of the smaller house. They start to rent the smaller house to families with nine people or less. Each time the small house to the right gets more than nine people in it, ten people move to the big house next door and leave the remainder in the smaller house. So," Simone was looking at Jenna's problem, "if you take these two numbers—25 and 27—think about those houses. Twenty-five means you have 20 living in the big house and five in the small one on the right. Twenty-seven want to join this first group, so how do you do it? When the seven try to join the five, they make too many—12. So ten move next door and two stay in the small house." Simone made this diagram:

House of Tens	House of Ones	(Numbers)
2	5	(25)
+ 2	7	(27)
4 tens	12 ones there's not enough room, so 10 move next door, leaving	
5 tens	2 ones	(52)

Then she went on, "So you add that ten to the 20 plus 20 and you get 50 in the big house and two in the small house. Fifty-two!"

Without realizing it, Simone has used storytelling to help her friend understand how to regroup in addition. She's created an imaginary situation of houses, each having a place value that corresponds with the actual place value Jenna has to learn for her addition problem.

If Jenna understands her friend's fictional scenario, she will probably be able to transfer this understanding to the problem she's working on and will comprehend, in a concrete way, the kinds of operations she performs to get her answer. Carrying a one over to the tens column will stick in her mind as another ten people moving into the big house next door. Simone has also benefited from this process. In telling the story, she's gained new perspectives on an operation that she has grown used to doing mechanically.

Creative Learning as a Link to Higher-Level Conceptual Thinking

In order to translate a math or science concept in this way, a child first has to understand it fully. Many students—both gifted and average—who may feel disinclined to pursue a particular subject (or may be confused by it) often become motivated when they see a way to give life to the parts. For gifted children, this process provides opportunities to explore relationships and test hypotheses in new ways. Integrating language arts and other arts with math and science presents new perspectives on the concepts students are learning and new ways to manipulate them. It's the difference between saying "Here's how the process works—follow it like this" and "Here's how the process works—now see if you can perform it through a story (poem, painting, dance, skit)."

In this chapter, we'll use some of the creative strategies discussed in Chapters 4 and 5 and demonstrate how you can apply them to primary math and science lessons. One of the greatest assets of creativity is its capacity to *involve and motivate* students. This is especially true in subjects that are abstract or seem to be confined within a

rigid set of rules and principles. Imagination restores wonder to the world of math and science, revealing elements of surprise and adventure that delight young children and engage them in higher levels of critical and conceptual thinking.

Creative representations of mathematical concepts tend to make thought more flexible. Take the example of Simone and Jenna. A student might ask, "Why is everything done in tens?" Knowledge of *how* and *why* certain rules work as they do can give children a stronger grasp of logic and the different ways to apply it. Math problems evolve from set formulas children repeat and record into intriguing phenomena they can create and manipulate.

This approach coincides with some recent shifts in the way children are learning math and science. In 1989, the National Council of Teachers of Mathematics (NCTM) adopted a set of 54 standards for teaching and evaluating students from kindergarten through 12th grade. Among the key assumptions that guided NCTM's development of the 13 standards for kindergarten through fourth grade are that the curriculum should:

- be conceptually oriented
- actively involve children in mathematical processes
- emphasize the application of mathematics (problem solving and reasoning)
- include a broad range of content.*

These tenets constitute a shift in math instruction to methods that involve greater student participation and opportunities for creative learning. We wholeheartedly support the notion that children need different ways of relating to math and science concepts. Primary math and science should not be merely sets of rules and procedures for children to memorize and follow. Rather, they should be "sense-making" experiences that invite students to create and contribute to their growing knowledge. In this chapter, we suggest several avenues by which you might guide children to do this, including exploration of properties and processes in everyday life, experimentation, manipulation of ideas for new inventions, and imaginative translations of mathematical and scientific

---

* National Council of Teachers of Mathematics. *Curriculum and Evaluation Standards for School Mathematics.* Reston, VA: National Council of Teachers of Mathematics, 1989, pp. 17-19.

concepts. Our intent is to help you guide children to see the math and science all around them and to use new applications in innovative ways.

To present these ideas, we've divided children's study into explorations of *properties* and *processes*. At times, these explorations overlap. For example, in a geometry lesson, students could learn the basic characteristics (properties) of two- and three-dimensional shapes and might then investigate more about both properties and processes by doing some of the following:

- Experiment with these shapes to create their own environments.
- Explore ways that geometric shapes can compose a wide variety of patterns.
- Express their ideas and insights about shapes through art, creative writing, and drama.

In a similar fashion, students could begin a science lesson by learning some of the basic characteristics of bird life and then proceed with one of the following:

- Study one or several principles of flight, relating the flight of birds to that of aircraft.
- Write stories from the birds' perspective.
- Imagine how they could construct wings for people to imitate the flight of birds.

Through this approach, math and science become more than means to understand the world; they become means to imagine it.

Discovering Properties

The creative imagination is a powerful source for exploring the *properties* of an object, a living thing, a concept, or even a symbol. In the last two chapters, we've seen the value of having students identify themselves imaginatively with someone (or something) they are studying. Pretending is a very natural activity for young children—one that expands conceptual thinking. When you empower your students to draw on their creative resources, you can deepen what they've already learned and help them explore their knowledge in new ways.

As students begin to understand scientific and mathematical properties, you can encourage them (especially those who don't yet write much) to use a variety of media for their work—visual arts, short skits, mimes, or dictated stories and poems. Your goal is to allow students to step into the world of a math or science topic and explore its properties and attributes through the arts.

As a warm-up, you might want to begin with some "mind-benders"—questions or activities that help children stretch their imaginations. Analogies are useful aids to innovative thinking. You can create them in isolation or relate them specifically to whatever the class is studying on a particular day. Here are some examples:*

- How are you like a flower?
- How is third grade like a tree?
- How is a flower like a star?
- How is a story like a river?
- How is a computer like an animal?

You can adapt this line of thinking to different grade levels and subjects within your math or science curriculum. For our purposes here, analogies encourage children to make unusual connections between themselves and the subject they're studying. This will prove useful when the students begin to explore math and science concepts and to elaborate on many of the properties and processes they are learning.

Science: A Study of Animals

Kwami had always loved reptiles and amphibians. As a three-year-old, he'd pored over pictures of lizards, frogs, and snakes, asking for their names and learning to identify them himself. At four, he'd spent hours in the backyard looking for toads and garter snakes. In kindergarten, Kwami and his class were exploring a variety of animals and habitats. Kwami seemed less than enthusiastic about the activities the children were doing. During free time, he would head for the back of the room and absorb himself in picture books about amphibians.

With gifted children like Kwami, you might try a process that allows students to delve deeply into a subject they feel keenly about. In-depth creative and scientific work on a *single* animal can often impart more knowledge to students than teaching them a few facts about a whole spectrum of animals.

---

* Carol D. Creighton, primary classroom teacher, Northbrook, IL. Used with permission of Carol D. Creighton.

Let's explore some ways in which you might undertake this type of study. You could begin by asking all the children to choose a species they would like to investigate. The value of creative exploration is its flexibility, allowing students of different ability levels to advance at their own pace. Tell the class they're going to explore one animal and will then turn their knowledge into a creative story. In this story, they'll pretend they are the creature themselves. Provide books and magazines for the children to thumb through while they decide.* Like Kwami, the students should feel some curiosity, delight, or fascination for the creature they choose in order for this activity to work effectively.

1. Set the Stage: Investigate

Once the children have decided which animal they wish to investigate, have them write down (or if they don't write, dictate) any facts they already know about it. Even if they can report only what the animal looks like, and whether it has fur or scales or feathers, it's always a good practice to begin with the *students'* impressions and insights. You could have the children share some of their thoughts and begin to discuss basic animal categories according to habitats, types of food the animals eat, comparisons to different species, and other distinguishing features. Use questions similar to the following to guide children before, during, and after their research:

- Is your animal warm-blooded or cold-blooded?
- Does it eat meat, plants, or both?
- Is it a mammal like humans? Why or why not? Does it belong to another animal group?
- What does your animal look like? Does it have hair? Is it big or small? Does it have claws or feet? A mouth or a beak? Does it fly, swim, crawl, jump, or run?
- What kind of place does it live in?
- What do you like most about your animal?
- What is your animal's most unusual feature?
- Is there something you don't like about your animal?

* You'll find some resources related to the activities discussed in this chapter in the "References and Resources" section beginning on page 117, in Appendix B beginning on page 198, and in Appendix C beginning on page 211.

2. Imagine

Once the children have collected some facts they know about their animal, explain that you want them to create a story about it. The point of the story is not for the students to make up a complicated plot, but to try explaining their animal's world from the standpoint of the animal itself. Here you're guiding children to use the art of story-making to enhance their scientific knowledge of the animal they select. Rather than simply gathering information for an assignment, they'll be seeking facts they need in order to write their story.

Two story starters we like to use are "A Day in the Life" and "What Would It Be Like?"

A Day in the Life

Make available a variety of books, posters, and other resources for students to use in learning about their animal. Ask the students to describe their day as if they were this animal. Encourage them to talk with the word "I." To help them choose details to include, you might ask questions such as these:

- What kind of place do you live in? Is it hot or cold? Wet or dry? Above ground or below?
- What does your body look like? How does it feel to live in that body?
- What do you eat? Where do you find food? Where do you find water?
- Where do you sleep? What do you use to build your home?
- How do you spend your day? Do you gather food? Hunt? Sleep? Move from one place to another (migrate)?
- Are you a mother? A father? A child?
- How do you get along with other animals who live near you?
- What is the name of your group or species? Are you part of a pod? A herd? A flock? A school?
- How do you communicate with other animals in your group?
- What dangers do you face from other animals? From humans?
- How do you defend yourself? What do you do if you or other animals in your family are in danger?
- What's special about animals like you? Why is your species important in nature? In the world?

For students who can read, you may want to write these questions on the board. The children could follow them as they design their "day in the life" story. For younger children who aren't yet reading independently, you could provide resource books with fewer words and more pictures. Your focus for these children would be to help them acquire a number of scientific facts about the animal. Most video stores have a good selection of wildlife films you could show the class. With very young children, we often turn down the narration and talk to the class ourselves—asking them questions and reviewing the concepts they are learning.

You can also encourage more creative thinking by asking the children to visualize their animals in unusual environments: "If you were an elephant, how would you like living in a city? Where would you go? Where would you look for food?" "If you were an otter, how would you like living in a nearby stream? Would you be happy?" These alternative scenarios are fun and can help children use their imaginations to gain more precise knowledge and understanding.

Ask nonwriters to draw or sketch different scenes of a story. The story could unfold in steps or sequences, which students could then share with the class. Guide children as they explain their stories. Ask questions about their pictures, and encourage the other students to ask questions too: "How fast can you run (swim, fly)?" "What do you do when you're afraid and need to escape quickly?" "Where do you look for food?" "Where will you sleep tonight?" The whole class can learn from this process.

Occasionally, a few students may realize they don't know exactly how their species behaves in certain circumstances. Sharing their work and responding to questions will stimulate critical thinking and the desire to discover and know more. The children will enjoy using each new fact they learn as a source for additional artistic and imaginative details.

Allow for flexibility in how children express their ideas. This is a chance for them to think about and share science creatively. For example, some children may want to write a free-verse poem to describe their animal. (For suggestions on helping children write free-verse poetry, see "Creative Composition: Free-Verse Poetry" beginning on page 92.) Younger nonreaders may enjoy expressing their ideas through mime, dance, or some other form of creative movement. If you have several children working on the same animal, you could group them together so they can pool resources and ideas. They might also collaborate: one could write, another draw, another compose a poem, and so forth.

Here is an example of how a fourth-grader named Jeff translated his interest in nature into two poems:*

A bald eagle soars up high
an enormous wing span
flies to a nest of baby chicks
noble brown-white head
shows fish of all kinds he is not afraid
swooping down in the water grabbing his meal
feeding the chicks then himself eating the whole
    thing
soaring down to meet his mate
Soon the babies are on their own, so are the
    parents.

———

The mighty tree stands over the bushes
Like a mighty king
Standing proud and tall
Swaying with joy in the wind
the bushes quivering
in the presence of this character
its once green leaves turn bright yellow and red
falling one by one on the dark soil
for it is fall now, the leaves raked up
but its green leaves will come again

What Would It Be Like?

The story starter "What Would It Be Like?" will spark many children's imaginations. To give you a feel for how appealing this can be for students, we'll use the chameleon as an example.

The chameleon lives primarily in Africa and Asia. Because it's too slow to escape predators *or* catch insects, nature has bestowed a unique asset: camouflage. The chameleon's natural skin color blends perfectly with its surroundings, yet it can change in a matter of seconds when the chameleon needs to communicate with others in

---

* These poems were written in a creative writing class taught by Joan Franklin Smutny at the "Worlds of Wisdom and Wonder" program, which is conducted through The Center for Gifted at National-Louis University, Evanston, Illinois. The poems are reprinted here with the permission of the child and his family.

its species. Some varieties of chameleons can also alter patterns as well as colors on their skin's surface. For example, the skin of a Senegalese chameleon can change from a smooth, uniform green to black and gray with triangles and polka dots displayed on either side of the body! Nature has also provided the chameleon with an amazing tongue that is both long and quick. The tongue extends in length farther than the animal's entire body, and its speed more than compensates for the chameleon's otherwise slow movements.

We've provided this description to illustrate how and why this imaginative process could appeal to young children. For an investigation of chameleons, students might create a story about what it would be like to wear the skin of a chameleon. Students could investigate ideas and questions like the following:

- A chameleon can use one eye to look at a juicy insect and the other to watch for danger. What it is like to have two eyes that can each see different things?
- How does it feel to be able to change your skin color and patterns?
- How do you use changing colors to "talk" to others in your species?
- What does it feel like to have a body temperature that's exactly the same as the temperature of the air around you?

Most children will enjoy doing something as imaginative as internalizing the experience of being a chameleon. It gives life to the scientific facts they learn about animals. Gifted children may wish to go further with the activity, finding more facts on their animal and incorporating them into their stories or visual representations in different ways. Be flexible with this. Just as you adjust your methods to the needs of children who may struggle with reading and writing, you'll want to encourage young gifted students to pursue their research and creative representations to new dimensions.

Suggest to children that the more they learn about the *science* of their creature's life and habitat, the more interesting their stories will be. (To stimulate your own imagination, you might enjoy reading *The Color of Distance* by adult science-fiction writer Amy Thomson, who used her research on rain forests and lizards to create the

novel. In her book, human-like chameleons speak "skin speech," live in the canopy of the rain forest, and have an entire culture based on their unique physical needs and environment.)

3. Extend the Experience

Gifted children who quickly master the essentials of this process could attempt more challenging projects:

An Animal Culture: You might suggest that students create a "culture" based on scientific facts of an animal species. The students can depart from strict fact into fantasy, but they must ground their creation in actual biological and environmental attributes. (For more ideas on helping students do this, see "Originality: Creating Culture" on pages 67–72.)

Balance of Nature: You might have students analyze what they (as a given species) contribute to the balance of nature. One way to do this is by considering what would happen if the species disappeared entirely. Which other species might overpopulate as a result? Which species might also disappear? How would the air change? The plants and trees? The oceans? The weather? Or have students consider the opposite possibility: What would occur in nature if their species began to overpopulate?

Animal-Inspired Language: Encourage children to consider the influences an animal or species has had on human culture. In a study of chameleons, students might explore what people mean when they refer to someone as a chameleon, or what is meant by the concept of "camouflage." A wonderful source for this line of inquiry is *Nature Got There First: Inventions Inspired by Nature* by Phil Gates.

You can adapt this exploration of properties to a wide range of subjects and issues in the sciences. Transforming science into a fictional account motivates children by making learning personally meaningful. As they begin to take on the role of the animal species they have selected, they will naturally want to know more scientific details. Science then becomes a source for imaginative creation, and imagination becomes the engine for scientific discovery.

Math: A Study of Shapes

Desiree, a second grader, finished the class assignment and began fiddling with the shapes on her desk. She loved playing with geometric shapes. Soon she was constructing a scene of houses, yards, and cars out of the shapes in front of her. Watching Desiree, the teacher had an idea. Preschool and kindergarten children built with different-shaped blocks all the time. Why not extend that experience for her second graders by having them explore and construct with two- and three-dimensional shapes?

This is a wise teacher. Without more creative activities, the fun of geometry may disappear for a child like Desiree. And the possibilities for exploration are nearly endless! When learning basic principles of geometry, primary students enjoy investigating the different things they can do with shapes. Playing with shapes imaginatively invites critical thinking.

You can use role playing to explore properties in the mathematical universe as effectively as in the scientific one. Doing so offers a way for children to investigate the attributes of certain math concepts. At first, this approach may seem to be more of a stretch than the last one, since it involves making an environment out of inanimate shapes. As suggested earlier, you can use analogies to prepare children for the kind of flexible thinking they will do in this exercise. Ask the students to think of geometric shapes they like and about why they like them. Next, invite them to create analogies between themselves and a shape. For example, you could ask: "How are you like a triangle? How are triangles like people? If you became a triangle, how would you feel about yourself? What would you do with yourself?" We have found that, with a little encouragement, primary students easily make the mental leap that enables them to imagine their world in geometric terms.

1. Set the Stage: Investigate

To start the students on their imaginative journey, expose them to some books that will help them see the different possibilities of geometric shapes. Leonard Fisher's *Look Around! A Book about Shapes* is a wonderful source to help children make connections between geometry and the real-world shapes around them. Through discussion, the class will see shapes in ordinary objects (such as rectangles, squares, and triangles in the architectural structures of a skyscraper, a pyramid, and a house). Children could also consider how nongeometric objects resemble geometric ones (such as how a tree might look like a rectangle with a triangle on top, or how a rounded bush might be seen as circular).

You could also read and discuss math expert Marilyn Burns's *The Greedy Triangle*—a book that animates the life of a triangle in a way that provides a more creative approach to geometric properties. You could then invite students to write or tell similar stories. Have them begin with the statement "If I were a circle (triangle, square, rectangle), I would look like this." The children could draw themselves and go on to develop their story. Or they might begin in this way: "What I would like best about being a triangle is. . . ." Children could complete the sentence and diagram their ideas. Simple introductory activities like these are a good lead-in to creative projects in geometry. They provide some preliminary experiences for the class to explore mathematics imaginatively.

Continue by asking the children to choose a basic geometric shape such as a circle, square, or triangle. Group the students together according to the shapes they have chosen. Ask them to think of as many different uses as they can for their shape. At first, they'll list the obvious ones: a circle can make wheels, a square can make a box, and so forth. Keep encouraging new and unusual ideas. For example, discuss how they could make a shape with many sides and angles and why it would roll better than a square. You might say: "Imagine you have an unlimited supply of triangles. What would you make? What in your home or school or neighborhood would you change with this supply of shapes? How could you construct a merry-go-round made only of triangles? How could you have buildings, buses, or bicycles?" This will help students think flexibly about shapes that may seem—at first glance—inflexible and static.

Next, ask children to write down or talk about properties of the shape that they already know. Supply pictures of a variety of environments (both natural and human-made) so they can explore the different ways their shapes function in the world around them. Have three-dimensional shapes available for the children to handle while you ask questions such as these:

- Is this shape circular, or does it have sides?
- If it has sides, how many? Are they equal in length, or are they different lengths?
- What do you like about your shape? What can you do with it? Can you build or make anything with it?
- Why are many roofs triangular? What are some of the problems buildings with flat roofs might have? Why do you think more buildings aren't shaped like circles? Why are cans cylindrical—both round and straight—and not rectangular—straight on all sides?
- Can you imagine a world where all the doors are round and all the doorknobs are triangles? Where wheels are square? Where the sun and moon are square? Where cars are shaped like computer disks? Where airplane wings and sailboat sails are round?
- Can you imagine inventing a triangular door? If the point were at the top of the door, what would it be like for people coming and going? What would it be like if the point were at the bottom?

These questions encourage the children to perceive the uniqueness of the shapes they have chosen, and to experiment with this uniqueness.

2. Imagine a World of Triangles

Using the triangle as an example, you could have your students imagine that they are people with an overall triangular shape. They will have begun exploring this through Marilyn Burns's *The Greedy Triangle* and may already have created drawings or stories about themselves as triangular beings. Now ask them to explore their shape further. Explain that there are many different triangular shapes with a variety of angles and side lengths. Encourage children to explore the different possibilities of triangular bodies. Suggest that they sketch an entire family or a group of friends. Tell students that they may include arms, hands, legs, feet, and necks, but that the end result should be basically triangular human shapes.

Move on to a discussion of the furniture and living spaces for triangular people. Tell the class that the shapes we use in our own doors, chairs, tables, and beds are those that work best for *our shape*. You might ask: "How would you describe the basic shape of a human being? Are we most like a rectangle? A square? A circle?" To help

children visualize this, have them trace a shape over a person in a magazine picture.

Then have students look at a door and see the relationship between a person's shape and that of a door. Explain: "Doors are made to allow shapes that are basically tall and rectangular (*oblong*) to move through them. But what if we were shaped like triangles—wide at the bottom and very narrow at the top? What would be the best shape for a door then? For a bed? For a whole room?"

Next, ask children to imagine they are designers. It's their job to design a room, a vehicle, clothing, or a space that will be uniquely suited to triangular people. Follow the children's interests. They may like to explore transportation systems, kitchens, or playgrounds. The point is to foster critical and creative thinking about spatial relationships—in this case, the relationship of the triangular body to the environments that surround it.

Keep the activity simple. If it helps, you could write on the board a list of objects or spaces for the children to explore in depth. Ask questions:

- What are some of the main problems someone with a triangular body would have in our world?
- How would you like the rooms of your home arranged? Would you like a lot of rooms? Or would you like to have an open space with different sections?
- How would your house be shaped? What would your car look like?
- What would it be like to have enormous feet and a pointed head? What sort of clothes would you have? What sort of bed would you sleep in?

Be sure the students have enough visual aids and manipulatives so that they can experiment and explore. Offer assorted magazines with pictures of indoor and outdoor scenes as well as blocks, LEGOs, and shapes made by the children. Give students some choice in how they represent their designs; they might draw, paint, model with clay, create shoe-box dioramas, or even write stories. Have them label their creations: "Neighborhood of Triangular People," "Bedroom for Young Triangles," "Kitchen for a Triangle Family."

3. Extend the Experience

So far, the students have explored the properties of triangles by re-creating everyday objects and environments to fit the needs of triangular bodies. This is a fun way for young children to think critically about the basic triangular shape and its relation to other shapes and spaces around it.

To extend the experience, ask the children to pretend that the triangular people moved away. Now they need to re-create their objects and places for ordinary humans—using only triangles as building materials. Their job will be to try to build homes, furniture, vehicles, or other objects that resemble what people use in the real world, but to build them entirely out of triangles.

Transform the World of Triangles

This activity demands flexible thinking. The children will need plenty of two- and three-dimensional triangles to play around with. To help the class see the range of possibilities for *non*triangular shapes made from triangles, pose a few problems such as these:

- How could you make a regular four-sided door out of triangles?
- How could you use different-shaped triangles to draw a tree with branches?
- How could you make a skyscraper out of triangles?
- How could you make a wheel out of triangles?

As they work on these problems, the students will begin to investigate relationships among different kinds of triangles and to experiment with ways triangles can be combined to make other geometric shapes.

When you feel they are ready to tackle a complete environment, guide students through the same explorative steps. First, give them plenty of options. They don't have to use the same idea they used when they made their triangle worlds—that's only one possibility. A number of your students may wish to try something completely different. To give them ideas, you might display children's work from the preceding activity ("Imagine a World of Triangles," page 107). Again, you can use pictures from magazines as well. Or ask the children to think of their own homes, neighborhoods, schoolrooms, and playgrounds as sources for their choices.

Give yourself options, too. You may decide that your students would benefit most by choosing one environment to work on together. You might even wish to start by asking the class to try

a series of experiments. Let's say you choose the classroom as an environment to re-create with triangles. You could guide children by asking questions like these:

- Look at the tables or desks. Is there a way you can make a table out of triangles?
- What kinds of triangles can you use to make walls that look like our walls?
- How can you construct a door out of triangles?
- Can you make something nearly round—like a doorknob—out of triangles?
- If we had a huge plant in this room, what would it look like? Can you make the plant's leaves out of triangles?
- Can you make three-sided windows?
- Can you make a person—you, me, or another student—out of triangles? Can you make the person look like an ordinary human being rather than a triangular one?
- Can you draw a human face made of triangles? Is there a way you can draw the legs, arms, and other body parts so the person looks something like you or me?

Allow children to work on other scenes or objects if they wish. Once they begin to experiment with triangles in this way, they'll be able to continue on their own. They can make cars, streets, or outdoor parks using triangles in unique ways.

Referring to artists is also helpful here. Picasso's cubist paintings are an obvious choice; Monet's landscapes offer another good visual reference. Calendars are a wonderful source of many artists' reproductions. Hang the calendar pictures up around the room and have the children walk up close to the paintings, then back up slowly to see the overall effect. In the case of Monet, you could show the children how the artist created an entire landscape using nothing but dots. This may suggest ideas for creating similar "impressions" out of triangles.

These are all creative—and very instructional—ways for primary children to explore triangles. You can also have students follow this process for other polygons (such as squares, rectangles, or hexagons). The experience of moving one shape around in various directions and combining and recombining shapes gives children many insights into the properties of a particular shape and how it relates to other ones.

As much as possible, let the children choose the medium for their project. Some students may like to create models using three-dimensional triangles they've created. Others may prefer to paint or draw. Children could also cut out and glue different-colored shapes to create images of their ideas in a kind of origami picture. Hang the models as mobiles; this will enable the children to see them from different angles. Display students' paintings and drawings so that the rest of the class can observe them. These displays will come in handy as you continue to work with the class on geometry. When you use children's work in this way, they'll feel that they are making a valuable contribution to the learning of the class.

Build a Bridge to Fractions

You can extend the reasoning children are learning to other mathematical concepts, such as the relationship of parts to the whole. For example, when the students used triangles to form new shapes, they put parts together to make another kind of whole. From here, you could ask them to look at some of the new shapes they have made, particularly those that form rectangles or squares.

Suppose a few children made a rectangle or square with two triangles. You could show them that each triangle is one half of the rectangle or square. In the same way, the children could cut paper triangles into smaller ones, color in a few of them, and figure what portion of the whole square or rectangle the colored pieces are. Children will probably adapt to this activity after the earlier creative process, because they have already discovered how to place certain shapes together to create other ones.

Most gifted children enjoy the challenge of creating new and unusual shapes through one fixed type of shape. If they complete the process quickly and are ready to tackle a more difficult one, encourage them to draw or construct a scene, using the shapes they've made and any others they like. The scene could be a natural one, or a school, home community, or other place. If they have worked for the most part in plane (flat) geometry, have them draw or construct three-dimensional cubes, prisms, cylinders, cones, and spheres. Have the students experiment with three-dimensional objects, using whatever manipulatives you have in class or they bring from home. Talk about and explore how cylinders are like tree trunks, how houses are like squares or rectangles.

Another approach would be to ask children to look for the shapes they see (or can imagine) *inside* objects and forms around them—the clock, the chair, or even their own hand, which has curves, lines, and angles.

As you guide the class through this process, you can add another creative dimension by displaying some of Picasso's cubist paintings and sketches in which he configured human faces and other natural objects in striking geometric forms. A wonderful tactile activity is to have students examine and touch objects that have a lot of texture—trees, fabrics, certain kinds of wood. They could then try and reproduce the images geometrically.

Discovering Processes

A similar creative approach can expand young children's understanding of scientific and mathematical processes. A *process* is a series of sequential actions or changes that produces a specific effect. When you bring creativity to bear on the study of a scientific or mathematical process, three immediate benefits result:

1. The children feel more motivated to study the process.
2. They tend to remember the process, and the logic or reasoning behind it, much better.
3. With this deeper understanding, students (especially those who are gifted) develop the confidence and freedom to apply the process to other contexts; they can then make discoveries of their own.

Science: A Study of Growth and Change in the Natural World

Colin was always very sensitive about the natural world. He loved sitting in trees, searching beneath stones and leaves, and studying how things grow. His mother taught him how to prepare soil, plant seeds, and care for the seedlings after they sprouted. Colin also enjoyed creating terrariums—natural environments he made and contained in a number of large jars in his room. When his class began studying trees, Colin was excited. But he wanted to do more than the rest of the class, because he already knew much of what they were studying.

For children like Colin, who have already acquired some fundamental knowledge of what the class is studying, imaginative activity related to the subject will both sustain and propel their interest. Such activity will allow them to move from general principles and rules to specifics—specific trees, specific places, and specific circumstances. Rather than learn a few processes in given circumstances, the children can explore them in environments *they choose* and under conditions *they imagine*. As in other creative work, students become producers as well as recipients of knowledge—and producing is vital to their growth. All children can benefit from learning in this way; gifted children especially will enjoy experiencing the processes in a variety of contexts and creating hypotheses of their own.

In Chapter 5, we introduced Thomas Locker and Candace Christiansen's *Sky Tree Portfolio* and mentioned the science elements integrated within this collection of 14 exquisite paintings of one tree. In our workshops for gifted student writers, we have found that the paintings serve as powerful catalysts for children of all ages. The posters can also provide a way to imaginatively and creatively extend the scientific study of a tree's life cycle.

Let's assume that you want to expand on the class's understanding of photosynthesis—the process by which trees produce oxygen on the planet—and of other related tree facts. Paintings from the *Sky Tree Portfolio* (or other prints and pictures you find) can enhance what children understand about the science of a tree. Students can begin creating stories, writing poems, and rendering their ideas in sketches, movement, or drama. The purpose here is to give children the freedom to invent. Using the scientific facts you have taught them, they can build fictional narratives that enable them to deepen their study and research.

1. Set the Stage: Investigate

The easiest way to begin this process is to have the children choose a tree species they like. Students may want to delve into different environments for their trees—a tropical rain forest, a redwood or sequoia forest, or one of many seacoasts. Provide resources they can use to make their selection. You might display several pictures of different species of trees and discuss their unique features—the climates in which they grow, their colors, the shapes of their leaves, their life spans,

and so forth. You could also ask the children to tell you about different trees they have seen in their neighborhoods or travels. Ask questions such as these:

- Do you have a favorite climbing tree? Why is it your favorite?
- What changes do you notice in your tree in spring? In summer? In fall? In winter?
- What's the most unusual tree you've seen? Why is it unusual?
- How is your favorite tree like other kinds of trees? How is it different?

Encourage students to think about what aspects of tree life they want to "research." To do this, they need exposure to different kinds of trees, climates, and environments to see what interests them.

Once your students choose their tree, you can guide them through a series of leading questions. Ask them to pretend they are the tree they have selected. You could stimulate their imagination by asking:

- Where do you live?
- What kind of climate do you live in? Is it dry? Rainy? Cold? Warm?
- What kind of land surrounds you? Woods? Rocks? Desert? Hills?
- What kind of bark do you have? What do your leaves look like? How tall do you get?
- What kinds of animals live around you? Inside you? Who crawls or hops around in your branches?
- What do you have that helps the animals around you?
- Are there other trees around you? How tall are they? How thick are their trunks and branches?
- What are the greatest needs of trees like you?

Give the children time to think through and sketch out whatever they already know about their tree species and its basic needs.

2. Imagine: Stimulate Further Discovery

It's more difficult to assume the life of a tree than to pretend to be an animal. Catalysts are critical here. The *Sky Tree Portfolio* is an excellent stimulus. It provides many aids for teachers who would like to entice their primary-age students into the daily life of trees. On the back of "The Summer Tree" painting, for example, is this question: "What does the tree do during the long summer days?" Here is the answer provided:*

"All summer the tree bathes its leaves in the light of the sun. The leaves also take in air. The roots are actively absorbing water and minerals from the soil. The water, air and minerals meet in the green leaves and with the help of the sunlight, the tree creates its own food: sugars. No human being or animal can create sugar out of air, earth and water. It must be interesting to be a tree!"

These are fascinating details for young children immersing themselves in the new world of trees. Also on the poster "The Summer Tree," explanations of photosynthesis provide more information that gifted children (especially the "science bugs") will enjoy incorporating into their imaginative work.

The whole process of the tree's converting the energy of the sun and carbon dioxide from the air, absorbing water and minerals from the soil, and storing sugars and starches for its own food and growth is a rich and intriguing one. Here is a species that produces its own food without moving in any direction! Furthermore, as the *Sky Tree Portfolio* authors point out, "all life is directly or indirectly dependent upon plants for the food they eat. So the tree standing on the hill by the river, is actually very busy all summer long."**

This combination of science and artistry will enable young students to see the different possibilities of rendering scientific facts creatively. Pictures of trees will inspire them to draw some of their own, sketch environments, and write anecdotes or short poems from the trees' perspective. Students can represent the daily process of making food for themselves; of the kinds of animals, birds, and insects that surround them; and of their feelings about seasonal and other changes.

To successfully integrate science facts and creative imagination in a way that encourages critical thinking and discovery, you could ask your

students to focus on several fundamental aspects of tree life in their representations. For example, they could choose a few of the following topics:

- How does the tree makes its own food?
- What animals get their food, home, or shelter from the tree?
- How is the tree affected by climate and seasonal changes?
- How does the tree survive the hardships of its environment?
- How does the tree reproduce? What part do animals and birds play in this process?

3. Extend the Experience

You can help children extend these concepts artistically by asking them to think about trees in terms of color, feeling, story, and movement:

- What color would you give a tree in winter? The sky?
- What feeling would you give it?
- What is a typical day like for your tree?
- Can you show us what your roots do when it rains?

You can also use analogies:

- How is the tree like the stars?
- How are branches of a tree like the arms of a person?
- How are leaves like clothes?

This kind of questioning will loosen the borders between science and art, scientific principle and poetic or artistic expression, fact and fiction.

Ideally, you'll want to have a display of books or posters that show trees in diverse seasons, conditions, and environments. Other excellent resources besides the *Sky Tree Portfolio* are *Trees and Forests* from Scholastic's "Voyages of Discovery" series, Theresa Greenaway's *Tree Life*, and Joanne Oppenheim's *Have You Seen Trees?* The students can begin simply and move ahead to more complex work according to their ability and understanding. To give them a visual image of the processes they describe, encourage children to make sketches or drawings with arrows that indicate the process they wish to represent. Depending on their ages and abilities, the students could add captions identifying the tree

---

* Thomas Locker and Candace Christiansen. *Sky Tree Portfolio*. Stuyvesant, NY: Sky Tree Press, 1995.
** Locker and Christiansen, 1995.

species they are depicting and what the tree is undergoing to make food; to store food for the winter; to protect itself against drought, wind, or frigid temperatures; or to reproduce.

Your gifted students will enjoy the mental exercise of using scientific processes to make creative tree stories. It will be a challenge for them to make the life of a tree—which appears on the surface to be static and even dull—lively and adventurous. To help all your students step into the role, guide them with these ideas and questions:

- Look down at the ground. See how far down your trunk goes. How do your roots feel? How deep are they? Feel the rain. Feel your roots soaking in the water. How does that feel? Can you feel the water seeping up into your trunk? Is the soil healthy? Do you get enough "food" from the earth and the water to feed you so you can grow and be strong?
- Stretch up to the sky, as high as you can. Look up at the sun. Feel your leaves taking in the sun for you, taking in the energy and the carbon dioxide. What does this feel like? Like breathing? Like taking a shower?
- Feel the sun, the carbon dioxide, and the moisture in the earth combining to make sugars for food. Can you taste these sugars? Are there any animals who want some of this sugar?
- It's summer (fall). How does the air feel around your branches and leaves? Is it warm? How long are the days now? What changes do you feel happening? (Here children could focus on the breakdown of green chlorophyll, allowing other pigments to become more visible.)
- How old are the trees around you? Are they ancient trees? Seedlings? Young saplings? How old are *you?*
- What animals live in your branches? Tell some stories about these animals. How do they help you and the other trees in your "neighborhood?"
- How long have you lived? What are some of the changes you have seen happen around you?

While they are thinking about these questions, the students can also integrate paintings or sketches into this exploration. Studying their tree in books, magazines, or outdoors will give them new insights to include in their drawings; they'll notice details they hadn't observed before. This experience will be especially rich if the students choose trees from different environments around the world. The whole class will benefit from studying these basic science principles in different contexts. Gifted students will enjoy comparing how trees function in diverse settings and how they devise unique responses to the challenges of weather conditions, seasonal changes, density, drought, and other climatic hardships.

Math: Turning Symbols into Stories

Mattie loved playing with numbers. When she went shopping with her dad, she liked checking the prices of items and adding them up. She also enjoyed comparing prices of various brands to see how much money her dad could save. Sometimes Mattie would pretend to be different characters who had come to the store to buy things. She would make up stories to herself as she went up and down the aisles. In the store, numbers had a real life for Mattie that they didn't always have in school. Mattie didn't like doing word problems as much as she liked creating them. She enjoyed inventing scenarios that took her to the limits of her mathematical understanding and posed new problems.

In children's earliest years, the world of numbers has a wondrous, almost magical quality. Who hasn't seen the earnest face of a toddler as she points and counts or proudly displays her age with two or three fingers? Yet numbers often lose their appeal in school, where the priorities of acquiring certain skills take precedence over this early creative play.

When you try more creative approaches, number processes can assume new dimensions for children. More than providing entertainment or diversion, these approaches give students an opportunity to analyze the processes in completely new ways. This in turn encourages students, especially those who are gifted, to pursue their understanding in new, more challenging contexts.

1. Set the Stage: Tell a Story

At the beginning of this chapter, we saw how vividly Simone was able to translate the concept of place value into a concrete, memorable story (see pages 100–101). Using stories to revitalize the number world not only breathes life into mathematical concepts and processes but also reframes them in familiar, understandable terms.

Let's say you're teaching children to regroup when subtracting two-digit numbers from two-digit numbers. The example you're using is 47 from 95. You could use manipulatives if you'd like, but along with these you could add this explanation and story:

> "Even though 95 is a bigger number than 47, when you subtract it bit by bit, some of the numbers have to borrow from their neighbors. Okay, do you see *Seven,* here? She's a big bully and wants to scare *Five* by taking his five ones and then asking for more. That would put *Five* in debt. So *Five* has to come up with a plan. He goes over to his banker friend, *Nine*—here in the tens column—and says, 'Hey, you have 90 ones—nine tens. Would you lend me some?'
>
> "Now, anyone who wants to live in the tens column has to follow this rule that when they lend ones, they can only lend ten at a time—no more, no less. So *Nine* agrees to give *Five* ten ones (which leaves *Nine* 80 ones, or eight tens, which means *Nine* is now *Eight*). *Five* goes back with the ten ones and joins them to the *five* he already has, making *fifteen.*
>
> "Now, when *Seven* comes back the next day, *Five* won't be scared because he can give her the *seven* she wants and still have *eight* left over. Now we move over to the left, where the bankers all hang out. The *four* in the tens column (40 ones) comes to the *eight* in the tens column and takes *four* away. The final answer, then, is 48."

A story is a wonderful way to make mathematical concepts more accessible to young children. You can draw a diagram on the board or have the children enact the story as you tell it. Through this experience, the students will begin to connect mathematics with story situations. Rather than remaining processes for children to perform mechanically, math problems become plot lines for stories. Before you invite the students to create stories of their own, begin another addition problem for the class to do together; work the problem and create the story for it together. The value of this method of teaching is that children learn certain concepts inductively. By exploring stories to the limits of their knowledge, they prepare themselves for the next logical development.

Gifted children may like to turn a problem into a story on their own and then add some additional elements to their story. For example, Simone might move more and more people into her House of Tens, perhaps to the point where it fills up. As the teacher, you could use Simone's story with the class and guide children to move from two-digit numbers to computations with three-digit numbers. To do this, you could introduce a new column and a new "house"—the Mansion of Hundreds. Once students become comfortable with the three fictional houses, the principle of subtraction could evolve in similar story fashion. The idea of people moving out will seem as natural as that of people moving in. Keep reminding children that the people from the House of Tens can only move in groups of ten. When the House of Ones needs to borrow in order to subtract, a whole group of ten ones will have to move in to the House of Ones temporarily. Then students can subtract the numbers with the same logic they used for adding.

After children become more comfortable with these basic steps, they can invent stories of their own. This creative strategy tests and strengthens students' knowledge of the concrete process and gives them a chance to discover how it works in different fictional contexts.

Once you break out of the strict divisions between math and art, math and language arts, math and creative thinking, you and the class will find yourselves inventing some wonderful stories around number operations. Gifted children will love this. They frequently seek new and innovative applications for the knowledge they so quickly acquire. They'll especially value the process of translating the representation of numbers and symbols into imaginary worlds.

2. Create Fairy Tales with Numbers

An approach we like to use is to turn number operations into fairy tales. Fairy tales are an excellent genre for this purpose because they are so familiar to young children. Here are some ideas for getting your students started on number fairy tales:

A Fraction Fairy Tale

Once upon a time, there was a greedy detective who was looking for treasure in a field. Now, this detective *really* wanted to have this treasure all to himself. As luck would have it, he was also a magician. So he came up with a clever plan: He would divide himself into pieces and have each piece look in a different part of the field. This would ensure that the detective—at least, some part of him—would find the treasure before someone else did. The detective told the pieces of himself that whichever piece found the treasure should hop up and down to call attention to itself. Then the dividing began. The man divided himself in half, and then those halves divided themselves in half. Each of the four pieces went into a different part of the field looking for the treasure. Finally, one of the pieces found it! But instead of hopping up and down, what do you think it did? It grabbed the treasure and ran off as fast as a piece of a person could run!

Using this fairy tale, the children can play with the idea of fractions. Have them draw the story, perhaps in a cartoon frame format, so they can visualize it. Then have them make symbolic representations under the different segments of the story. Beneath the picture of the detective dividing himself into four pieces, students could write one or both of these notations:

$$1 = \frac{4}{4} \qquad\qquad 1 = \frac{1}{4} + \frac{1}{4} + \frac{1}{4} + \frac{1}{4}$$

In the segment where one piece runs off with the treasure, they could write this:

$$\frac{4}{4} - \frac{1}{4} = \frac{3}{4}$$

A Division Fairy Tale

Once upon a time, there was a famous cookie maker who had a bakery called "24 Cookies." She made 24 cookies an hour—no more, no less. One day, eight hungry trolls came in and demanded all the cookies. The cook looked at her cookie sheet of 24. She told the trolls, "I have 24 cookies. There are eight of you, so I can give each of you three cookies." But the eight trolls were hungry; they wanted more than three cookies apiece. So they started arguing with each other about who could have how many cookies. Four of the trolls got tired of arguing and ran off. "Now how many can we have?" said the trolls to the baker. "I still have 24 cookies," the baker replied. "But now there are four of you, so I can give each of you six."

The students can go on from here, inventing more and more operations. But you'll need to monitor this process to maintain a balance between invention and actual mathematical learning. Students may create plots that exceed their math knowledge considerably! In some cases, this can be counterproductive. The plots should stretch children's understanding and encourage flexibility in mathematical thinking, not overwhelm them with convoluted twists and turns.

Gifted children, on the other hand, may introduce all sorts of added complications that they are able to handle mathematically. For example, three instead of four trolls could run off, leaving five to divide up the 24 cookies. This would then lead to a remainder—four cookies for the baker! Or perhaps the five trolls would divide the extra four cookies up into smaller and smaller fractions. As before, you can have the students draw cartoon-like sketches and write the operations beneath their pictures. The fun of all this is that math operations occur in the course of a story, and there are infinite possibilities for the kinds of problems children can create.

A Multiplication Fairy Tale

Once upon a time, there was a young boy who could weave cloth into gold blankets. The boy was trapped high in a tower by six dragons. "Please release me!" pleaded the boy. "I must get home to my family!" The head dragon replied, "All right, we will release you—but first you must weave two beautiful gold blankets for me." So the boy wove two blankets. It took a little time, and when he was finished they were gold and beautiful. But when the other dragons saw the blankets, they each wanted two blankets as well. The head dragon said to the boy, "You must make all the blankets my dragon friends want, or I will not release you!" The boy cried bitterly, for he knew that if he made the blankets one by one, it would take him months to finish.

Just when the boy thought all was lost, a little elf appeared on the floor at his feet. The elf said, "Fear not, child, for I am the multiplier elf. If you have made the right number of blankets for one dragon, I can multiply that number for the rest." So the boy put the two blankets in front of the elf, who waved her hands six times. And, lo! Six piles of two blankets each appeared on the floor! The dragons took their twelve beautiful gold blankets, and the boy thanked the elf and headed home.

In the beginning, you'll need to give the students story ideas like these. Doing so will help them make the mental leap from math operations to fictional illustrations—which, in turn, will lead to more explorations. We have found that children have a wonderful time concocting stories about the multiplier elf—stories that lead to unexpected mathematical discovery and learning.

Given a start with a story like this, many children will quickly elaborate, inventing twists and turns in the plot that have corresponding mathematical formulas. At some point, gifted children (even those as young as four) will begin creating story ideas themselves.

You can also adjust the stories and operations for younger students who may be learning more basic math concepts than those described here. After children have learned a new concept, you can have them generate a fairy tale about it. To help students begin their stories, you might want to give them some starter ideas. Here are some situations you could pose:

• A mouse enters a bakery and finds five cupcakes and five cookies.
• Four hungry giants come to a school cafeteria asking for hot dogs.
• In a toy store, a row of 12 teddy bears hope a child will take them home.
• Four worms meet inside an apple; each of them wants to eat some of it.

Have children make their own suggestions. As different students offer ideas, write them on the board. In a short while, the class will have compiled a variety of scenarios for mathematical explorations. As they work on their stories, encourage students to sketch or dramatize their inventions. This will help them actualize the "math plots" they are inventing and identify the parts for which they may need help.

For young children just learning about numbers, you can use a simpler version of the fairy tale idea:

An Addition and Subtraction Fairy Tale

Once upon a time, four kangaroo moms went for a walk. Each had a baby in her pouch. The babies were happy while their mothers hopped along. But soon the moms met two friends in a field and stopped to talk. The grownups talked and talked. The babies started to fidget. Finally, two baby kangaroos jumped out of their pouches and hopped off into the woods to play. The other two followed them. Soon the moms realized their babies were gone. With their friends, they called and called, hopping all around the woods. They found the four babies in a shady glen, happily dancing and leaping. The four moms took their babies and put them back in their pouches. Then they said goodbye to their two friends and went home.

This is a very simple scenario for addition and subtraction. The children can easily act it out, or you can talk them through it while sketching the story on the board. Four kangaroo moms plus four babies equal eight kangaroos ($4 + 4 = 8$). Then they meet their two friends ($8 + 2 = 10$). For a while, there are ten kangaroos. Two babies leave ($10 - 2 = 8$). Then two more babies leave ($8 - 2 = 6$). The moms and their friends look for the babies, and find all four playing ($6 + 4 = 10$). Then the two friends leave ($10 - 2 = 8$) and the moms and babies go back home.

Young children can easily add to this story. As they speak, you can write the plot in math form. Each time a child adds another piece to the story and the number of kangaroos changes, ask: "How would I write that? How many kangaroos did we have before this happened? How many are there now?" This process unites mathematics with imagination. It can involve even very young children in creative reasoning that enables them to explore math problems of their own making.

3. Extend the Experience

As the children become more involved in a story, they will find more and more elaborate mathematical "situations" they can create through the plot. At times, they may find themselves in a math scene they can't quite figure out. This gives you a natural opportunity to explore with students the complex mathematical dimensions their story has developed. Jon Scieszka and Lane Smith's *Math Curse* is a wonderful example of a story that uses mathematics imaginatively

Because the field of exploration is virtually limitless, gifted children will delight in this activity. It gives them the freedom to test their knowledge and integrate it with other math operations they have already learned, creating unique and complex scenarios.

Give all of the students opportunities to explore their ideas through a variety of means. They can draw, create models, or even act out the processes with classmates to see how they can solve the problems they've invented.

When the activity draws to a close, be sure to display students' work. Sharing the many different scenarios the class has created will allow you to significantly extend children's learning. Through this process, they will become more flexible and innovative in their thinking and be able to create as well as solve mathematical computations.

Questions and Answers

"Will I accomplish by using the creative arts to help me teach math and science?"

There are many stimulating and imaginative new ideas for teaching math and science today. A number of the publications cited in "References and Resources" (pages 117–120) present rationales, teaching strategies, and activities for integrating the arts and sciences. We know that children learn and master math and science concepts in a variety of ways. The more avenues we can find to help young learners grasp and really "own" their knowledge of a process, the better

the chance that they will do so. And by integrating lessons on new concepts with creative activities, we foster a higher level of critical thinking in children—and the flexibility to explore a whole new dimension in math and science.

Even students who are talented in math or science will explore new directions through this integration. It's an approach that can also create real breakthroughs for children who resist or struggle with either subject by enabling them to enter its world from a more imaginative, artistic framework.

"What should I do if the children create mathematical or scientific problems beyond their ability to solve?"

This is a legitimate concern. An imaginative child could easily create a math fairy tale that involves concepts and activities far in advance of the curriculum. How you respond depends on the ability of the child and the level of the problem she has created. Sometimes you'll have to encourage students to make changes in their stories. There will be other times, however, when you may find it appropriate to teach the whole class a new concept, using a student's tale as a catalyst. Generally speaking, discourage the class from developing convoluted or irrational plot twists. Remind students that their creations need to occur within the bounds of the math and science facts they know.

"What can I do with children who have trouble making the mental leap from a math or science concept to a language arts context?"

Some children are so accustomed to the conventional approach to subjects that they may find these approaches difficult. How can ordinary life be conceived in terms of triangles? How can we humans put ourselves in the position of a tree? It's one thing to get students thinking in interdisciplinary terms within general themes; it's quite another to ask them to convert a mathematical concept into a fairy tale, or to dramatize the inner life of an ordinary tree. However, if you provide sufficient catalysts—questions, suggestions, and examples—you'll find that children will begin to perceive relationships among concepts that once seemed unrelated. Be sure to give yourself and the class enough time and preparation to warm up to these ideas.

"Do you recommend these kinds of activities as enrichment or as a core part of the lessons?"

Both. We understand the pressures that all classroom teachers have in working within a set curriculum. We don't want to upset the natural rhythm you establish throughout the year. Start by trying a few simple integrated activities. You might spend several days teaching a basic math operation and then introduce a creative activity to enhance students' new knowledge. All of the examples we've described require a certain amount of prior knowledge of a property or process. They enhance the children's understanding of the new knowledge they have gained and prompt them to exceed that knowledge by applying it in new directions.

Conclusion

The creative imagination recaptures for young children the wonder they once felt for the fascinating world of science and math. Rather than merely "jazzing up" the subjects, imaginative approaches encourage higher-level thinking by allowing the children to invent their own contexts for the phenomena they study. Creativity softens the rigidity that students sometimes feel in math and science. It can transform those subjects into intriguing possibilities to be discovered and explored, rather than isolated facts to be memorized. Even word problems or lab experiments can be made more vivid and meaningful when children can take them beyond the confines of their specific subject matter. When science and math traverse the world of the arts, young children discover new possibilities and avenues for self-expression.

Creatively gifted children especially will benefit. These students can find release from the restrictions of narrow logic and rules, processes and principles. They are hungry for more—more exploration and discovery, more knowledge and mastery, more unique perspectives. Creative learning satisfies this hunger. Bright, imaginative children can discern the poetry of mathematical logic, the magical qualities of nature's rhythmic processes, the circuitous routes of number operations within fairy tales, and the amazing transformations of the geometric universe. As Albert Einstein so aptly observed: "Imagination is more important than knowledge."

References and Resources

Abruscato, Joe, and Jack Hassard. *The Whole Cosmos Catalog of Science Activities for Kids of All Ages.* Glenview, IL: GoodYear Books, 1991. Complete with illustrations, explanations, and poetry, this book is a giant-sized collection of over 275 science activities for adults and children to explore together.

AGS Math Manipulatives. This package of different types of manipulatives includes 60 attribute blocks in a variety of shapes and sizes along with manuals and activities. Write to AGS, 4201 Woodland Road, Circle Pines, MN 55014-1796. Toll-free phone: 1-800-328-2560.

Anno, Masaichiro, and Mitsumasa Anno. *Anno's Mysterious Multiplying Jar.* New York: Philomel Books, 1983. Simple text and pictures introduce the complex mathematical concept of *factorials* in a context both beautiful and mysterious.

Bowden, Marcia. *Nature for the Very Young: A Handbook of Indoor and Outdoor Activities.* Illustrated by Marilyn Rishel. New York: John Wiley & Sons, 1989. Designed for home or school, this book offers a lively and interesting collection of activities that educate and delight young children from preschool age to second grade, using nature as the catalyst for learning.

Branley, Franklyn M. *Sunshine Makes the Seasons.* Illustrated by Giulio Maestro. New York: Harper & Row, 1985. An introduction to the sun and how it affects the earth, this book includes useful experiments to help children understand seasonal transformations.

Burns, Marilyn. *The Greedy Triangle.* Illustrated by Gordon Silveria. New York: Scholastic, 1994. One of Burns's "Brainy Day Books," this volume ushers the young reader into the wondrous world of mathematical ideas and properties, integrating them into a whimsical and lively story.
———. "How to Make the Most of Math Manipulatives." *Instructor* 105:7 (April 1996), pp. 45-51. A recognized expert in the field of early childhood mathematics offers helpful advice and suggestions on strategies she uses to avoid common problems and pitfalls with math manipulatives. Her ideas are clearly explained and easy to follow.

Butterfield, Moira. *1000 Facts about Wild Animals.* New York: Scholastic, 1993. While focusing on animals, the author also examines volcanoes, rivers, deserts, rain forests, weather, and other facets of our planet. A good resource for science units.

Cassidy, John. *Earthsearch: A Kid's Geography Museum in a Book*. Palo Alto, CA: Klutz Press, 1994. Coauthored by selected teachers, this volume brings geography alive through a range of hands-on experiences.

————. *Explorabook: A Kids' Science Museum in a Book*. Palo Alto, CA: Klutz Press, 1991. Coauthored with the world-famous San Francisco Museum of Science, Art, and Human Perception, this excellent book is a complete museum visit for children. Winner of a 1992 Parents' Choice Award.

Cherry, Lynne. *The Great Kapok Tree: A Tale of the Amazon Rain Forest*. New York: Harcourt Brace & Co., 1990. This story about a lush rain forest has captivated children of all ages since its publication. Named a 1991 IRA Teacher's Choice as well as an NSTA-CBC Outstanding Science Trade Book for Children.

Chevat, Richard. *The Magic School Bus Science Explorations*. New York: Scholastic, 1994. A gentle introduction to a variety of science topics such as sound, weather, and seeds, this book integrates explanations with short activities to stimulate discussion.

Cook, Carole, and Jody Carlisle. *Challenges for Children: Creative Activities for Gifted and Talented Primary Students*. Illustrated by Dave Dillon. West Nyack, NY: The Center for Applied Research in Education, 1985. Designed for K–3 teachers, this volume offers a unique and vast collection of activities in social studies, language arts, math, and science as well as in specialized areas such as library skills, creative arts, and independent learning. You can select activities to support the curriculum, a specific skill, or a particular content area in meeting the individual needs of talented young children in the classroom.

Eckert, Sharon, and Judy Leimbach. *Primarily Math: A Problem Solving Approach*. Illustrated by Annelise Palouda. San Luis Obispo, CA: Dandy Lion Publications, 1993. A pioneer work in math education, this book offers teachers strategies that will help students in grades 2–4 reason, develop problem-solving skills, and expand their ability to communicate mathematical concepts.

Ferrier, Jean-Louis. *Picasso*. Paris: Finest S.A./Editions Pierre Terrail, 1996. This paperback volume is a comprehensive and engaging exploration of Pablo Picasso's genius. It contains a wide range of his styles and reproductions, including both sculptures and paintings.

Fisher, Leonard. *Look Around! A Book about Shapes*. New York: Viking Kestrel, 1987. An imaginative resource for primary teachers and their students that makes the geometric universe accessible and alive for young learners.

Fogarty, Robin, and Kay Opeka. *Start Them Thinking: A Handbook of Classroom Strategies for the Early Years*.

Palatine, IL: IRI SkyLight Publishing, 1988. This volume includes a wide range of activities for K–3 children that develop skills in critical and creative thinking, problem solving, and decision making. The activities are easy to integrate into the existing curriculum.

Fogarty, Robin, and Judy Stoehr. *The Mindful School: Integrating Curricula with Multiple Intelligences*. Palatine, IL: IRI SkyLight Publishing, 1995. This unique and practical book offers strategies for developing relevant integrated units as well as ideas for connecting themes to intelligences. Teachers can select activities and explore ways to integrate subject matter content in a variety of ways.

Gates, Phil. *Nature Got There First: Inventions Inspired by Nature*. New York: Larousse Kingfisher Chambers Inc., 1995. An extraordinary resource for teachers seeking creative applications for science concepts, this book shows how nature (plant and animal life) has inspired the modern world's most ingenious inventions.

Graham, Terry. *Let Loose on Mother Goose: Activities to Teach Math, Science, Art, Music, Life Skills, and Language Development*. Nashville, TN: Incentive Publications, 1982. This book transforms the popular and well-known Mother Goose rhymes into a source for integrated learning with activities that you can easily incorporate into your curriculum. Students will love using the enjoyable and familiar rhymes for their work in class.

Greenaway, Theresa. *Tree Life*. Photographs by Kim Taylor. New York: Dorling Kindersley, 1992. Part of the "Look Closer" series, this book invites children to explore the wide range of animal species that inhabit trees all around the world. A valuable resource for helping students appreciate what trees contribute to life on our planet.

Grover, Max. *Amazing and Incredible Counting Stories! A Number of Tall Tales*. San Diego: Harcourt Brace & Co., 1995. Through a series of sensational (and improbable) newspaper stories, readers can count giant banjos, pickle balloons, and timesaving jelly faucets. A witty introduction to the world of numbers for the very young child.

Hammerman, Elizabeth, and Diann Musial. *Classroom 2061: Activity-Based Assessments in Science Integrated with Mathematics and Language Arts*. Palatine, IL: IRI SkyLight Publishing, 1995. This volume offers a set of carefully crafted, integrated performance assessments and practical guidelines for educators to develop similar assessments of their own. A vital resource.

Leimbach, Judy. *Enrichment Units in Math*. Illustrated by Elisa Ahlin. San Luis Obispo, CA: Dandy Lion Publications, 1995. This collection of math materials is ideal for students ready to go beyond practicing computational skills and other basic concepts taught in the regular curriculum.

Locker, Thomas, and Candace Christiansen. *Sky Tree Portfolio.* Stuyvesant, NY: Sky Tree Press, 1995. An exciting and original resource for integrating science concepts with creative activities in the visual and language arts. Each of the fourteen 16″ x 20″ full-color posters invites the interest and response of students of all ability levels, scientific interests, and aesthetic sensibilities. Adapted from the book by Locker and Christiansen, *Sky Tree* (New York: HarperCollins, 1995). To order the portfolio, write to The Center for Gifted, National-Louis University, Evanston, IL 60201-1796, or call (847) 251-2661.

National Council of Teachers of Mathematics. *Curriculum and Evaluation Standards for School Mathematics.* Reston, VA: National Council of Teachers of Mathematics, 1989. This document presents 54 standards divided among four categories: grades K–4, 5–8, 9–12, and evaluation.

Oppenheim, Joanne. *Have You Seen Trees?* Illustrated by Jean Tseng and Mou-Sien Tseng. New York: Scholastic, 1995. Told in the form of a poem with lush illustrations, this book is especially suited to young children just learning about trees and the different ways they support animals and people. An effective and graceful integration of poetry, artistry, and science.

Perdue, Peggy K. *Science Is an Action Word!* Glenview, IL: Scott, Foresman & Co., 1991. This collection of science activities for grades 1–3 focuses on four general areas: scientific method, earth science, life science, and physical science. All the activities are classroom-tested, open-ended, and process-oriented. They show teachers how to turn their classrooms into fascinating laboratories with inexpensive and easily available materials.

Pinczes, Elinor. *One Hundred Hungry Ants.* New York: Houghton Mifflin Co., 1993. An entertaining way to introduce children to the principles of division, this book will entice any child with a love of rhyme, picnics, and bugs (even if he doesn't like math).

Pollock, Steve. *Ecology.* New York: DK Publishing, 1993. One of the "Eyewitness" books, this volume explores how animals, plants, energy, and matter interconnect in habitats around the world. A rich resource for teachers to integrate with other science curricula.

Pope, Joyce. *Animal Homes.* Mahwah, NJ: Troll Associates, 1994. An imaginative introduction to the habitats of nature's various animals.

Poppe, Carol A., and Nancy A. Van Matre. *K–3 Science Activities Kit.* West Nyack, NY: The Center for Applied Research in Education, 1988. A well-sequenced and comprehensive sourcebook for all ability levels, this volume offers five science units—weather, nutrition, birds, trees, and pets—and a total of 40 activities. Includes illustrations, reproducible materials, management suggestions, and charts of critical-thinking skills required for each activity.

Rohmann, Eric. *Time Flies.* New York: Crown Publishers, 1994. Inspired by the theory that birds are modern relatives of dinosaurs, this wordless book involves young students in a thrilling journey through time with a series of oil paintings that will spur creative imagination.

Schneck, Marcus. *Patterns in Nature: A World of Color, Shape, and Light.* New York: Crescent Books, 1991. A marvelous source for exploring shapes and patterns in nature, this book includes more than 120 full-color photographs that inspire original thinking and insight in children of all ages.

Scieszka, Jon, and Lane Smith. *Math Curse.* New York: Viking, 1995. Through bold illustrations and a witty text, the authors entice both students and teacher into the wonders of mathematics and its applications in everyday living.

Svedberg, Ulf. *Nicky the Nature Detective.* Translated by Ingrid Selberg. Illustrated by Lena Anderson. New York: R&S Books, 1988. This charming book is an informative and entertaining guide for the beginning naturalist, describing changes in flora and fauna from season to season while also offering exciting ideas for nature activities.

Taylor, Barbara. *Forest Life.* Photographs by Kim Taylor and Jane Burton. New York: Dorling Kindersley, 1993. Part of the "Look Closer" series, this volume gives young children an intimate view of forest life that provides insights into plants and animals in original and creative ways.

Terrell, Sandy. *Roberto's Rainforest.* El Cajon, CA: Interaction Publishers, 1995. This innovative and activity-filled book is a scientific "canoe trip" that allows young naturalists to explore a tropical rain forest in South America.

Thomson, Amy. *The Color of Distance.* New York: Ace Books, 1995. Written for adult readers, this novel is an excellent example of how a professional author used her research on the ecology of a rain forest and the biology of reptilian species for a work of fiction.

Torrance, E. Paul, and H. Tammy Safter. *Incubation Model of Teaching: Getting Beyond Aha!* Buffalo, NY: Bearly Limited, 1990. This trailblazing book offers a conceptual knowledge of creative "incubation" and of how to design more innovative teaching approaches that will tap children's natural curiosity, playfulness, spontaneity, and invention.

Trees and Forests. New York: Scholastic, 1995. Part of the "Voyages of Discovery" series, this volume covers a great deal of content on tree life around the world. Through art and text, as well as intriguing graphics and special effects, it provides a powerful catalyst and interactive guide for exploration and discovery.

Van Der Meer, Ron, and Bob Gardner. *The Math Kit: A Three-Dimensional Tour Through Mathematics.* New

York: Macmillan Publishing Co., 1994. A captivating approach to the study of mathematics, this book includes graphic representations of the properties of simple arithmetic, multiplication tables, and decimal places; three-dimensional models of the Pythagorean theorem, solid polygons, and trigonometric angles; games; and a complete glossary of math terms.

Van De Walle, John A. *Elementary School Mathematics: Teaching Developmentally,* 2d ed. White Plains, NY: Longman, 1994. Based on NCTM standards, this exceptional volume for K–8 teachers offers a developmental approach to mathematics that emphasizes problem-solving and the conceptualization of mathematical ideas rather than a system of rules and procedures.

Wilkes, Angela. *The Amazing Outdoor Activity Book.* New York: Dorling Kindersley, 1996. An action-packed book, with more than 50 creative outdoor projects for children to build, grow, collect, draw, make, and bake. A good resource for parents or teachers that includes easy-to-follow instructions.

Winebrenner, Susan. *Teaching Gifted Kids in the Regular Classroom.* Minneapolis, MN: Free Spirit Publishing Inc., 1992. Winebrenner discusses what to do with the child who already knows what you are going to teach. She presents specific strategies with step-by-step instructions and reproducible forms.

Wood, John Norris. *Woods and Forests: Nature Hide and Seek Book.* Illustrated by Maggie Silver. New York: Alfred A. Knopf, 1993. A visually beautiful introduction to the wonderful creatures hiding behind bushes, under rocks, and inside holes in the tree, this book presents many important facts about animals and the habitats—American and European woodlands—they occupy.

7

Assessing and Documenting Development

*L*ouis, usually bouncy and boisterous, quietly walked into the kitchen and sat down. He stared at his report card and tried to figure out what the words said. He knew that this piece of paper was very important. Its purpose was to tell his mom how well he was doing in school. Worriedly, Louis eyed the single row of letters. Had his teacher remembered everything he'd done? How would his mom react? Could this small piece of paper really tell all the things he was doing and learning?

The Assessment Conundrum

The issue of assessment and evaluation brings out a wide range of emotions in everyone involved. There's pressure on students to earn good marks; there's pressure on teachers to be fair. The problem of grading young children has never been easy. What do letter grades—S or U, A or C—really mean? Is it "satisfactory" to do work similar to that of other students? Or to sit and "fill time"? Is the child evaluated on paper-and-pencil exercises alone? If so, what happens to the child whose fine motor skills are weak? Does that mean his work can't be satisfactory—or better than satisfactory?

Tracking each child's work in the beginning years is very important. Documentation showing what the child *knows* and *is able to do* should be maintained and passed along from teacher to

teacher. This assures continuity. Each new teacher can use the information to plan projects, avoid needless repetition, and find and value areas of expertise.

Planning Activities for Broad-Based Assessment

In assessing young children, nontraditional methods that show how the child *is intelligent,* as well as *how intelligent* the child is, are essential. As a teacher, you'll want to plan assessment experiences that meaningfully show what each child knows and can do. For best results, plan activities that fit the following criteria:

1. They are natural rather than contrived. The activities need to flow with the lesson rather than be added on.
2. They are open-ended. Each child needs opportunities to show all that she is capable of doing. Too often, a ceiling is put on the activity: the gifted child may get all the answers correct, but you are still left to guess what she really knows. Open-ended assessment is more likely to elicit the child's higher level of response.
3. They incorporate all areas of the curriculum. In evaluating children's knowledge and ability, we need to consider what the child can do in language arts, math, art, science, social studies, drama, physical games, and music.

4. They are age-appropriate. In planning an activity, ask: What's the purpose of the activity? Has it been taught, or have the children had the opportunity to learn it? Is it clear? Do the people reading or scoring the performance know what they're looking for?

5. They reflect the many ways in which children learn. Whenever possible, give choices to the child about how to present knowledge: through drawing, writing, singing, role-playing, speaking, or physically demonstrating. Choose experiences that allow the use of varied learning styles and multiple intelligences. Chapters 1 and 2 describe different intelligence preferences and learning styles and discuss ways to help children learn and perform within their most comfortable modes. See "A Type and Degree of Intelligence" (pages 6–7) and "Individual Learning Styles" (pages 28–30).

Assessment needs to be *formative*—occurring daily—as well as *cumulative* (summative)—occurring at the end of the unit, topic, area, or year of study. Evaluation should be based on growth and learning styles. It must allow you to move beyond and away from rigid assessment situations to those that are more flexible and open-ended.

Sound, authentic assessment provides the basis for building activities and experiences that challenge the child who already knows the information and can do the regular work. At the same time, it gives us information about which children need additional teaching or a different format in order to learn the material.

Mali liked complex things. If work was too easy for her, she added her own special flair. Quite often, she doodled on the sides of the workbook pages. Her imagination sometimes ran on overtime.

Mali could easily count from 1 to 100, something her teacher wasn't aware of. One day, while completing a dot-to-dot sheet, Mali decided the picture was "too plain." When her teacher saw Mali's completed dot-to-dot, she found the numbers 1, 1¼, 1½, 1¾, 2, 2¼, 2½, and so on, up to 10. The additions did, indeed, make the picture more interesting!

Observing this precocity, the teacher decided to meet with Mali's parents. They agreed on broad-based assessment. A standardized test showed that Mali was at least two grade levels ahead in all math areas. The teacher reviewed Mali's portfolio and saw that Mali had mastered the specific math work the class was currently doing. The teacher began to offer Mali the opportunity to work and

Moving Toward Open-Ended Evaluation*

Rigid evaluation relies on:	*Open-ended evaluation relies on:*
right/wrong answers	open-ended opportunities for multiple answers
quiet	appropriate level of noise
paper-and-pencil tasks	hands-on tasks
teacher talking	child participation
negative criticism	positive, growth-producing comments
desk activities	activities within a variety of settings

* Adapted from Joan Franklin Smutny, Kathleen Veenker, and Stephen Veenker. *Your Gifted Child: How to Recognize and Develop the Special Talents in Your Child from Birth to Age Seven.* New York: Ballantine Books, 1989, pp. 97-98. Used with permission of Joan Franklin Smutny.

progress with math games and manipulatives more suited to her ability.

This example points out three tools of broad-based, authentic assessment: standardized testing, portfolio assessment, and observation. Let's look at each one more closely.

Standardized Testing as a Measure of Intelligence*

Children deserve to learn in school. In order to teach them, we need to find out how they learn best and at what pace they learn. We also need to find out what they already know. Traditionally, standardized testing offers a means for doing this. Testing complements and creates a basis for teaching.

Tests Don't Give the Whole Picture

Tests, however, can be misused. Often, achievement tests of specific academic subjects are interpreted as intelligence tests. Group tests usually record only what children can do with pencils in hand. That leaves out many components of achievement, ability, and intelligence. Another limitation of group tests is that they're likely to penalize highly gifted children. On these tests, a score in the 98th or 99th percentile may not depict the extent of the gifted child's functioning level, especially if it's normed for the student's grade. In fact, any test that is "on-level" is probably inappropriate for gifted children. An "off-level" test, one designed for older students, has a higher ceiling and is less likely to limit the highest possible score.

When Brad was four, his first individually administered IQ test score was 139 on the Wechsler Preschool and Primary Scale of Intelligence–Revised (WPPSI–R). *When he was six, his school used a group test, the* Otis-Lennon Mental Abilities Test; *Brad scored 132. Further testing, this time with the individualized* Wechsler Intelligence

Scale for Children–Third Edition (WISC–III), *resulted in a score of 152. Then Brad scored 180 on yet another individually administered test with a higher ceiling—the* Stanford-Binet Intelligence Scale, Form L–M. *How could this happen? And what could it mean?*

As is commonly done, the first IQ scores obtained through Brad's school were determined by group testing. Like many group tests given in schools, Brad's early tests measured academic aptitude or achievement more than abstract reasoning abilities. Such group tests generally require one right answer; they sometimes confuse children who consider many possible answers. Also, group tests usually include only a few items at the higher ranges of difficulty. This creates a "ceiling" effect and tends to limit children's possible scores.

Measuring intelligence is complex because children's intelligence is expressed in many ways. Intellectual differences among young gifted children are vast and varied. That is why standardized tests designed to accommodate the huge majority give only a limited view into gifted children's capabilities and ways of functioning.

Although an individually administered IQ test is usually more comprehensive as a single measure of intelligence, scores for individualized tests aren't completely reliable either. And these need to be considered within a range of five to ten points above and below the given score (for example, a specific score of 130 means that the child's IQ is between 124 and 136). Most individually administered IQ tests measure many abilities and then find the average of those diverse skills for a single score of *general* intellectual ability.

Regardless of whether a test is administered within a group or individually, there's much that an IQ score *doesn't* tell about a child. For example, if a child has extremely high verbal skills but lags some in spatial and fine motor development, he might attain an IQ score in the average range, despite having many intellectual abilities that are far above average.

It's usually safe to assume that any test score is probably an *underestimation* of a child's abilities. There are many reasons why this might be the case. At the moment of a testing situation, a child might:

• say "I don't know" rather than risk saying something wrong

---

* For a list of standardized tests and their descriptions, see Appendix A, pages 196–197.

- wonder what a parent or sibling is doing or what he is missing on TV
- be distracted by the noise in the next room
- want to avoid creating higher performance expectations in parents and teachers
- want to avert the possibility of being placed in a gifted program that will separate him from friends
- have an ear infection and not hear clearly
- be ill (or becoming ill), hungry, tired, or low on energy and therefore not fully alert
- be reacting to an allergen, known or unknown, and thus feel tired, hyper, or unable to fully focus.

In contrast, it's impossible for children to perform on a test *beyond* what they know or what they can do. A child can't fake a right answer. He can't pretend to say a series of numbers backward. He can't cheat on putting a puzzle together.

Other factors are also involved in testing any child. Sound intelligence testing must look for specific abilities and strengths and test for limits. Learning and thinking styles come into play.

At age five, Mario was a complex thinker. He questioned everything. His powers of observation were fantastic. However, he didn't perform well on standardized tests. Sometimes his thoughts went beyond the test. He thought of different answers that should have been given but weren't. In many instances, the choices on the paper seemed too simplistic. At other times, Mario read more into the question than the test maker had intended, so his responses were frequently "wrong." One test question asked, "What is the color of coal?" The choices were black, purple, or gray. Mario marked all three. When the examiner asked him why, he responded, "It's black when I see it inside, it's purple when I see it in the sun, and after it's burned it's gray."

Here, the examiner needed to ask Mario how he arrived at his answer. By Mario's reasoning, the answer was logical and correct—although, according to test regulations, it would be scored as wrong.

The Role of the Examiner

Another critical ingredient in valid testing is the child's rapport with the examiner. When children feel safe and encouraged, they're more likely to risk showing examiners who they are and what they know. They're more likely to guess—and to tap into their subconscious—when they're not absolutely certain about an answer.

But what if a child simply doesn't like the examiner? Perhaps the adult reminds the child of someone she doesn't like. Perhaps the child is even afraid of the examiner. One child told the tester that she couldn't talk to her examiner because he was a stranger and her mother had told her never to talk to strangers!

Here are some ways to create a more comfortable situation for both the child and the examiner:

- Before the scheduled examination, explain to the child that she will meet with a man or woman who will do activities with her to find out how she learns best.
- Request that the child bring a snack to eat during the testing process. This might provide essential brain fuel, or it might be "comfort food."
- Be flexible enough to reschedule at the last minute if necessary. This flexibility is important. The child might not feel well; noisy demolition work might suddenly begin just outside the window; the child could discover that she'll miss a birthday party if she takes the examination. In any of these cases, her scores may not be valid.
- Use this "trade secret" to establish an easy give-and-take between child and examiner: Ask the child to select and bring several photographs or pictures to show the examiner. This invites the child to invest something in the process, to quickly become accustomed to how the examiner responds to her, and to start off with a positive association.

Testing Culturally Diverse Children

Nearly all tests have some bias toward the majority culture. When a child from outside of that culture is tested, the results of standardized intelligence tests should not be used as an absolute sign of cognitive ability. Instead, they should be viewed as a general estimate of the child's current level of measurable functioning and as a benchmark for further testing. Testing can also help teachers identify the best learning approaches for the child and plan procedures that will engage the child's strengths.

Some children from cultural minorities may have fewer test-taking skills and different problem-solving strategies. Some may even sabotage themselves by working slowly to avoid competition and gain acceptance. Here are some suggestions to consider when assessing a child from an ethnic or other cultural minority:

- Determine the child's preferred language.
- Use a multiple-method assessment approach. Don't assume that a single score or a small collection of scores can fully portray the child's intellectual abilities.
- Integrate other types of assessment, such as informal observations or actual work samples and anecdotes from the child's portfolio. (Portfolios are discussed beginning on page 126. You will find information on informal observation on page 129, and forms to use for this purpose on pages 131–138.)
- If possible, compare the child's scores with those of other children in the same group. National norms are likely to be inappropriate for judging most minority children.
- Take into account the child's degree of acculturation.
- Be cautious about drawing generalizations from any test score.
- Try to be aware of any personal biases you might have, and guard against letting these affect your interaction with or assessment of the child.

A few tests are less culturally biased than others. Here are some we recommend (the tests are fully described in Appendix A beginning on page 196):

Wechsler: In the *Wechsler Scales,* the *Performance Scale* is less dependent on cultural and language knowledge than the *Verbal Scale.* The Block Design subtest correlates significantly with classroom performance and with mathematical ability. Also, the Digit Span subtest can be used to assess short-term auditory memory, attention span, and ability to concentrate. A Spanish adaptation of the *Wechsler Intelligence Scale for Children–Revised* (WISC–R) is available.

Stanford-Binet: Use the Abstract/Visual Reasoning Area subtests of the *Stanford-Binet Intelligence Scale, Fourth Edition.*

K–ABC: Use the Nonverbal subtests of the *Kaufman Assessment Battery for Children (K–ABC).*

Note that the *Peabody Picture Vocabulary Test–Revised (PPVT–R)* is a measure of receptive vocabulary only and should *not* be used to determine intelligence of Hispanic-American preschool and kindergarten children.

Ethnicity is only one type of difference. Children who come from low socioeconomic groups of *any* ethnicity are likely to test differently than the cultural norm. Children of poverty are the most vulnerable. Their adaptive strategies may not "fit" the tests. Tests are also misused if they cast out children with special differences and personal problems.

Another important caution in interpreting IQ scores: Gifted children, because of their exceptional cognitive abilities, may exhibit great discrepancies between their measures of performance/fine motor abilities and those of verbal and other cognitive skills. For example, using the *Wechsler,* differences of 20, 30, and even 40 points between Verbal and Performance scores indicate learning disabilities in most average and high-average children. *This may not hold true for gifted children.* Such disparity *does* show that gifted children might be frustrated by their fine motor lag and might need alternative ways to express what they know. However, the children are probably not "learning disabled."

Outside Consultants

Sometimes it's necessary to use outside help to become aware of children's exceptional learning styles and needs. When a private professional assessment is made, these are some questions to consider before and after testing:

- Is the agency or examiner/interpreter widely experienced in testing gifted children?
- Does the examiner/interpreter have a respected reputation among those in your "gifted community"?
- Did the child enjoy the testing experience?

- Were the scores adequately interpreted to the parents? Were behavioral, emotional, social, and academic recommendations discussed? Were parents clearly told what the numbers mean and don't mean?
- Do the test scores accurately reflect the child's abilities?

What Standardized Tests Tell Us

Standardized tests give information about some areas of strength and weakness. They help us know how a child compares with others of the same age. However, they often don't assess the wide range of talent or abilities of the child and may focus only on intellectual development, reading ability, visual-spatial acumen, or thinking skills. For some children of minority cultures or economic groups, the test may cover material with which they have no prior experience, thus placing them in an invalid assessment situation.

Questions to Ask About Discrepancies

Any discrepancies between test scores and performance need to be carefully analyzed. The following questions may give you helpful information about the validity of a particular test.

When the child performs far better on a test than in the classroom, ask:

- Are the lessons too easy, or are they repetitious?
- Is the child not challenged in the classroom?
- Does the child usually or often feel stressed or fearful in the classroom?
- Are there problems outside of school that affect the child's learning?
- How is the child's health? Could there be a physical problem? Is the child getting enough rest?
- Are the directions given in the classroom clear?

When a tester was testing four-year-old Robby, she asked him to count backward from ten. Robby promptly rose from his seat, turned his back to the tester, and began to count, "10, 11, 12, 13. . . ." Robby did what he was asked to do—literally.

When the child performs far better in the classroom than on a test, ask:

- Was the test appropriate for the child?
- Was the child motivated to take the test?
- Did the child feel anxious about the test?
- Was the test administered by a stranger in an unfamiliar environment?
- Did the test involve only paper-and-pencil tasks?
- Are the child's strengths obvious in areas not covered by the test?
- Was the child tired or ill during the test?
- Is the child a perfectionist? (The slow, methodical thinker may need more than the required time to perform the tasks.)
- Was the child distracted during the test? (Sometimes being with other children or in a stimulating environment may pull the child's attention away from the task at hand.)
- Did the child appear to think with more complexity than the test required?

Using Portfolios to Document and Evaluate Progress

For some children, tests will be inappropriate. Mario's case (page 124) provides an example. Mario's low score was in no way indicative of his knowledge. A simple interview documenting his responses needs to replace or append the test score. "Real-life" assessment is much more appropriate for the child whose ability far exceeds the boundaries of the testing situation.

Even when testing is appropriate, more broad-based, authentic assessment is an important and useful means of documenting children's abilities and progress. One of the most promising methods for collecting and evaluating the child's work is a portfolio. Author and gifted educator Bertie Kingore defines portfolios as "systematic collections of student work selected to provide information about students' attitudes and motivation, level of development and growth over time."*

Chapter 1 discusses creating portfolios and using them as a means of getting to know your

---

* Bertie Kingore. *Portfolios: Enriching and Assessing All Students, Identifying the Gifted, Grades K–6.* Des Moines, IA: Leadership Publishers, 1993, p. 1. Used with permission of Bertie Kingore.

students (see "Portfolios" beginning on page 9). The same portfolio you compile for this purpose can also be an excellent tool for ongoing assessment. Its effectiveness requires careful planning and clear organization. It must be more than a random collection; you'll need to establish goals for the portfolio and make decisions about what it will contain in order to serve its purpose of helping you evaluate a student's progress. The portfolio should reflect the child's growth and learning over time.

You might consider including a small collection of work that represents the young child. For example, at the start of the school year, you might ask the child to create a self-portrait or a family portrait. Then you could have the student repeat the task in the middle of the year and again at the conclusion of the year. This will show growth and be affirming for the child.

The same type of assignment can be given in math, writing, and problem solving—each showing how the child grows in ability. You might also choose an item that represents a student's unique characteristics or interests. For example, a child may love horses and draw pictures of them during all of his free time. One of those drawings, included in his portfolio, can be a kind of snapshot of his special "love."

Involving Children

Save children's work or pictures of their work. Each week, have them select a piece that they wish to put into their portfolio. Some teachers find it easiest to have children start with one or two content areas. Encourage students to select not only their "best" work, but also things that were hard for them to do or required a lot of effort. Add to the portfolio work that represents new information that the child has just learned. Include the "draft" copy along with the finished product; you 'll then have excellent examples of multiple stages of growth.

You might also include products students have done in their free time or at home. These spontaneous products will be different for each child and will be a prime source of information about the child's special interests and abilities. They may show excellence or indicate areas where the child needs special help. Not every child will have a spontaneous product; some children may have several.

Involving Parents

If you like, suggest to parents that they maintain their own portfolio for their child. Parents could, for example, collect:

- items that commemorate special occasions
- notes about "firsts" for the child
- photographs of the child at different stages
- drawings the child has made
- pictures of, or notes about, the child's collections or hobbies
- a list of books read by and to the child
- medical notes
- anecdotes or observations made by child-care providers.

Keeping a home portfolio gives parents a way to share with you what the child is like or what the child has done at home. Chapter 1 includes several family letters and forms to assist you in learning more about children at home: "Your Child's Pictures" (page 18), "Information, Please" (page 19), "About My Child" (pages 20–21), "Checklist of My Child's Strengths" (pages 22–23), and "Your Child's Personal Exhibit" (page 24).

Children can make and maintain their own portfolios. (See "Child-Created Portfolios," page 12.) A child-created portfolio can complement the one that you keep, offering a window on what the child enjoys and values and on the ways in which she is excelling or growing.

Maintaining the Portfolio*

Date each new entry and file it at the back of the portfolio. This allows you to see growth and to keep a chronological record of the work. You can teach the child to do most of this filing. It then becomes the child's responsibility to add to the portfolio. You may need to write the date on the board or provide a stamp that the student can use to date work. To be meaningful, portfolios need to be manageable, easily identifiable, and readily accessible for the child.

Each entry should include an explanation of why the piece was selected. Young children who aren't yet able to write can dictate their reason to

---

* Many of the suggestions included here for maintaining students' portfolios are from Kingore, p. 3. Used with permission of Bertie Kingore.

an older child or an adult. This can be a simple note: "I chose this because _____." This aids the decision-making process and allows you and any portfolio reader to see why the work was considered significant enough to be included.

Talking with the Child About the Portfolio

It's very important that you talk with the child about her portfolio. A portfolio conference gives you the opportunity to highlight work and gives the student a chance to value her work and see progress. You're building on success and providing encouragement and motivation to keep on learning.

Open the lines of communication with statements and questions such as the following:

- Tell me about your work.
- How did you do that?
- Explain what you did.
- How did you figure that out?

This is a time for sharing information, not for interrogation. Recognize effort as well as any end result. Be positive. Build on what the student has done, and set goals for what she'll attempt to accomplish next. This encourages the child to take responsibility for successes and needed improvements. Self-esteem is a natural byproduct here—it thrives on growth and success! The conference also opens a door for increased understanding between you and the child and provides an opportunity for you to become more sensitive to her needs and strengths.

Conferences need to take place apart from other children, yet still in clear view of the rest of the class. We suggest that you meet while the remaining students are working in learning centers or using free time. Help the others in the class to understand and respect that this is your special time with one student. Knowing that they, too, will have time alone with you will support them as they learn to do this.

Effective Portfolio Assessment

For portfolios to be educationally effective, they must emphasize content, process, and product as well as effort and achievement. They also must include student ownership and self-evaluation. Bertie Kingore writes:*

"Portfolios must be developed so they:
- are a natural part of daily classroom activities rather than contrived;
- are thoroughly integrated into the instructional program;
- encourage student responsibility, ownership, and pride of accomplishment;
- allow students to polish and refine their craft—to build upon what they are learning to do well;
- focus discussions about learning and development among students, teachers, and parents;
- incorporate learning tasks and also students' ideas, interests, and attitudes;
- invite challenge and complexity in students' thinking and in the works they produce; and
- encourage student metacognition and increase their awareness of their capacity for self-reflection and making judgments."

Children become so proud of their portfolios that they need the opportunity to share them. You might want to arrange a "portfolio party." Children can display their portfolios and explain what they have done and learned to parents, relatives, neighbors, and community members. This is a chance to inform stakeholders in your school about the wonderful things your students are doing—things that aren't adequately reflected in test scores alone. The portfolio party might occur in conjunction with parent night, parent conferences, open house, or a school learning fair. Be sure to invite the local press and get media coverage!

---

* Kingore, p. 3. Used with permission of Bertie Kingore.

Documenting Development Through Observations

Observations are yet another way you can assess the young child. To make accurate, reliable observations that are objective, fair, and consistent, you need to establish what you are looking for and the degree to which a particular behavior or skill is evidenced.

A checklist is an easy and efficient way to document what you have observed. When the child shows evidence of a behavior or skill, you note it, along with the date. You can record and date more detailed observations on note cards and file them in the child's portfolio.

Checklists are especially effective when they not only list behaviors and skills, but also provide brief descriptions and standards by which to measure them. For example:

>***Includes detail in writing***
>Not yet evidenced: *Gives no detail.*
>Developing: *Includes some detail.*
>Age-appropriate: *Includes appropriate detail.*
>Outstanding: *Uses elaborate, descriptive, rich detail.*

This gives bright children who have achieved the level of "age-appropriate" a goal or direction to grow in so mediocrity won't be established as the norm. You'll want to date your notations; then you can reassess the child periodically, each time noting both *what* level has been reached and *when* the child reached it.

The "Student Observation Forms" (pages 131–138) are detailed checklists that can help you to evaluate young children's performance or skills in specific areas.*

When the child has finished a piece of work or when an area of study comes to a close, the child may be able to give you valuable information about what he has learned. You may want to have

the child report on this by using the "What I Learned" self-evaluation form (page 139).** Older students will be able to complete the form on their own. With younger students who aren't yet comfortable reading or writing, ask each child those questions on the form that you think will give you helpful information.

Questions and Answers

"If the gifted student moves ahead in the material, won't other students feel bad?"

Since most evaluation is done on an individual basis, there's no need for children to be aware of a comparison. Also, there may be an area in which a gifted child's performance is "average" or even "below average." To celebrate growth in all children, use the portfolio to show you how best to use your time to extend, teach, and remediate.

"My children want to take their work home with them. How can I keep it for their portfolio?"

If the children really want to bring their work home, make photocopies for them. However, you may find that once the children really "get into" the portfolio process, your problem may not be about what goes home, but about how to limit what goes into the portfolio. Be sure to communicate with parents so they understand that everything the students work on in class won't be coming home. And make an effort to share children's portfolios with parents at conferences and open house.

"What if the child wants to put many examples of the same thing into the portfolio?"

Explain to the child that you value his ability to do that particular thing very well, and you recognize that he's trying to perfect his skill. Say that you'll keep one example of that favorite subject each month, or that he can choose one example for September, one for January, and one for May. Then make it clear that you expect him to also select other items that represent other areas of learning.

"Won't all this assessment and evaluation take time? How can I do it all?"

It will take time, but time that is spread across the school year. Your goal is to have ongoing information to aid you in designing classroom instruction. It's initially time-consuming to teach

---

* The checklists are adapted from Bertie Kingore, *The Kingore Observation Inventory (KOI)* (Des Moines, IA: Leadership Publishers, 1990), and from Smutny, Veenker, and Veenker. Used with permission of the authors.
** The "What I Learned?" form is adapted from a self-evaluation tool developed by Dodie Merritt, a teacher of gifted children at Genoa-Kingston School in Genoa, IL. Used with permission of Dodie Merritt.

children portfolio management skills, but as these skills are mastered, your burden lessens. It's also important that you structure your time for what's important.

Tests take time to give and to score. Portfolios can be integrated into the lesson and classroom routine so they don't necessarily take *more* time, but *different* time. Practice "selective abandonment" with things that are time-consuming and unproductive.

Also, think creatively. Is there a parent, a community volunteer, an older child, or an aide who's willing to help you do some of the evaluation on a one-on-one basis with your students? Could you work with *one* child for a few minutes each day during students' free time? Keep in mind that this process is continuous and comprehensive. By doing a little bit each day, you can help yourself stay on top of things.

Conclusion

When young gifted students come into the school setting, they are excited about learning new things. Your task is to make sure that you extend the excitement and nourish the curiosity, without leaving gaps in children's knowledge and skills. To do this, you need to constantly assess and evaluate what each student *knows* and *can do*. Documenting growth validates achievement and rewards excellence. Your own payback comes when you observe children thrilled at learning, busy working on new things that match their abilities and potential.

References and Resources

Gellman, E.S. *School Testing: What Parents and Educators Need to Know.* Westport, CT: Praeger Publishers, 1995. This excellent resource for anyone involved in making children's educational decisions explains tests and their uses and misuses. Written for those with little or no training in testing.

Kingore, Bertie. *The Kingore Observation Inventory (KOI).* Des Moines, IA: Leadership Publishers, 1990. Presents a structure of observations that young gifted children typically demonstrate. The observations can be incorporated into an identification process or used to set an instructional focus.

———. *Portfolios: Enriching and Assessing All Students, Identifying the Gifted, Grades K–6.* Des Moines, IA: Leadership Publishers, 1993. Elaborates on purposes, practices, and implementations in creating portfolios for young gifted children.

Marland, Sidney, Jr. *Education of the Gifted and Talented: Report to the Congress of the United States by the U.S. Commissioner of Education.* Washington, DC: U.S. Government Printing Office, 1972. A significant report documenting the needs and lack of services to America's brightest children.

Roeper Review: A Journal on Gifted Education. The Roeper School, P.O. Box 329, Bloomfield Hills, MI 48303. Most issues of this quarterly journal include a "Testing" section that reviews instruments used for assessing gifted children. A collection of these articles, available from the Roeper School, would be a valuable resource for learning the intricacies of testing gifted children.

Sattler, Jerome M. *Assessment of Children.* San Diego, CA: Jerome M. Sattler, Publisher, Inc., 1992. The most comprehensive reference available on testing children.

Smutny, Joan Franklin, Kathleen Veenker, and Stephen Veenker. *Your Gifted Child: How to Recognize and Develop the Special Talents in Your Child from Birth to Age Seven.* New York: Ballantine Books, 1989. Comprehensive explanations to help parents and educators to understand the characteristics and needs of young gifted children.

Walker, Sally Y., and Lori Whitman. *Making Memories: A Parent Home Portfolio.* Beavercreek, OH: Pieces of Learning, 1997. Activities and pages for documenting a child's growth and development in portfolio form.

Webb, James T., and Patricia A. Kleine. "Assessing Gifted and Talented Children." In *Testing Young Children,* J.L. Culbertson and D.J. Willis, ed. Austin, TX: Pro-ed., 1993. This chapter examines the general process and some specific suggestions for testing gifted children.

STUDENT OBSERVATION FORM I

Learning and Cognitive Development

Student's Name: _____

To the teacher: Use this form several times throughout the year. On the line beside the appropriate item, write the date on which you assessed the child's level of development.

KEY TO LETTER SYMBOLS

N = Not yet evidenced   **A** = Age-appropriate

D = Developing   **O** = Outstanding

Analytical Thinking

Analyzes tasks:

_____ **N:** Approaches tasks with no evidence of prior thought.

_____ **D:** Begins tasks after some thought.

_____ **A:** Shows ability to think through task.

_____ **O:** Thinks through and analyzes tasks; can apply learning to new tasks.

Sees cause-and-effect relationships:

_____ **N:** Has no idea of cause and effect.

_____ **D:** Occasionally sees what caused reaction.

_____ **A:** Sees cause and effect when it occurs.

_____ **O:** Understands (can explain) cause and effect.

Ability to take apart and reassemble things:

_____ **N:** Is unaware of parts.

_____ **D:** Can disassemble, but has difficulty putting things back together.

_____ **A:** Can take apart and reassemble basic things or ideas.

_____ **O:** Is able to disassemble and reassemble things and ideas in novel, workable ways.

Expresses relationships between past/present experiences:

_____ **N:** Able to see only the present.

_____ **D:** Beginning to distinguish between past and present.

_____ **A:** Can distinguish past and present.

_____ **O:** Expresses relationship between past, present and future events.

➡

Makes up stories, songs, plays about experiences:

____ **N:** Does not tell stories, sing songs, or enact plays.

____ **D:** Repeats stories, songs, or plays as told.

____ **A:** Can make up short stories, songs, or plays.

____ **O:** Tells stories, sings songs, or acts out plays with elaborate details.

Organizes collections:

____ **N:** Does not see any organizational schema.

____ **D:** Is beginning to see simple organizational patterns.

____ **A:** Can organize simple collections in standard ways.

____ **O:** Is capable of organizing complex collections in different ways.

Motivation or Task Commitment

Keeps at task until it makes sense:

____ **N:** Flits from thing to thing; has short attention span.

____ **D:** Is able to stay with task for short while.

____ **A:** Stays with some tasks when they are of interest.

____ **O:** Shows persistence and commitment to getting task completed.

Asks penetrating questions:

____ **N:** Does not ask questions; asks unrelated questions.

____ **D:** Asks questions that relate to topic.

____ **A:** Asks questions that show evidence of understanding the topic.

____ **O:** Understands topic in-depth; asks questions that reflect thinking.

Is curious:

____ **N:** Has difficulty focusing on item.

____ **D:** Asks standard questions (who, what) relating to items.

____ **A:** Wants to know how things work.

____ **O:** Asks why and what if.

Displays unexpected depth of knowledge in one or more areas:

____ **N:** Shows only superficial knowledge.

____ **D:** Has an area of interest.

____ **A:** Wants to know more about an area of interest; asks questions or searches for more information.

____ **O:** Is a resident expert in a specific area.

Remembers:

____ **N:** Has difficulty recalling information or details.

____ **D:** Remembers some details while other information may be hazy or lacking.

____ **A:** Recalls details of things that pertain to self.

____ **O:** Can clearly recall and recount past events, promises, and minute details.

➡

Displays energy and excitement when learning:
____ **N:** Is reluctant to try anything new; shows little enthusiasm.
____ **D:** Shows interest in learning.
____ **A:** Is energetic about topic that interests him/her.
____ **O:** Becomes very enthusiastic about learning; does not want to quit.

Wants to do things on own; shows independence:
____ **N:** Wants teacher to do things for her/him.
____ **D:** Does some things on own.
____ **A:** Prefers to do things on own.
____ **O:** Does not want help; asks to be left to do things in own way.

Learning

Number of repetitions needed to learn:
____ More than 30
____ 15–25
____ 10 or less
____ 5 or less

Categorizes by more than one attribute:
____ **N:** Does not see attributes.
____ **D:** Observes attributes but has difficulty categorizing.
____ **A:** Can categorize one or two simple attributes.
____ **O:** Is capable of seeing and categorizing multiple attributes.

Is able to read and explain meaning of what was read:
____ **N:** Recalls a few details.
____ **D:** Knows literal meaning.
____ **A:** Comprehends written material.
____ **O:** Makes inferences and/or analyzes reading.

Comprehends symbols (note all that apply):
____ Letters
____ Numbers
____ Maps
____ Music

Understands these mathematical concepts (note all that apply):

____ One-to-one correspondence	____ Division
____ Addition	____ Making change
____ Subtraction	____ Telling time
____ Regrouping	____ Measurement
____ Multiplication	____ Graphs and charts

For Teachers

Writing and Language Development

Student's Name: _____

To the teacher: Use this form several times throughout the year. On the line beside the appropriate item, write the date on which you assessed the child's level of development.

KEY TO LETTER SYMBOLS

N = Not yet evidenced   **A** = Age-appropriate

D = Developing   **O** = Outstanding

Writing Skill Development

Writes sentences:
- ____ **N:** Does not write in complete sentences.
- ____ **D:** Writes in complete sentences.
- ____ **A:** Writes fully developed sentences.
- ____ **O:** Writes exemplary sentences well above those of age peers.

Includes detail in writing:
- ____ **N:** Gives no detail.
- ____ **D:** Includes some detail.
- ____ **A:** Includes appropriate detail.
- ____ **O:** Uses elaborate, descriptive, rich detail.

Predicts:
- ____ **N:** Thinks and predicts inaccurately.
- ____ **D:** Predicts some with minimal accuracy.
- ____ **A:** Has made a prediction based on thinking through information.
- ____ **O:** Shows thoughtful reflection; makes reasonable, accurate predictions.

Shows comprehension:
- ____ **N:** Shows foggy comprehension.
- ____ **D:** Shows some comprehension.
- ____ **A:** Comprehends information.
- ____ **O:** Shows strong, complete comprehension; applies comprehension beyond lesson and to other situations.

STUDENT OBSERVATION FORM II
(CONTINUED)

Language Development

Is able to do the following (note all that apply):

_____ Use multisyllabic words.

_____ Use similes, metaphors, and analogies.

_____ Modify language for less mature children.

_____ Use language to teach other children.

_____ Express similarities and difference among unrelated objects.

_____ Use time concepts.

STUDENT OBSERVATION FORM III

For Teachers

Social and Emotional Development

Student's Name: _____

To the teacher: Use this form several times throughout the year. On the line beside the appropriate item, write the date on which you assessed the child's level of development.

+--+
| **KEY TO LETTER SYMBOLS** |
| |
| **N** = Not yet evidenced   **A** = Age-appropriate |
| **D** = Developing   **O** = Outstanding |
+--+

Sensitivity

Takes action to help someone in need:
____ **N:** Is not aware of others' needs.
____ **D:** Sees others' needs but is not sure what to do.
____ **A:** Sees others' needs and attempts to respond.
____ **O:** Sensitive to others' needs and responds with appropriate action.

Shows nonverbal awareness of others' needs:
____ **N:** Is not aware of others' needs.
____ **D:** Sees others' needs but is not sure what to do.
____ **A:** Sees others' needs and attempts to respond.
____ **O:** Sensitive to others' needs and responds with appropriate action.

Shows sensitivity in these ways (note all that apply):
____ Uses empathic statements.
____ Has a sense of justice.
____ Has high expectations of self.
____ Has high expectations of others.

STUDENT OBSERVATION FORM III
(CONTINUED)

Sense of Humor

Catches on to subtle humor:
____ **N:** Does not get the point of jokes.
____ **D:** Laughs at simple jokes.
____ **A:** Understands jokes.
____ **O:** Understands puns and subtle jokes/humor.

Likes to "play" with language:
____ **N:** Understands only literal language.
____ **D:** Understands simple riddles and jokes.
____ **A:** Makes up simple riddles and jokes.
____ **O:** Makes up puns, riddles, and jokes with double meanings; shows mature sense of humor.

Personal-Social Development

Does the following (note all that apply):
____ Expresses feelings in words.
____ Works and plays cooperatively with other children.
____ Participates with others in large groups.
____ Takes turns and shares.
____ Shows concern for others and their property.
____ Takes initiative in learning.
____ Pays attention and concentrates on a task.
____ Consistently completes a task.
____ Works cooperatively with adults.
____ Feels good about self.
____ Is courteous to others.
____ Resolves peer conflicts with language.
____ Can separate from parent and engage in activity.
____ Reunites well with parent.

STUDENT OBSERVATION FORM IV

Fine Motor Development

Student's Name: _____

To the teacher: Use this form several times throughout the year. On the line beside the appropriate item, write the date on which you assessed the child's level of development.

____ Follows top-to-bottom progression.

____ Follows left-to-right progression.

____ Folds paper into halves.

____ Folds paper into quarters.

____ Folds paper into diagonals.

____ Uses crayon or pencil with control within a defined area.

____ Controls brush and paint.

____ Uses scissors with control to cut a straight line.

____ Uses scissors with control to cut a curved line.

____ Connects a dotted outline to make a shape.

____ Pastes using one finger.

____ Holds a pencil correctly.

____ Works a previously unseen puzzle of ten or more pieces.

____ In drawing a person, includes a major body part and features.

____ Traces objects.

____ Copies a pattern from board to paper.

____ Writes basic strokes.

WHAT I LEARNED

My Name: _____ **Date:** _____

This is what I studied:

Here's what I did:

Here's what I learned:

WHAT I LEARNED (CONTINUED)

Here's what I enjoyed most:

Here's what I enjoyed least:

If I did it all over again, here's what I'd change:

Here's how I rate what I did (*circle one*):

Needs More Work   OK   Good   **Excellent**   The BEST

Here's the grade I would give myself: _____

8

Cluster Grouping to Help All Children Learn Cooperatively

Rosa came home from school and told her mom about how her teacher always moved her from one group to another. Rosa enjoyed certain groups more than others. In some groups she was "teacher," while in others she learned new things. Rosa explained that sometimes teaching was fun, but that she really liked learning new things better.

For several years, *cooperative learning* has been seen by some educators as a solution to the classroom problem of the ever-widening range of student abilities. Traditional cooperative learning divides students into groups comprised of one child of high ability, two of average ability, and one of low ability. Many schools and teachers use this arrangement to help students learn efficiently and to improve socialization skills.

For gifted children, being placed in traditional cooperative learning groups can present problems. Rosa's feelings about "teaching" and "learning" reflect what we know about this. Students learn better by motivating each other—by sharing ideas and pooling resources toward a common learning goal. Placing a child in the role of "teacher" can eliminate many opportunities for discovery and growth.

Drawbacks of Traditional Cooperative Learning

For all students, traditional cooperative learning presents mixed results. A child who is highly able may provide some leadership and help the other students in constructive ways; however, he may also become frustrated by a group that relegates most of the work to him. In practice, both the brighter students and the more assertive ones (who aren't necessarily one and the same) often end up doing most, if not all, of the decision making and work.

This is unfair to everyone. In many cases, it teaches the group "leader" how to dominate a group. This can reinforce a negative sense of superiority, which can be intimidating to others in the group. A gifted or bright child may perceive points more quickly and comprehensively and become impatient with other students' slower pace. We want to guide assertive and bright children to learn tolerance, humility, flexibility, and patience. At the same time, we must find ways to meet these students' needs for academic, creative, and intellectual fulfillment.

Meanwhile, students in the middle—those with average ability—may lose their chance to "shine." These children may feel intimidated or resentful. Children of lesser ability may have their weaknesses reinforced. In a supportive learning environment, children of generally lower ability often show unexpected strengths at surprising moments. Grouped with students who are so much faster than they are, they may learn not to try. It's discouraging and even painful to work with a classmate who thinks more quickly and who is looked to as the source of all the best ideas.

Six-year-old Mark's mother called the teacher. She was distraught. A few months ago, Mark could hardly wait to start school. Now he was crying and feigning illness so he wouldn't have to go. His mother couldn't understand what had happened. Mark was a serious boy who loved learning. He had been reading since the age of four. His math skills were superb. Mark enjoyed watching the evening news and discussing current events with his parents. At times, his questioning skills and level of understanding made him seem almost a miniature adult. Why wouldn't he love school?

Mark's teacher, Mrs. Costino, was also upset. In her classroom, she used cooperative learning a good deal of the time. But Mark was uncooperative in his group. He had little patience with the other students. Sometimes he tried to take over the group and boss the children, who in turn grew resentful. At other times, he became quiet and sullen. Mrs. Costino spent much of her energy trying to coax Mark to be more cooperative. It was a situation in which everyone seemed to be losing.

After talking to Mark's mother and consulting with some of her teaching colleagues, Mrs. Costino decided to try a new approach: She grouped Mark with other high-ability students, matching their experience with a separate, challenging task. At the same time, she kept the rest of the class in mixed cooperative learning groups.

Although Mrs. Costino had worried that the groups would founder without a role model, to her surprise and delight, new leaders emerged—in both Mark's group and the others. And Mark's mother reported that her son's attitude toward school was greatly improved.

Originally, Mrs. Costino was using a group strategy that didn't allow Mark to go beyond what he already knew. Mark was frustrated and felt he had to either tutor the other children or adapt by withdrawing. When she grouped Mark with other

highly able children, the teacher saw many benefits—not only for Mark, but for the rest of the class as well.

Cluster Grouping: A Flexible Alternative

Experts in the field of gifted education agree that high-ability children need to spend at least part of their day interacting and learning with other children of similar ability. To make this happen, we recommend that you use cluster grouping. Cluster grouping allows you to place gifted children together while simultaneously placing the other students in heterogeneous groups. This provides the best cooperative grouping situation for all children.

With cluster grouping, children who have been identified as gifted are placed in a small group of four to six students and are clustered in one teacher's class. With very young children, when identification has not yet occurred, it is possible to group children based on their skill levels, work styles, and interests.*

A kindergarten child who is already reading needs to be grouped with others who are reading at a similar level so their instructional time is spent *learning more* rather than coasting while other students learn readiness skills. A child who already knows math facts needs to be grouped with other children who understand more complex math concepts and can solve problems on an advanced level. It's deadening for children to repeat simple reading and math tasks that provide no opportunities for growth or creativity. These children need challenging "instead of" work (see Chapter 3, "Compacting the Curriculum and Extending Learning," pages 41–56)—related work that sparks their curiosity, interest, and motivation.

Cluster grouping provides the best cooperative learning situation. Gifted children feel less isolated or different, more free to take risks and rise to the challenges of further learning.

---

* We encourage early identification whenever possible. See Chapter 1, "Identifying the Young Gifted Child" (pages 5–24), for ways to work with parents and others to identify preferred intelligences and unique abilities and talents. Chapter 2, "Creating the Learning Environment" (pages 25–40), discusses learning styles. Chapter 7, "Assessing and Documenting Development" (pages 121–140), presents information on testing and ongoing evaluation.

Some teachers worry that this arrangement is somehow "elitist." It truly isn't. With cluster grouping, we recognize that children don't all learn in the same way or in the same time frame. We aren't providing something "better" for the gifted students; we're creating an appropriate opportunity for them to experience challenge, to learn, and to grow. This is what we want to provide for every child and what most programs already provide routinely for the majority of students. High-ability children simply require something different at times.

Guidelines for Grouping Young Children

Most teachers find that cluster grouping provides the most productive situation for young gifted children. However, there may be times when other arrangements will also work. These others might include interest groups, cooperative learning groups in which the children's strengths complement each other well, or groups formed to focus on creative or imaginative processes. What follows are some guidelines you can use to help all children gain the most benefits from working cooperatively.

Provide Variety

Provide opportunities for children to work with a variety of other students on many different subjects. If at all feasible, each child should have the chance to work with several others in the class. This will ensure that no one is "stuck" with a difficult combination over and over again. It will also open opportunities for children to collaborate in unexpected ways.

The approach you use to group work (structured, open, creative, divergent, or content-based) should serve the learning goals you've established for each classroom activity. The first question to ask yourself is: "What kind of learning process have I planned for the children?" Your answer should direct you in determining the types of groups you'll create. For example, group processes can be more flexible and open-ended in interdisciplinary units in which students explore a subject from multiple perspectives. If the class

is studying the ecology of the rain forest, you can organize groups according to interests (what aspect of the forest children wish to explore), study sources (such as science books, stories, paintings, or drama), ability levels, motivations, or a combination of all four.

Feel free, too, to use group work as a catalyst for individual projects. Sharing ideas can provide an impetus for students to achieve in unique ways. Periodically, you can use instructional groups as a resource to reignite the class when children run out of ideas or need inspiration to consider other approaches to their study.

Offer Choices

Cooperative grouping works better when children help choose groupmates and topics and assist in designing the project's structure. For practical reasons, you'll sometimes need to make these decisions. Whenever possible, however, try to offer the students as much input as possible. At the very least, consider their personal preferences. Children will be far more invested in the project and excited about the process if they have helped to choose partners, subjects, and format.

It's fine to negotiate with students in setting up activities. This doesn't mean that you should simply let children have their own way, or that you should avoid areas in which they really need practice and experience. But it's both appropriate and desirable to offer students some degree of input in designing and defining a task or project. Start by deciding where you can be flexible and where you need to set limits. How you use group work and the kinds of parameters you set will depend on the time available, the nature of the task, and the composition of your class (children's level of maturity, their strengths and weaknesses, and so forth). If you want your students to master certain math concepts, you can encourage them to choose resources, activities, and media for exploring their ideas. But you'll also need to set limits on the amount of time they spend experimenting, the number of options they explore, and the media they use.

Feel free to make adjustments as you go along. For example, sometimes you may find that children benefit from occasionally working on their own rather than completing their ideas together. This is fine. Remember, group work should serve the learning needs of the class, not create a situation in which you and the class are constrained by the group work.

Set Clear Parameters

Young children are used to spending time with other children, but not necessarily to working cooperatively within a group to meet individual and group goals. As mentioned before, you'll need to set parameters that are clear, but not stifling. You have three objectives:

1. To provide a specified framework in which children can operate confidently without feeling overwhelmed, confused, underdirected, or discouraged.
2. To allow as much latitude as possible to accommodate individual strengths and interests.
3. To encourage and accommodate a wide range of decision making and plenty of creativity.

Ground Rules for Children Working in Groups

By the time they begin school, most children have a wealth of experience playing in groups. You can draw on what your students have learned from this experience while you prepare them to work in learning groups.

Take some time to discuss behavior expectations. One way to begin this discussion is by asking students to think of times when they most enjoyed playing with their friends. Try to get them to identify what made those play activities work for them, using questions such as these:

- How did your friends act while you were playing?
- How did you feel when they acted like that? Why did you feel that way?
- How did you act?
- How do you think your friends felt when you acted like that? Why?
- Did anyone lead your group of friends in your game? Or did everyone share in leading?

In the same way, you can invite children to consider an experience they *didn't* like. Use questions such as these to help students think about what they found difficult:

- Did you feel overwhelmed—lost or alone—in the group?
- Did you feel bored or left out? Why do you think you felt that way?
- Did anyone take over the game?
- Were everyone's ideas respected?
- What happened when friends disagreed?

The questions and discussion will help your students identify *specifically* what has and hasn't worked in their experience with others. This process serves two additional purposes: It informs you about students' sensitivities and experiences, and it puts the children in touch with qualities they value in themselves and others when working or playing in groups.

Exploring these questions will prepare the class for a discussion of ground rules. We recommend that, in setting rules, you use children's ideas and suggestions wherever possible. Students are more apt to follow rules they feel they've helped create than those arbitrarily set by the teacher.

In essence, you're modeling the very behavior you want children to adopt in their own groups. While setting the rules together, keep referring back to children's own play experiences. Explain the importance of finding ways to make groups fair for everyone. Let your students think of ways to monitor themselves, to prevent anyone from taking over the group, and to ensure that everyone has opportunities to explore ideas. Gifted children are particularly sensitive to issues of justice; they may suggest policies that even you haven't considered.

We use the following ground rules. Feel free to adapt them to your students' ideas and to the ages, abilities, and unique circumstances of the children in your own classroom:

- Decide what you want to do.
- If you can't all agree, see if you can try more than one idea.
- Take turns sharing ideas.
- Listen to others in your group.
- Make your best effort.
- Help each other.
- If you don't understand or agree about something, talk about it with your group.
- Get the teacher's help if you need it.

You may find it useful to create a role of "group monitor"—someone in the group who has the job of upholding the ground rules. The student who has this role will feel empowered to speak up. Having a group monitor also helps keep the volume down: there won't be a cacophony of voices every time a child breaks a rule! Allow children to take turns with this role. That way, no one becomes the "group boss"—and every child has the experience of upholding the rules he or she helped create.

When a Group Doesn't "Click"

Sometimes a group simply won't "click." Two or more children may be obviously mismatched in temperament or ability. If you have done your best to help them stick together productively and the group is simply not connecting, let the students (and yourself) off the hook. It's particularly important to do this if the learning goal is an academic one.

Separate the children who are in conflict and allow them to finish alone. Do this matter-of-factly, without condemnation or punishment. Simply say to the students: "I feel you could do a better job if you each finished this project on your own." Often, conflict can be legitimate and can indicate the need for students to move in separate directions. Let the children know you honor this need. They will probably complete the work far more effectively! Forcing groups to stay together to the "bitter end" is usually counterproductive. There will be plenty of other opportunities to insist that children carry through and finish projects together—projects in which it's not essential that major academic learning take place.

We have found that one of the most effective ways to use group work, particularly for gifted students, is as a catalyst for individual learning. This is often true when group members are struggling to agree on what to do. You can expect them to share ideas and coordinate their efforts for part of the assignment. Then offer children the option of following through by working in pairs or threes or by pursuing their ideas on their own. Be flexible at all stages of the learning process. Improvise with your students. If, at any point, group work stops producing results for children, conclude the joint activity and allow each student to continue working independently.

Evaluate Students Individually

When children work in groups, it's important that you assess the degree to which each child has met the academic goals for the activity and what new learning has taken place. Whatever methods you use (mastery tests, portfolios, checklists, oral responses to questions, or others), you'll need to document that each student has acquired new learning through the group's project. Be sure that every child has plenty of opportunities to design and develop ideas. Even if your students are producing a project together, provide some way that the children can write, draw, or sketch their own *individual* ideas so you can see how each student has responded to the assignment.

This is a situation in which "group grades" aren't appropriate. At best, a group grade on a project intended to produce individual learning, creative expression, and discovery is unfair; at worst, it's damaging to future motivation, self-esteem, academic progress, and confidence. Working in groups is an aid to the learning process. Obviously, those who take full advantage of group work will acquire more ideas than those who do little or who never even attempt to participate. Evaluations, however, should focus on each individual's learning and growth rather than on how much the student contributed to the group. Otherwise, you'll be grading the child on cooperative learning skills rather than on knowledge and conceptual growth.

When evaluating, remember that appearances can be misleading. Shy children may not say very much in a group, but they will still learn a great deal from listening to the ideas of others. Creatively gifted children may misbehave because they're bored or because they want to approach an assignment differently than the more academically gifted students.

The last thing you want is for group work to decrease students' motivation to stretch their knowledge and imagination because they think doing so will affect their "group grade." Be sure students understand that they will be evaluated on what they, as individuals, learn and produce.

Avoid Group Homework

We strongly recommend that you not give cooperative learning assignments for homework unless they are truly optional. These assignments can be unfair to children and parents alike. Families are busy; many parents will find it difficult, if not impossible, to arrange the time, transportation, and supervision young children's group homework requires. Moreover, your students gain the most when you closely monitor group or partner work in class. There, you can circulate from group to group to ensure the ground rules are met. You can observe, check for understanding, and help iron out difficulties. You're able to teach the skills students need to work with others and to assess whether individual children are getting the activity's full benefit.

Let the Goals Determine the Group Size

Let the goals for each activity determine the group's size and scope. If the major goals are for children to learn to work together and make group decisions, the activity should be one that calls for group problem solving, such as planning a science experiment, producing a puppet show or simple play, or creating a picture or mural. While individual students will take responsibility for the various components of projects such as these, group cooperation is still important and appropriate.

If the goals involve learning cognitive skills, understanding advanced concepts, or mastering complex subject matter, grouping children in pairs will be more effective than forming larger groups. In partner learning situations, each child will have more ownership of the outcome and more accountability for learning. There won't be so many distractions and personality conflicts, and the mastery of the material will be more manageable. It is easier, too, to compatibly pair students of similar interests and abilities than it is to arrange a whole class of fully productive groups.

Most important, allow plenty of opportunities for the children to work on their own. Children need to do this for many reasons: to learn accountability, self-discipline, and responsibility; to build a sense of self-worth through achievement; and to grow in self-reliance. Working independently is highly important for both gifted children

and students who are of average or lower ability. The team spirit resulting from working cooperatively has many benefits, and much learning can take place in a group setting. But the sense of self-worth that a student gains through *individual* achievement is absolutely essential for every student's continued personal progress.

Questions and Answers

"In my district, we aren't allowed to do any tracking. Isn't cluster grouping a form of tracking?"

No, there's a difference. Tracking is based solely on ability level and keeps children with the same group all day, every day of the year. Cluster grouping is more flexible: Children are temporarily grouped according to their mutual interests, talents, or ability levels. Teachers can create cluster groups for specific learning goals and then dismantle them later, allowing children to work independently.

"With young children, is ability grouping always the best approach? Aren't there times when I will want to group for other reasons?"

If the group's topic is of great interest, children of various levels can come together and learn productively, each contributing her own strengths, curiosity, enthusiasm, and creativity. Sometimes, too, children of widely discrepant abilities will choose to work together and will engage in much in-depth learning. If a keen interest or a close friendship is there, the children often instinctively supplement each other's weaknesses and complement each other's strengths. It will be up to you as the teacher to use your intuition, observation, and judgment in arranging groups that bring out the best in everyone.

"Won't the children in a cluster group feel singled out?"

If they're grouped with children who have similar abilities, gifted students will feel more a part of a group than if each student is all alone, the only one who is different. Gifted children *know* they're different, even if no one says anything. They may wrongly perceive that to be different is to be "bad," and they may try to hide or play down what they know so they'll fit into the class. If this happens, they may never realize their hidden potential.

"What kinds of activities can I provide for high-ability children?"

It's important to provide every child with an appropriate opportunities to learn and grow. You'll first need to look at the objective of the cooperative learning task and then assess whether each child has met the objective. If a particular child or group of children has already mastered a concept or skill, you can assign something connected to that concept that is more advanced. You'll find many ideas for doing this in Chapter 3, "Compacting the Curriculum and Extending Learning" (pages 41–56).

"It sounds like cluster grouping means putting all the gifted children together in one classroom. At my school, each teacher has one or two gifted children. How can we make cluster grouping work?"

Cluster grouping can mean placing higher-ability children together, but not always. It can also mean forming groups of children with similar interests and motivation levels. Don't assume that all talented children will automatically work well together. Be creative in how you combine students, and let them have as much input into the process as possible. You may find that a couple of gifted students will work well with a couple of highly motivated students when the special strengths or interests of both sets of children mesh.

Therefore, if you have only two or three gifted students in your classroom, you can still create a cluster group. Place them together in a small group, or join them with one or two other enthusiastic average or above-average learners. Sometimes this works better than placing all gifted students together. Highly motivated "regular" students can often keep up with gifted children and offer unique strengths of their own.

Conclusion

Any kind of instructional grouping must serve the educational needs of the children involved, regardless of their ability level. While heterogeneous grouping can sometimes benefit everyone, it frequently fails to meet the needs of students on either side of the ability spectrum—especially those who are gifted.

In this chapter, we have recommended *flexible* grouping based on ability, interest, and motivation. We advocate the use of instructional groups solely as a means to promote growth and learning. As new requirements arise, you should feel free to improvise with the group process by making adjustments and creating different kinds of groups. It's also important that you give students opportunities to work independently to develop the ideas that spring from their group collaborations.

With instructional grouping, students' learning is what is most important. Always ask: Are *all* children benefiting from the experience? Are they growing as a result of their collective efforts? Student achievement is more critical than the successful performance of the group. Cooperative groups may work well and yet not result in significant individual learning. A more creative approach to clustering will inspire students to develop their abilities freely. Rather than stifle children's ideas, flexible grouping can encourage them to expand in a context that does not impose inhibiting roles or restrictive boundaries, but instead gives students the confidence and freedom to be themselves.

References and Resources

Bellanca, James, and Robin Fogarty. *Blueprints for Thinking in the Cooperative Classroom.* Palatine, IL: IRI SkyLight Publishing, 1991. Applies a cooperative team approach to critical and creative thinking in the classroom.

Kulik, James, and Chen-Lin Kulik. "Ability Grouping and Gifted Students." In *Handbook of Gifted Education*, Nicholas Colangelo and Gary A. Davis, eds. Boston: Allyn & Bacon, 1991. Research-based information about the effects of ability grouping on gifted students.

Robinson, Ann. "Cooperation or Exploitation: The Arguments against Cooperative Learning for Talented Students." *Journal for the Education of Gifted* 14(1), pp. 9-27. Robinson presents compelling arguments as to why gifted students may dislike and rebel against cooperative learning.

Rogers, Karen. *The Relationship of Grouping Practices to the Education of the Gifted and Talented Learner: Research-Based Decision Making.* Storrs, CT: National Research Center on the Gifted and Talented, 1991. This book does a splendid job of explaining current research on grouping practices and relating it to the specific educational needs of gifted students. While remaining sensitive to all populations, the author addresses a range of critical issues and concerns, focusing on the dilemma many bright students face in cooperative learning situations.

Winebrenner, Susan. *Teaching Gifted Kids in the Regular Classroom.* Minneapolis, MN: Free Spirit publishing, 1992. Winebrenner discusses what to do with the child who already knows what you are going to teach. She presents specific strategies with step-by-step instructions and reproducible forms.

9

Building Partnerships
with Parents

It was the first day of third grade. Down the hall marched Mrs. Johnson with her third grader, Chad. She picked out his desk, then unpacked his backpack and supplies. As the teacher asked Chad questions to get acquainted, his mother answered for him.

For the first six weeks of third grade, Chad seldom spoke. Every morning, his mother hovered. Every week, she called the teacher or wrote notes touting Chad's abilities. Mrs. Johnson was already labeled in the school as a "pushy" parent. Just the mention of her name made the principal's eyes roll. Chad, however, had always been quiet in school. Extreme boredom had turned him into a daydreamer. When called on, he rarely knew the answer because he never paid attention. Though his kindergarten, first-grade, and second-grade teachers recognized that he was bright, none of them saw proof of his mother's claims that he was highly gifted.

But Mrs. Johnson was right about her son. Chad was brilliant. Before too long, his astute third-grade teacher could clearly read the signs. She met with Mrs. Johnson and assured her that she, too, recognized Chad's gifts, and that she would challenge him in her class. Mrs. Johnson was happy and relieved. She stopped hovering, ceased bragging, and ended her intrusions for the rest of the year. Chad began to speak for himself and to use and expand his many intellectual gifts.

What It's Like for Parents

Parents of gifted children often feel caught in a maze of conflicting emotions. They may feel proud, excited, and awed by their child's abilities; at the same time, they may feel doubt and anxiety, worry that they are being "pushy," or fear that they're not up to the task of parenting a gifted child.

In their book *Bringing Out the Best*, Jacqulyn Saunders and Pamela Espeland describe some of the typical worries shared by parents of young gifted children:*

- "I think my child may be gifted, but I'm not sure."
- "I feel like I'm being presumptuous to even care whether my child is gifted."
- "Sometimes I feel intimidated by my own child."
- "Sometimes I'm frightened for my child."
- "I feel overwhelmed by the responsibility of raising a gifted child."
- "There are times when I feel so isolated."

Many parents of gifted students know that their child is "different" and perhaps bored at

---

* Jacqulyn Saunders and Pamela Espeland. *Bringing Out the Best: A Resource Guide for Parents of Young Gifted Children.* Minneapolis, MN: Free Spirit Publishing Inc., 1991, pp. 40-45. Used with permission.

school, but are uncertain how to go about obtaining the level of educational experience they intuitively feel their child needs. And once a gifted child is identified, parenting can suddenly seem a good deal more complicated. Since their child has uncommon qualities, conventional wisdom about childrearing often falls short of their unique parenting needs. Parents can experience confusion and anxiety about resources (of their finances, intellect, or time) and about their parental roles. Although studies show that giftedness has a strong genetic component, most parents of gifted children don't view themselves as gifted.* Yet, quite often, these parents share some of the qualities of their children:

• acute sensitivity and focus
• intense feelings and reactions
• strong internal sense of control
• keen awareness
• creative imagination
• probing, analytical curiosity
• extraordinary memory.

Parents wonder and worry about many things: about the effects of labeling their child as gifted; about socialization, acceleration, emotional well-being, and sibling relationships; about their roles and responsibilities as the parents of a gifted child; about the many aspects of gifted programming that didn't exist for them as children and still don't exist for the majority of children today.

Like their children, parents need to understand the reasons for practices and policies. They, too, need to feel a sense of justice and fairness. They're confused about what it means to be gifted—and about what it doesn't mean. Sometimes, when told that their child has scored in the top five percent of all students, parents develop an array of new expectations for the child. Parents (and teachers, too) often confuse intellectual precocity with emotional maturity, organizational abilities, or the level of responsibility they expect from the child. It isn't easy to deal with a second grader who can discuss world politics at dinner but acts the silliest of all his friends at a birthday party.

Parents of gifted children face particular stresses that require some focused guidance:

* Kathryn S. Keirouz. "Concerns of Parents of Gifted Children: A Research Review." In *Gifted Child Quarterly* 34:2 (1990), p. 57.

• What they experience may contradict everything they've ever heard about childrearing. Faced with a challenging child, these parents have nowhere to turn, no resources or "experts" to consult.
• Their child may oppose or undermine every assertion of parental authority in such plausible ways that these parents are rendered speechless or confused. Gifted children may have perfectly rational answers for every reprimand, and seemingly logical reasons for doing everything they're asked not to do. Parents and other adults often perceive verbally talented children—especially those with a flair for the dramatic—as arrogant or starved for attention.
• These parents may expect too little or too much of their gifted child, or they may find it difficult to reconcile disparities in the child's intellectual and emotional development.
• Finding the advice of experts conflicting, these parents may feel unable to create or choose effective options. Which teacher or school administrator should they believe after hearing varying explanations for their child's unusual, inadequate, or troublesome school behavior?
• Families may become overwhelmed by seeing their special child poorly served, and feel unable to help or to find help.

Parents of gifted students need support from other parents and from educators and other professionals who understand the challenges of living with highly able and creative children. They need to know that they are not alone and that there are people who are willing to help them. As a teacher, you can be one of those people. These parents already know that their child isn't perfect, that the child is, in fact, often extremely difficult for the teacher and the school to deal with. They're usually only too glad to receive suggestions for dealing with the "down side" of giftedness as long as their child's positive traits are recognized and the need for academic challenge is met.

Success at school is more likely if parents are understanding and encouraging with their children at home. To cultivate this understanding, schools and teachers have a role to play in informing parents about characteristics of gifted children. As the teacher, you may be their first (and possibly the only!) source for this information. After one father learned that some of his son's troublesome behaviors also characterized giftedness, he sighed with relief and explained, "Now instead of reacting to him as someone who's always trying to drive me crazy, I can see him as someone special who has ideas that are different from mine."

Examining Your Own Feelings

With so many students and so much to teach, it's easy to sometimes feel impatient or even resentful about the needs of special students. After a long and frustrating day, you may find it challenging to consider new strategies for dealing with a particular child or to talk with a concerned parent. Keep in mind that without a conscious effort on your part to show empathy and interest, your underlying irritation is likely to come through. Something in your body language, facial expression, choice of words, or tone of voice will probably reveal your feelings. This can hurt the relationship you've worked hard to cultivate.

If you struggle from time to time with negative feelings about gifted students and their parents, you are not alone. Yet you want to treat all children and families with respect, and to open all possible doors to children's growth and learning. To help yourself maintain and communicate a positive perspective, you may find it helpful to examine your feelings and the "self-talk" you use when your enthusiasm begins to wane:

- When a student knows more than you do about dinosaurs or can recite the Latin names for flowers, how do you feel about yourself as a teacher? Do you hear yourself thinking: "How on earth does Darryl know all that?" Try to shift that thinking: "How exciting that Darryl knows and cares so much about that!"
- What's your mental attitude toward children's uneven development? Instead of "Maisie can't be gifted—she'd leave her head at home if it wasn't attached," you could ask yourself, "I wonder what's going on in Maisie's head. How can I help her explore and express all of her ideas?"
- Are you ambivalent about labeling and providing special support to gifted children? Try reminding yourself of the importance of helping all students reach their full potential.

- How do you feel when parents criticize or offer suggestions? Uncomfortable? Irritated? Defensive? Try to find a way to productively redirect your thinking: "Mr. Royko cares so much about Callie's education. Is there a way he can help me work with her?"
- Do you become defensive when parents disagree with you regarding assessment, methods, or advice? Could you focus instead on acknowledging your shared concern for their child?

If you've made an effort to grapple with these attitudes and feelings honestly, you should congratulate yourself. By working through these kinds of issues for yourself, you'll be much better prepared to build a positive relationship with parents of gifted children. If you find yourself feeling "stuck," you might want to return to the first two chapters of this book or to some of the suggested readings in the "References and Resources" for Chapter 1 (pages 16–17), Chapter 2 (page 39), and Chapter 9 (pages 156–157). There you may find the inspirational boost you need to get yourself back into balance.

You Can't Overcommunicate

A child's parents are likely to be the most enthusiastic and valuable source of support and resources available to a teacher. Since they tend to be most involved with their children's education during the early primary grades, parents can provide you with abundant information and assistance. Connecting with parents allows you to become acquainted with a child's interests and abilities outside the boundaries of your classroom. As each person shares and receives ideas, everyone benefits: you, the parent, and the child.

Opening a Dialogue

You can open and sustain a dialogue with parents by inviting their input and offering a variety of ways for them to provide it. Chapter 1 includes several family letters and forms to help you dialogue with parents about their children's abilities, interests, and needs: "Your Child's Pictures" (page 18), "Information, Please" (page 19), "About My Child" (pages 20–21), and "Checklist of My Child's Strengths" (pages 22–23). To invite parents to communicate easily and regularly about concerns for their child, Chapter 2 suggests that you send home the "Help Me Help You" family letter (page 40) at the beginning of each month or school term.

For students in kindergarten and first grade, an intake interview is common. Here's your opportunity to excel as a good listener. Ask parents to tell you about their child's special interests and abilities. Take notes! Also, find out how much parents know about what goes on in your classroom. Pay attention to body language, and stay alert. Even offhand comments may give insights into family dynamics. Although intake interviews are less common in older grades, they can be very helpful—especially when information from previous teachers doesn't jibe with the child's behavior and performance in your classroom.

To promote parental cooperation, helping must be reciprocal. This means that you'll want to update parents on your current projects, goals, and needs. If you don't identify your needs, parents are less able to support you. Parents can loan or donate materials, share skills, and help you connect to others in the community; they can be your best "cheerleaders" when aware of the extensive and exciting learning going on in your classroom. To invite this kind of participation, you can send home either of the "Can You Help?" family letters. Use the first letter (page 158) to ask for materials and assistance for your general classroom program; use the second letter (page 159) to request contributions to a particular theme or topic of study. You'll find samples of completed forms below and on page 153. Send either letter as often as you feel it's appropriate and necessary.

CAN YOU HELP?

For Parents

Child's Name: _Margarita Rojas_

Dear Parent/Caregiver:

Do you have a special skill or talent to share with our class? Do you have any time to help out in our classroom? We need parents who are willing to help with: _____
_____ _keyboarding, music activities, art projects_ _____

We also need the following materials for our class. Are there any you could loan or donate? If not, can you suggest people or organizations in the community who might do so? We need: _____
_____ _baby food jars with lids_   _computers_ _____
_____ _musical instruments—any type_ _____

Please let me know how you can help by completing the brief form at the bottom of this sheet and sending it to school with your child.

Thank you for your interest in your child's classroom. If you have any questions, be sure to stop by or call.

Teacher's Signature: _Mrs. Allemagnie_
Phone: _555-1234_

- -

Child's Name: _____

To: _Mrs. Allemagnie_   **From:** _____
Date: _____

Here's how I can help: _____
_____
_____

Days available: _____
Times available: (morning) _____ (afternoon) _____
Phone: (daytime) _____ (evening) _____
Comments:

CAN YOU HELP?

For Parents

Child's Name: _Bjorn Nelson_

Dear Parent/Caregiver:

This term, our class will study: ___An interdisciplinary unit on East Asia—social studies,_ _science, literature, music, culture_

I'm wondering if you have any items related to this unit that you would be willing to donate or loan. We could use items such as: ___postcards, recorded music or musical instruments,_ ___clothing, stories, poems, books, or information about people and language___

Please let me know how you can help by completing the brief form at the bottom of this sheet and sending it to school with your child.

Thank you for your interest in your child's classroom. If you have any questions, be sure to stop by or call.

Teacher's Signature: ___Mr. Murlowski___
Phone: ___555-0031___

- -

Child's Name: _____

To: ___Mr. Murlowski___   **From:** _____
Date: _____

I can donate these items: _____
I can loan these items: _____
Days available: _____
Times available: (morning) _____ (afternoon) _____
Phone: (daytime) _____ (evening) _____
Comments:

The Parent-Teacher Conference

The parent-teacher conference is an opportunity to cooperate with parents in identifying each child's particular abilities and social-emotional characteristics. Give parents enough notice so they can prepare for the conference. You might want to send home a copy of "Questions for Your Child's Parent-Teacher Conference" (page 160).*

---

* This form is adapted from the "Parent-Teacher Questionnaire" in Susan Winebrenner, *Teaching Kids with Learning Difficulties in the Regular Classroom* (Minneapolis: Free Spirit Publishing Inc., 1996), p. 212. Used with permission.

Guidelines for Parent-Teacher Conferences

Follow basic good conference practices:

- Allow sufficient time (at least 20 minutes).
- Begin with a look at what's good; emphasize the positive throughout the conference.
- Invite parents to talk first or early on.
- Be accessible and receptive to information and suggestions; respond sincerely to parental concerns.
- Note any points or requests parents make; plan to follow through on any requests, and keep parents informed.

- Let parents know that you welcome their input at any time during the school year.
- At the close of the conference, summarize the main points, concerns, or agreements you've discussed.

It would be hard to overemphasize the importance of being positive. However, never minimize problems either. Glossing over situations that need immediate attention isn't wholesome for the child or you and only perpetuates a bad situation. Nonetheless, the conference should be a positive experience overall for the parents, or you risk losing them as your best allies in helping their child. If a child has a host of problems, choose one or two to focus on. Help parents view the problem as solvable, not overwhelming. By the end of the conference, make sure you have said several positive things for each negative one. This will lay firm groundwork for good parent relations over the remainder of the school year.

Conferences with Parents of Gifted Children

For the gifted child, the purpose of the conference is not to glorify giftedness, but to explore the child's particular abilities and needs. Rather than take a narrow "gifted vs. nongifted" view, let the conference focus instead on the child's particular abilities, sensitivities, special needs, personality, and interests. You'll encounter in parents a vast range of responses and emotional reactions to their child's giftedness, from insecurity about acknowledging special abilities to clear assumptions that, of course, their child has exceptional qualities! Remember that parents know more about their child's life out of school than you do, and that you know more about the child's life at school than the parents do. Share that knowledge so that together you will all know more about the child than you did before.

Although formal programs to identify giftedness in young children rarely exist in schools, this can work to the *advantage* of your students, their parents, and you. It's likely that you can be more inclusive in acknowledging exceptional qualities, rather than needing to limit your focus to only those abilities served by the school's gifted program. If your school does have a gifted program that starts in a higher grade, remember that children don't "begin to be gifted" when they enter the program. You may have a great opportunity to be a young student's gifted program for as long as the child is in your room!

In most cases, parents come to you as the expert for advice, counsel, and validation. This is especially true for parents of young gifted children. Often, these folks are having an unusually difficult time. At worst, they may be experiencing difficulties in disciplining or handling an active, creative, inventive, strong-willed child; at best, they are scrambling to keep up with their child's insatiable curiosity, drive, thirst for knowledge, and hunger for novel experiences. The parents are likely to look to the school (and thus to you, the teacher and first point of contact) for advice, coping strategies, ideas, and guidance in finding additional resources.

You will want to be able to give them information that will be helpful. This chapter includes four reproducible forms with information for parents: "Books for Parents of Young Gifted Children" (page 161), "Organizations for Parents of Young Gifted Children" (page 162), "Computer Software for Young Gifted Children" (page 163), and "Online Resources for Parents of Young Gifted Children" (page 164). You may want to make copies of these forms before the parent-teacher conference and offer one or more of them to parents who seem interested. In addition, call your State Department of Education and ask about state programs or organizations for parents of gifted and talented children.*

The more you know or can learn about giftedness and related resources in your school and community, the more you can help parents and, ultimately, the children you serve. Are there parent groups, enrichment programs, counselors with expertise in giftedness, or local organizations to which you can refer parents?

Because the general awareness of giftedness is relatively low, you may find that you're the first person ever to suggest that misbehavior or other problems might be due to the fact that the child is extremely bright.

---

* As of this writing, information on state programs is also available on the World Wide Web (at http://www.eskimo.com/ user/kids.html). Click on "Organizations and Societies" and find information under "State (USA) Associations for the Gifted." If you are outside of the United States, click on "Organizations and Societies" and find information under "Associations for the Gifted outside USA."

By third grade, Ramón already had a notorious reputation in his school for being the class clown, wisecracking, and leading other kids astray. Ramón was always getting in trouble on the playground. He had lazy study habits and generally showed little interest in school. Ramón's parents thought he was just mischievous. His perceptive third-grade teacher, however, thought he might be bored and so assigned him higher-level work. With a good deal of discipline from the teacher, Ramón's attitude and schoolwork began to change markedly. It became evident that he had an extraordinary talent for creative writing. The teacher had few further behavior problems with Ramón for the rest of the school year.

"Smartness" is often associated with the child who thinks quickly, speaks articulately, and always has the right answer. Because of this, many children's gifts remain unrecognized by both parents and teachers.

At a conference with her daughter Sue's second-grade teacher, Mrs. Kim explained that Sue seemed to be having trouble in math. She wondered if Sue needed a tutor or should be tested for learning disabilities. The teacher, Mr. Marquette, asked Mrs. Kim for some more time before making a recommendation. He began to pay particular attention to Sue's behavior during math. He soon realized that Sue was very bright in math, but lacked confidence. Though she couldn't do computations quickly, she had fantastic reasoning abilities. Sue was clearly intimidated by the boisterous boys in the class who shouted out correct answers almost immediately. She wasn't aggressive in that way, and so she had concluded that she was "dumb" in math.

Mr. Marquette made some changes. He no longer allowed students to shout out answers, and he waited longer before calling on anyone for solutions to problems. Gradually, Sue began to excel. Her confidence returned. Months later, she became the first child in the district to achieve a perfect score on the state achievement test in math.

Sue's gradual transformation provides a wonderful window into the value of parent-teacher communication. Without hearing Mrs. Kim's concern, Mr. Marquette might not have stopped to observe Kim more closely and may not have changed his classroom procedures. Without her teacher's thoughtful intervention, Kim's unusually high ability would probably have gone unrecognized and unchallenged.

Questions and Answers

"If I go to the trouble of asking parents what they think their child needs, how will I find the time to manage my regular curriculum?"

Any change in your style or approach will take some time at first. But if children are given the opportunity to pursue their interests and to be challenged at a level that engages their thinking processes, your job is likely to become easier. With parent support, children often become generally more cooperative. Also, you don't need to accommodate all of the suggestions and requests a parent makes. Start with only one adjustment, and see if the child's day—and yours—gets any better.

"I have a parent who really wants to get involved. What should I suggest?"

Here are a few ideas. You might suggest that the parent:

- learn about gifted children and different ways to enhance their development
- research the resources available at the school about educating gifted children, and spearhead the development of a gifted child resource library including books, computer software, and periodicals
- help other parents of gifted children get involved or even start a parent support group
- identify and contact local mentors or tutors
- start an artist-in-residence program for your classroom or school.

Conclusion

Parent involvement in any child's schooling can be a significant positive force. To effectively contribute to their child's education, however, parents need the cooperation and support of school personnel as well.

We're all pioneers in developing awareness and support for young gifted children. If you can spark in your school or community any small interest in developing a child's exceptional strengths, that effort has the potential to multiply. You will have established a precedent for the future, a basis upon which to build adaptations for other children. Reaching parents is essential to this cause. Welcome and promote parent involvement! Doing so is a precious investment in all young children.

References and Resources

Alvarado, Nancy. "Adjustment of Adults Who Are Gifted." *Advanced Development* 1 (1989), pp. 77-86. Insightful and helpful for parents of gifted children who may not acknowledge their own exceptional qualities and the effects these have on their lives.

ERIC Clearinghouse on Disabilities and Gifted Education. *Supporting Gifted Education through Advocacy.* Reston, VA: Council for Exceptional Children (CEC), ERIC Digest No. E494. Concise and directly applicable suggestions for parents and educators. This four-page digest may be freely reproduced and distributed. Write to CEC, 1920 Association Drive, Reston, VA 22091-1589. Toll-free phone: 1-800-486-5773.

Dinkmeyer, Don, and Gary D. McKay. *Systematic Training for Effective Parenting (STEP)*, 2d rev. ed. Circle Pines, MN: American Guidance Service, 1997. A complete parenting program that includes a handbook for parents, videos, and leader's materials. The *Leader's Resource Guide* includes an excellent short course in facilitating parent groups and group dynamics ("Part One: STEP Group Leadership," pp. 16-30). *STEP* publications are often available in libraries or through schools. Write to AGS, 4201 Woodland Road, Circle Pines, MN 55014-1796. Toll-free phone: 1-800-328-2560.

Keirouz, Kathryn S. "Concerns of Parents of Gifted Children: A Research Review." *Gifted Child Quarterly* 34:2 (1990), pp. 56-63. An excellent, concise source.

Knopper, Dorothy. *Parent Education: Parents as Partners.* Boulder, CO: Open Space Communications, 1994. A monograph in the "Professional Development Series: Current Themes in Gifted Education," edited by Elinor Katz. Presents a concise, useful reference and action guide supported with anecdotes and interpretations. Useful for busy professionals and parents. Write to Open Space Communications, 1900 Folsom, Suite 108, Boulder, CO 80302. Or call (303) 444-7020.

Kurcinka, Mary Sheedy. *Raising Your Spirited Child: A Guide for Parents Whose Child Is More Intense, Sensitive, Perceptive, Persistent, Energetic.* New York: HarperCollins, 1991. A valuable, practical, and popular resource for teachers and parents. Includes hundreds of specific suggestions to help children monitor themselves and develop self-control.

Meckstroth, Elizabeth A. "Guiding the Parents of Gifted Children." In *Counseling Gifted and Talented Children: A Guide for Teachers, Counselors, and Parents,* Roberta M. Milgram, ed. Norwood, NJ: Ablex Publishing, 1991, pp. 95-120. Specific information on teacher-parent conferences, involving parents in identifying gifted children, helping parents acknowledge and understand giftedness, and organizing and facilitating parent discussion groups.
———. "Paradigm Shifts into Giftedness." *Roeper Review* 15:2 (1992), pp. 91-92. Explores how a gifted child affects the family.

Mitchell, Patty Bruce, ed. *An Advocate's Guide to Building Support for Gifted and Talented Education.* Washington, DC: National Association of State Boards of Education, 1981. A classic handbook for effective advocacy with numerous resources to support gifted education at all levels and stages. Write to NASBE, 444 N. Capital St. NW, Washington, DC 20001.

Smutny, Joan Franklin, Kathleen Veenker, and Stephen Veenker. *Your Gifted Child: How to Recognize and Develop the Special Talents in Your Child from Birth to Age Seven.* New York: Ballantine Books, 1989. Includes an extensive chapter on advocacy and intervention to benefit young students. Offers parents specific suggestions and examples for supplementing their child's formal education.

U.S. Department of Education, Office of Educational Research and Improvement. *National Excellence: A Case for Developing America's Talent.* Washington, DC: U.S. Government Printing Office, 1993. A valuable document explaining the urgency for providing appropriate education for gifted and talented children. Every chapter includes persuasive references and useful information.

Walker, Sally Yahnke. *The Survival Guide for Parents of Gifted Kids: How to Understand, Live with, and Stick Up for Your Gifted Child.* Minneapolis, MN: Free Spirit Publishing Inc., 1991. The chapter titled "Advocacy: Working for Improvement" provides sensible suggestions for influencing schools to be more "user-friendly" toward gifted children. Topics range from consulting with the classroom teacher to effecting change at the state level.

Webb, James T., and Arlene DeVries. *Training Manual for Facilitators of SENG Model Guided Discussion Groups for Parents of Talented Children.* Dayton, OH: Ohio Psychology Press, 1993. Gives a detailed description of both content and process for developing and conducting guided discussion groups for parents of gifted children.

Webb, James T., Elizabeth A. Meckstroth, and Stephanie S. Tolan. *Guiding the Gifted Child: A Practical Source for Parents and Teachers,* rev. ed. Scottsdale, AZ: Gifted Psychology Press, forthcoming. A primer on understanding and nurturing gifted children that includes chapters on motivation, discipline, peer and sibling relations, stress management, and depression. The original edition won the American Psychological Association's Best Book Award.

CAN YOU HELP?

Child's Name: _____

Dear Parent/Caregiver:

Do you have a special skill or talent to share with our class? Do you have any time to help out in our classroom? We need parents who are willing to help with: _____

_____

_____

We also need the following materials for our class. Are there any you could loan or donate? If not, can you suggest people or organizations in the community who might do so? We need: _____

_____

_____

Please let me know how you can help by completing the brief form at the bottom of this sheet and sending it to school with your child.

Thank you for your interest in your child's classroom. If you have any questions, be sure to stop by or call.

Teacher's Signature: _____

Phone: _____

- ✂ **cut here** -

Child's Name: _____

To: _____   **From:** _____

Date: _____

Here's how I can help: _____

_____

_____

Days available: _____

Times available: (morning) _____ (afternoon) _____

Phone: (daytime) _____ (evening) _____

Comments:

CAN YOU HELP?

For Parents

Child's Name: _____

Dear Parent/Caregiver:

This term, our class will study: _____

_____

I'm wondering if you have any items related to this unit that you would be willing to donate or loan. We could use items such as: _____

_____

_____

Please let me know how you can help by completing the brief form at the bottom of this sheet and sending it to school with your child.

Thank you for your interest in your child's classroom. If you have any questions, be sure to stop by or call.

Teacher's Signature: _____
Phone: _____

- ✂ **cut here** -

Child's Name: _____

To: _____   **From:** _____
Date: _____

I can donate these items: _____
I can loan these items: _____
Days available: _____
Times available: (morning) _____ (afternoon) _____
Phone: (daytime) _____ (evening) _____
Comments:

QUESTIONS FOR YOUR CHILD'S PARENT-TEACHER CONFERENCE

For Parents

Child's Name: _____

Dear Parent/Caregiver:

Our parent-teacher conference is scheduled for _____ (date) at _____ (time). Before the conference, it would be helpful if you could take a few minutes to think about and respond to the following questions. Please bring the completed sheet to our conference.

1. At home, what are your child's strengths? What does she or he do best? _____
   _____
   _____

2. What chores does your child do? _____
   _____
   _____

3. At home, what does your child like to do? What are his or her hobbies or special interests?
   _____
   _____

4. How would you describe your child's personality outside of school? _____
   _____
   _____

5. What is it like to live with your child? _____
   _____
   _____

6. How does your child get along with other children outside of school? With adults?
   _____
   _____

7. How does your child feel about school? _____
   _____

8. What problems do you have with your child at home?_____
   _____

On the back of this form, please list any questions or concerns you would like to talk about during our conference.

Thank you for taking time to answer these questions! I look forward to seeing you at the conference.

Teacher's Signature: _____
Phone: _____

Dreyer, Sharon Spredemann. *The Bookfinder: A Guide to Children's Literature about the Needs and Problems of Youth Aged 2–15,* vols. 1–5. Circle Pines, MN: American Guidance Service, 1977-1994. A wonderful resource tool you can use to track down books that will offer your child (and you) insights on how to cope with a wide range of stressful situations. Provides a comprehensive subject index to match children with books they'll want to read. Includes age interest range and synopsis of every book. Check with your library or write to AGS, 4201 Woodland Road, Circle Pines, MN 55014-1796. Toll-free phone: 1-800-328-2560.

Galbraith, Judy. *The Gifted Kids Survival Guide (For Ages 10 & Under).* Minneapolis, MN: Free Spirit Publishing Inc., 1984. Helps young gifted children understand and cope with the stresses, benefits, and demands of being gifted. For many elementary-aged children, this book is their first exposure to the fact that they're not alone and they're not "weird." Includes advice from hundreds of gifted kids.

Kurcinka, Mary Sheedy. *Raising Your Spirited Child: A Guide for Parents Whose Child Is More Intense, Sensitive, Perceptive, Persistent, Energetic.* New York: HarperCollins, 1991. A valuable, practical, and popular resource for teachers and parents. Includes hundreds of specific suggestions to help children monitor themselves and develop self-control.

Saunders, Jacqulyn, with Pamela Espeland. *Bringing Out the Best: A Resource Guide for Parents of Young Gifted Children.* Minneapolis, MN: Free Spirit Publishing Inc., 1991. Suggests hundreds of ways to promote creativity and intellectual development—without pushing. Explains how to tell if a child is gifted, how to choose the right school, how to deal with teachers, and how to avoid parent burnout. Includes activities to do together.

Smutny, Joan Franklin, Kathleen Veenker, and Stephen Veenker. *Your Gifted Child: How to Recognize and Develop the Special Talents in Your Child from Birth to Age Seven.* New York: Ballantine Books, 1989. Designed especially for parents and teachers of the young child, with an added focus on gifted toddlers and pre-primary children. Includes many specific suggestions and examples to support your child's growth and early education.

Walker, Sally Yahnke. *The Survival Guide for Parents of Gifted Kids: How to Understand, Live with, and Stick Up for Your Gifted Child.* Minneapolis, MN: Free Spirit Publishing Inc., 1991. The chapter titled "Advocacy: Working for Improvement" provides sensible suggestions for influencing schools to be more "user-friendly" toward gifted children. Topics range from consulting with the classroom teacher to effecting change at the state level. A Parent's Choice Award winner.

Webb, James T., Elizabeth A. Meckstroth, and Stephanie S. Tolan. *Guiding the Gifted Child: A Practical Source for Parents and Teachers,* rev. ed. Scottsdale, AZ: Gifted Psychology Press, forthcoming. Based on information from guided parent discussion groups, this book speaks from people's personal experiences of living with and learning from gifted children. It describes qualities of gifted children in a manner that helps readers become familiar with the ways they can help children develop their best "selves." Includes chapters on motivation, discipline, peer and sibling relations, stress management, and depression. The original edition won the American Psychological Association's Best Book Award.

National Association for Gifted Children (NAGC)

1707 L Street NW, Suite 550

Washington, DC 20036

Telephone: (202) 785-4268

Join NAGC and receive their *Parenting for High Potential* magazine. NAGC's Gifted Children's Parent/Community Division might be of special interest to you. Write to NAGC and ask for the resource sheet for your state. Enclose a self-addressed, stamped business size envelope.

National Resource Center for the Gifted and Talented (NRC/GT)

University of Connecticut

362 Fairfield Road, U-7

Storrs, CT 06269-2007

Telephone: (860) 486-4676

This organization plans and conducts research about giftedness.

Gifted Child Society, Inc.

190 Rock Road

Glen Rock, NJ 07452-1736

Telephone: (201) 444-6530

Founded by parents, this organization sponsors many activities designed to assist gifted children and their parents, including programs and seminars related to LD, ADHD, behavior and social skills, school issues, and advocacy.

Council for Exceptional Children (CEC)

1920 Association Drive

Reston, VA 22091-1589

Toll-free phone: 1-800-486-5773

Located at CEC, the ERIC Clearinghouse on Disabilities and Gifted Education provides a valuable series called the ERIC Digests. Call the ERIC Clearinghouse directly at 1-800-328-0272 for a list of available Digests.

Parents of Gifted and Talented Learning-Disabled Children

2420 Eccleston Street

Silver Spring, MD 20902

Telephone: (301) 986-1422

Provides support and information regarding gifted children and children with learning differences.

Supporting the Emotional Needs of the Gifted (SENG)

Dr. James Delisle

SENG—College of Education

405 White Hall

Kent State University

Kent, OH 44242

Telephone: (216) 672-2294

An international organization that helps parents, educators, children, and teens better understand the high points and hassles of growning up gifted. Each annual SENG conference includes a program for children ages 8–14 staffed by local teachers of the gifted, graduate students, and certified counselors.

COMPUTER SOFTWARE FOR YOUNG GIFTED CHILDREN

Arthur's Teacher Troubles (ages 6–10). A humorous interactive spelling program developed by The Learning Company. Write to SoftKey, International, One Athenaeum Street, Cambridge, MA 02142. Toll-free phone: 1-800-227-5609. On the World Wide Web: http://www.softkey.com/

My First Encyclopedia (ages 3–6). Very easy to use, with no reading required! Offers fascinating and fun exploration of ten areas of learning. A Parents' Choice Award winner. Write to Knowledge Adventure, Inc., 1311 Grand Central Avenue, Glendale, CA 91201. Toll-free phone: 1-800-542-4240. On the World Wide Web: http://www.adventure.com/

Storybook Weaver (ages 6–10). A program to motivate children in creating their own personal stories. Developed by MECC. Write to SoftKey, International, One Athenaeum Street, Cambridge, MA 02142. Toll-free phone: 1-800-227-5609. On the World Wide Web: http://www.softkey.com/

Thinkin' Things Collection 1 (ages 4–8). Helps children use their own creativity to build skills in observation, memory, and problem solving. Write to Edmark Corporation, P.O. Box 97021, Redmond, WA 98073-9721. Toll-free phone: 1-800-426-0856. On the World Wide Web: http://www.edmark.com/

The Writing Center (ages 6–10). Helps children type, design, and print their own writing. Developed by The Learning Company. Write to SoftKey, International, One Athenaeum Street, Cambridge, MA 02142. Toll-free phone: 1-800-227-5609. On the World Wide Web: http://www.softkey.com/

ONLINE RESOURCES FOR PARENTS OF YOUNG GIFTED CHILDREN

For Parents

If you have access to a computer and the Internet, you can find all kinds of information about giftedness online—as well as support from other parents. Please note that electronic addresses often change. If you have difficulty reaching one of the sites listed here, try contacting another. Many sites offer links to other gifted resources.

Gifted Resources Home Page
http://www.eskimo.com/user/kids.html
Contains links to all online gifted resources, including state organizations and those outside the United States. Updated often.

National Association for Gifted Children (NAGC)
http://www.nagc.org/
Join NAGC and receive their *Parenting for High Potential* magazine. NAGC's Gifted Children's Parent/Community Division might be of special interest to you.

National Resource Center for the Gifted and Talented (NRC/GT)
http://www.ucc.uconn.edu/ wwwgt/nrcgt.html
This organization plans and conducts research about giftedness.

Gifted Child Society, Inc.
http://www.gifted.org/
Sponsors many activities designed to assist gifted children and their parents, including programs and seminars related to LD, ADHD, behavior and social skills, school issues, and advocacy.

TAGFAM
http://www.access.digex.net/ king/tagfam.html
A support group for families of gifted and talented children seeking workable solutions to problems related to giftedness.

YAHOO Resources for/about Gifted Youth K–12
http://www.yahoo.com/text/education/k_12/Gifted_Youth
Offers links to many online gifted resources.

10

Understanding and Meeting Children's Social and Emotional Needs

Usually Aparna eagerly joined group activities and wanted to lead whatever was going on. Lately, though, she seemed to be going through the motions. Her focus was somewhere else: she gazed out the window, picked at her cuticles, or traced wood-grain patterns with her finger. When the aide took the class out for recess, the teacher, Mrs. Lambert, invited Aparna to stay in and help water the plants. She talked to her student with gentle concern and learned that Aparna's family had recently given away their dog, Scoot, because her mom was going to have extensive surgery and needed a long period of bed rest for her recovery. Aparna had myriad worries: Why hadn't her parents told her they were going to give Scoot away? Was Scoot as confused and afraid as she was? Would the surgery hurt? Could her mom die? If her mom had to stay in bed, who would fix supper and help Aparna with her homework? Would her parents ever give her away?

In workshop presentations, we ask parents and teachers, "Who made a difference in your life? How did that person help you? Share this with someone seated near you." Then we watch respondents' faces light up and listen as the room becomes animated, filled with a noisy exuberance. More often than not, the person being described in these conversations is a loved and long-remembered teacher.

When adults reflect on someone who positively influenced their lives, it's often a teacher who believed in them, encouraged their attempts, listened to them, and expressed interest in them as people—not just in their achievements. This passing on of courage and hope is one of teaching's greatest rewards.

Meeting Children's Many Needs

As a teacher, your own professional fulfillment comes in some part from having the opportunity and the ability to affirm and motivate your students—not only in their intellectual growth, but also in their affective development. The gifted children in your classroom have unique social and emotional needs. Exceptional abilities have little value if children can't use them to feel happy and successful in their own lives. Perhaps only a small fraction of the ability to thrive in life is determined by intellectual intelligence. Other factors are more crucial in determining children's personal destinies. How children feel about themselves is far more important than what they know: "I can" is more significant than IQ.

What qualities lead children to personal fulfillment? Children need to be able to:

- be aware of themselves and of how they affect others
- understand and manage their emotions
- comfort themselves
- motivate themselves
- communicate and get along with others
- make thoughtful, constructive decisions.

Gifted Children Are Different

While all children need to develop in these aspects, the social and emotional characteristics of gifted children are often unique. Chapter 1 touched on several general qualities of highly intelligent and able children, including asynchronous development, enigmatic behavior, and a passionate and imaginative nature (see "What Are You Looking For?" on pages 6–9). For adults, and even for other children, the apparent contradictions between gifted children's rare abilities and their social and emotional behavior can be confusing. How can a child who is so intelligent be so out of step when it comes to fitting in with classmates?

Gifted children *are* different. It's only in the past 15 years or so that educators and mental health professionals have begun to give more attention to identifying and investigating the social and emotional aspects of giftedness, along with those of academic performance.

Gifted education can be an emotional, controversial issue. An enormous range of ideas exists about what's appropriate for young, highly able children. This confusion extends to gifted children's social and emotional needs—what these needs are, how they are demonstrated, and how teachers and parents can best respond to them.

Common Misconceptions About Young Gifted Children

Here are a few common, but for the most part inaccurate, assumptions about young gifted children:

1. They can succeed on their own.
2. They are self-motivated and therefore "teach themselves."
3. They love to teach other children.
4. They are proud to be held up as examples of model work and behavior.

5. They are naturally "loners."
6. They can't be identified until the third or fourth grade.
7. They should be held back so they won't suffer socially and emotionally.
8. They have no special needs because every child is gifted in some way.

When applied to a particular child, any one of these assumptions might be borne out in some way. None of them, however, pertains to all or even most gifted children.

A More Comprehensive View of Children's Needs

In caring about young gifted children, we can't simply apply a linear, cause-and-effect analysis about who they are and what they need. These children's intellectual and emotional lives are complex, created by an intricate interweaving of ideas, feelings, and situations.

Being gifted usually amplifies a child's emotional life in depth, degree, and intensity. For most young gifted children, high intelligence is an asset in their social and emotional adjustment. As a group, gifted children's overall self-concept and self-control levels are more highly developed than those of their age peers. Yet there remains enormous diversity among individual children. Gifted children have a vast range of social and emotional characteristics.

There are positive and negative aspects of high intelligence. As with people from any minority group, with gifted children it's often the *degree* of difference from the norm that creates vulnerability. As intelligence increases, so does the possibility for misunderstanding. To develop and enjoy their abilities, young gifted children need understanding and support.

When we consider gifted children's psychosocial adjustment, research and reports are contradictory. This reminds us that we can't broadly apply one set of answers to all gifted children. Instead, we can be fascinated and curious. We can wonder how each child sees and feels in a given situation. We can explore how and with what each student needs to be engaged to make a project worthwhile. We can discover what works for a particular child.

How Does It Feel to Be Gifted?

What does it feel like to be gifted? Most of us will never know. One of our students gave this explanation: "People expect me to be abnormally brilliant and brilliantly normal." For gifted children, it's normal to be abnormal. There's nothing we can "tweak" to change them into "normal" children. Just as a plant can't help turning toward light, these children can't deny their heightened awareness, sensitivity, curiosity, and intensity.

Judy Galbraith's research in identifying "The Six Great Gripes of Gifted Kids" helps us recognize and find ways to respond to children's special needs. Here's what she learned:*

1. No one explains what being gifted is all about—it's kept a big secret.
2. The stuff we do in school is too easy and it's boring.
3. Kids often tease us about being smart.
4. Friends who really understand us are few and far between.
5. Parents, teachers (and even friends) expect us to be perfect, to "do our best" all the time.
6. We feel too different and wish people would accept us for what we are.

Maybe the greatest handicap for young gifted students is that they're like square pegs trying to fit into round holes. There's nothing wrong with these children, but *who each child is*—and *what is expected of him*—is out of sync with who many of his age mates are and what's expected of *them*.

Social and Emotional Issues in Young Gifted Children's Lives

Let's look at some qualities that make young gifted students different, what drives these children, and how we can understand, support, and nurture them.

* Judy Galbraith, *The Gifted Kids Survival Guide (For Ages 10 & Under)*. Minneapolis, MN: Free Spirit Publishing Inc., 1984, p. 11. Used with permission.

Stress

Gifted students may feel the effects of stress for many reasons:

• Highly able children tend to feel and respond very intensely. Given the same taxing situation, young gifted kids will respond by *experiencing* more stress than most other children.
• Although in some ways gifted students are more developmentally advanced than their age mates, they are at times required to tolerate restrictions on their exploration and learning that feel stifling.
• Gifted children tend to be highly sensitive and to have deep emotional responses. A gifted child may wonder why things seem to bother her more than they bother other children, and may consequently view herself as less able to cope.
• Extremely bright young children are usually more conscious of a situation as a *whole* with many related components. They may experience more stress because they comprehend the complexities and multiple layers of an issue.
• Since gifted children are usually curious and have *more* questions, they may assume that they are *less* intelligent and knowledgeable than others. Because they are processing more information, highly able youngsters may also work more slowly than their classmates.
• With their vivid imaginations, young gifted children may be frustrated because they want to pursue a greater number of possibilities.
• Perceiving that adults and other children believe they should succeed without help, gifted children may hesitate to ask for help when they need it.
• Frustration comes when resources and available time place limits on what bright, creative children want to do. Then children often feel that they are compromising their ideals and abandoning more than they are producing.

Many activities in this chapter can be effective in helping your students reduce their stress level and change their attitude or situation. Consider especially the ideas discussed in "Coping Skills" beginning on page 171. You can also encourage children to reward themselves for any attempts they make to change their attitudes and behaviors in beneficial ways.

Sensitivity

Quesha came home from first grade, slammed the door, and declared, "I hate math!" "Honey, you're doing very well in math," her mother exclaimed. "Yeah," Quesha replied, "but some of the other kids are having a lot of trouble."

Like Quesha, many young gifted children are highly sensitive. Arriving at preschool, Keang clings to his mother, hides his face, and says nothing. Seeing that she's made a tiny mistake, Chelsea is distraught. Marcus seems to worry about everyone and everything: his family, his classmates, a child he saw crying in the supermarket, floods on the other side of the world. With Anna Maria, *everything* matters—a lost pencil, an accidentally dropped volleyball, a seemingly terse comment from the teacher. Brett is in second grade, yet he still cries in school.

Often, gifted children are angry because they think that other people just don't care. These students may take someone else's lack of sensitivity as an attack on *them.* What other children may not notice can have an immense impact on a gifted child. We need to help this student understand that it's not that other people don't care, but that others simply don't always see and feel things in the same way.

We can begin to help gifted students understand how and why other people's ideas and behavior might be different from their own. Analogies are one way to approach this:

- "Henry, you know some of us have to wear glasses to see well. Others see very well without glasses. Some people, like you, see and feel more than others. It's as if you're looking through a microscope."
- "If we were TV sets, some of us would get five channels. Some would be wired for cable and would pick up a lot more. Some people, like you, Sally, would seem to have a satellite dish and could pick up more information and ideas and feelings than many others."

Hearing these kinds of reassuring reminders regularly, over time, can help children understand and manage their sensitivity and respond to situations and events in a more balanced way. Class activities focused on appreciating differences can also be of help (see "Helping All Children Appreciate Differences" beginning on page 175).

Control

Studies show that intellectually gifted individuals at all ages exhibit the following characteristics:*

- self-sufficiency
- independence
- autonomy
- dominance and individualism
- nonconformity.

Add up these characteristics and you have *control.* Here's a brief example overheard by one preschool teacher: Four-year-old Lena announced, "I know everything!" "Okay," challenged Duncan, age five, "how much is three plus three?" Lena countered, "I'm not telling."

Understanding control issues can make your life as a teacher easier and more rewarding. We want our students to have control over themselves. For young gifted children, feeling that they have some sense of control over how they behave and think has a tremendous effect on their academic achievement and self-concept. The crux of self-control lies in children's perceiving that they have choices and can *make* choices that help them do what they want to do. Just because children have great ideas about how they *can* cooperate doesn't mean that they *will* act accordingly. Because a gifted child usually has astute awareness, vivid imagination, and excellent memory, you can help him learn to use his self-control to make wise choices.

From preschool on, many gifted children tend to exert more focused time, energy, willpower, and perseverance in achieving their constructive goals. In facing challenges and seeking goals, children need to become aware that they always have some choice over their behaviors and attitudes. They need to become conscious that their choices can work *for* them or *against* them.

How can you facilitate this? Appeal to the gifted child's sense of control:

- Tell the child what to expect. Allow lead time and give notice before an activity is to be terminated: "Rhea, you'll have ten more minutes with

---

* Paul M. Janos and Nancy M. Robinson. "Psychosocial Development in Intellectually Gifted Children," in *The Gifted and Talented: Developmental Perspectives,* Frances D. Horowitz and Marion O'Brien, ed. Washington, DC: The American Psychological Association, 1985, p. 165.

the microscope. Then it will be time for everyone to write in their journals."

- Give explanations and reasons for processes and jobs.

- Rather than automatically intervene to assist the child, ask, "How can I help?" Keep this in mind even with very young students.

- Separate parts of a situation and help the child distinguish between those she does have control over and those she doesn't: "You may write a story, a poem, or a skit—that's for you to decide. It must be about one of the four questions we just finished discussing."

- Teach and depend on shared control—both within small groups and with the class as a whole. Help students negotiate and reach a consensus on how they will cooperate.

- Define limits and help the children understand the consequences of possible choices. (Chapter 8 discusses ways to help groups of children cooperate and make choices. See "Guidelines for Grouping Young Children" beginning on page 143.)

- Teach creative decision making. (See pages 171–172 for a complete description of a creative decision-making process.)

Perfectionism

Many adults are concerned about perfectionism in gifted children. Although seeking perfection is gratifying, certain behaviors associated with doing so—anger, avoidance, and disruptiveness—are troublesome. For example, Tyrone may carefully trace *b*'s across his page until he turns a loop the wrong way. Then, seeing his mistake, he responds with rage, breaking his pencil and hurling it across the room.

Myriad factors contribute to such perfectionism. Often, more is expected from a gifted child. Adults and children also tend to impose high expectations on a student who has a particular ability or talent. It isn't unusual for gifted children to hear remarks such as: "For someone who already knows how to subtract, you sure ought to be able to remember to hang up your jacket!" Typically, too, there is a heavy emphasis on performance, both at home and at school. For instance, when neighbors visit four-year-old Leon's family, he's brought out to recite his alphabet monologue ("A is for artichoke, B is for banana. . ."). Many parents

and children are conditioned to see the value of intelligence reflected on paper, in the official terms of test scores and grades. If young children are put on display and praised only for their achievements, they may feel valued not for themselves but for what they can produce—for being "smart" and "right." These young children may conclude that they have to be perfect to be fully acceptable. Some move through the elementary years and into their teens thinking, "I am my parents' report card," or "I'm valued for what I can accomplish."

Perfectionism can be an adaptive behavior, an attempt by children to control their lives and their world. It can also be situational: a conflict might arise over a project that's more important to the child than to the teacher, or that interferes with the teacher's lesson plans. Situational perfectionism is sometimes mislabeled as "overachievement" when a child does more than we think is good for him—when we think he should be satisfied with less.

Easy skill mastery may condition gifted children to a relatively effortless existence. If students are developmentally advanced for their age, most of what they're expected to learn comes easily. They aren't accustomed to struggle. Then, faced with a task that is difficult to master, they may quickly reject the activity as something they just can't do. Gradually, these students internalize the expectation that they should "know better." Even very young children may deny themselves permission to make mistakes and avoid events that might show their flaws.

Perfectionism is usually not a pathological or compulsive behavior. It's rooted in caring about how something ought to be. But, especially in the early years, gifted children's resources, experiences, and fine motor skills can't accommodate the intricacies of their mental model. These children's asynchronous development impedes their accomplishing what they envision in their elaborate imaginations. This breach between performance and ideals can lead to frustration and sometimes disruptive behavior.

The following suggestions may be helpful to you in guiding each child to try new things and accept and learn from less-"perfect" attempts:

Teach courage. Transformation comes through trials. Tell the child, "I know you can try it."

Reward trying. Sometimes we're tempted to say, "It's okay how it turned out, as long as you did your best." With a bright child who might have complicated goals, this can imply that a project represents—or should represent—her best attempt. Not everything is worth a child's greatest effort and time investment. Encourage the student to try doing something new without being committed to high performance. This helps her motivate herself and persist in the face of frustrations.

Expect progress, not perfection. Remind the student and yourself that "finished" is sometimes a better goal than "perfect."

Applaud persistence. You might say: "Heroes keep on working at something, even when they don't believe it can be done. And look at you. You kept on trying, even when you weren't sure how it would turn out!"

Break down the task. At one time or another, we've all felt overwhelmed by a huge, all-encompassing goal. Help a child accomplish a larger project by defining and working through a series of small, attainable goals. In this way, you'll set the stage for a sense of "I can"—and for success. We tell our students, "Inch by inch, it's a cinch. Yard by yard, it's hard."

Acknowledge learning. Let a child know that you expect progress, not perfection. Ask: "What did you learn while you were doing this?" "What part did you enjoy most?" "What might you try next time?" "How might you do it differently next time?"

Ask, "What's good about it?" To turn the child's attention away from flaws and toward what he has learned and accomplished, you might say, "You've told me you're disappointed with some parts of your project. Now tell me what's right about it."

Help the child discover meaning. Notice choices the child makes and ask questions such as: "What were you thinking about when you were choosing which colors to use?" "Why do you think you enjoyed that so much?"

Honor the time invested. Tell the student, "You gave a lot of your time to this. It must have been important to you."

Focus on processes as well as products. You might ask, "How did you decide to change the experiment in the way you did?"

Make mistakes okay. Everyone makes mistakes. Help your students see that mistakes are inevitable and part of the learning process. You can call work "practice." You might comment on your own mistakes when they occur: "Oops—I cut all these shapes for our math project too small. Next time I'll know to measure more carefully. Who has an idea for how we can use shapes this size?"

Underachievement and Lack of Motivation

Children are always motivated. It's just that what *we* want and what *they* want are not always the same. Again, causes for an apparent lack of motivation among young gifted children are interwoven with self-concept, social adjustment, and environmental issues. A bright student who's an underachiever may be motivated by her own needs and rewards:

- It may be more challenging and interesting to work on something else than to fulfill other people's expectations.
- The rewards may not seem worth the effort.
- The purpose of the assignment may have little meaning to the child.
- The child may want to be independent.
- Refusing to comply may be a way for the child to wield power.
- The child may want to punish her parent or teacher.
- Underachievement may be a coping behavior the child uses to get her teacher or parent to expect less of her.
- The child may fear success because it could create higher expectations and pressures.
- By saying she didn't try something, the child can mask the fear of failure and save her ego.
- The school's program and the child's learning style may not be well matched.
- The child may be uninterested in projects that involve what she already knows.
- By not standing out as a high performer, the child may gain acceptance from peers.
- The child may use underachievement to get focused concern and help from parents and teachers.

• The child may feel misunderstood or even depressed.
• The child may have pent-up physical energy that she needs to release before she can focus on schoolwork.

To get at the root of a child's apparent lack of motivation, ask yourself: "What might be involved? What might I try?" Sometimes your questions will readily lead you to an answer. It may be a good idea to consult with the child's parent as well. The most valuable source of information is likely to be the child herself. Ask the student what her favorite and least favorite activities are and why she feels that way. Probe the child's interests. Learn about what's going on at home. You may gain valuable information that can help you guide the child to more productive, worthwhile school time.

Coping Skills

Most young children simply haven't lived long enough to have acquired coping skills. Their usual response to frustration is to withdraw or lash out. Yet childhood is a crucial time for shaping lifelong coping behaviors. As emotional habits become established, they're harder to change later in life. Children need to have some capacity to regulate their moods and keep distress from burdening their ability to think.

Coping Ideas to Share with Students

As a teacher, you can guide and reinforce children in finding positive ways to soothe their own feelings and sustain self-confidence. Here are some suggestions to offer your students:

Try it out in your mind. Tell children that their mind is a place to try out new experiences. Mentally walk them through what has happened, what might happen, or how else they might act or have acted. Review other possible behaviors and anticipate consequences.

Use positive self-talk. Teach children the value of positive thinking in instilling optimism: "I can manage." "I can do this." "Look how much I've done."

Change the channel. Help children recognize that their minds and behavior are instruments they can regulate. Introduce them to the idea that their thinking is like a TV set—it has pictures and words. Tell students to "watch" and see whether their thoughts are working for or against them. If they see that their thinking isn't helping them, they can "switch channels."

Read about it. Bibliotherapy is the use of books to help understand and cope with stressful events such as teasing, a friend's moving, or parents' divorce. Through reading, children can find reassurance that they are not alone in their problems and can gain useful information about how others have developed courage and made or found solutions. *The Bookfinder* by Sharon Spredemann Dreyer is an excellent resource you can use to track down books for children (or you) that will offer insights on how to cope with a wide range of stressful situations.

Use creative decision making. Because most gifted children reason at high levels, they're quite insightful. Help children follow a process to consider choices and experience control over situations. If you wish, give students a copy of "My Problem-Solving Plan" (pages 181–182) and go over the steps with them.

Using "My Problem-Solving Plan" with Young Children

Explain the steps in this way:

1. **Define the problem.** Have children ask themselves: "What would I like to be different? Is this my problem, or someone else's? Is it a problem I can solve? Can I solve it by myself, or will I need help?" Guide children to think of all aspects of the problem: what's happening, who's involved, and what consequences are occurring or could happen.
2. **Find the facts.** Help children learn what each person involved needs and wants and what led to the troublesome situation.
3. **Brainstorm ideas.** Explain that *brainstorming* means considering all the possible ways to solve the problem. Tell children to list all their ideas—even silly ones or those that don't seem possible to do. Suggest that they think of all their ideas first without judging any of them.

4. Consider the best ideas. Once students have no more ideas, help them evaluate each idea. Have them ask: "What might happen if I do that? How could I make this idea work? How might this idea help me? How might it help others? Could it hurt anyone?" Remind children to be "solution finders" rather than "fault finders." Help them see how they can move from *thinking* about the problem to *doing* something about it.

5. Make a plan. Encourage students to choose the idea that seems best. They should then decide to try it for a specific length of time, such as two times a day for a week.

6. Review how the plan has worked. Once children have given their idea a reasonable trial, help them evaluate the results. If the problem is solved, point out how the child has taken charge and made a positive change: "Good for you, Carla. You solved your problem! Now you know how to think things through." Be sure to have children think about what they've learned and what they might do in the future to avoid or solve a similar problem.

7. Try again. If the problem isn't solved yet, help children change the plan slightly or greatly and try again. Reassure students that some problems are tricky and take more work to solve than others. Express confidence in the students' ability to persevere and solve the problem. Support children in trying other ideas and, if necessary, in looking at the problem from different points of view.

Building Children's Self-Esteem

Another important way to help children learn coping skills is to support and nurture their sense of their own personal worth. Take some time for activities that build self-confidence and self-esteem. *Just Because I Am* and the companion *Leader's Guide* by Lauren Murphy Payne and Claudia Rohling are loaded with easy ideas and activities for you to use to foster children's self-esteem and confidence.

Introversion*

It's the fifth day of school, and five-year-old Gus is eager to get outside and play. Once outdoors, though, Gus lingers at the edge of the playground.

He shifts his focus from the shrieking commotion of his classmates and gazes around in a wandering, random fashion. After Gus's impatience for recess, his teacher is perplexed. This isn't the behavior she'd expected.

Understanding the social and emotional qualities and needs of young gifted children means being aware of introversion as a basic personality trait. Everyone's personality fits somewhere along a continuum from extroverted to introverted, and we all need both qualities to some degree. While extroverts are essentially energized by being with other people, introverts generally regain stamina by being alone. Many gifted people are introverts, a tendency that increases with intelligence. Because extroverts dominate American society, being introverted is another way in which gifted children can often seem out of step and difficult to understand. "Common Traits of Extroverts and Introverts" on page 173 compares some of the social preferences (not abilities) of children who are more outgoing and those who tend to look more inward.

For the introverted child, team sports, recess, or other active group activities can be especially difficult and even painful. These activities may feel too invasive. Inner-directed children often prefer individualized activities such as track, karate, or gymnastics.

There's nothing inherently antisocial about a child who prefers to be quietly reflective or to interact with others on a one-to-one basis. You can cultivate trust, sharing, and enthusiasm in this child by forging your relationship a little differently than you do with more outgoing children. To make your classroom more "user-friendly" for young introverts, you might do the following:

- Wait at least 3–10 seconds after asking a question and before repeating, rephrasing, or reposing the question or asking a different one. This allows needed time for gifted children (who usually sort through a greater number of possibilities than others in the class) and for introverts (who often prefer to think through their answers before responding).
- Provide private, quiet places such as a huge carton for a "quiet cabin" or a "private mat" in a corner.

---

* Chapter 1 includes additional information about introversion in gifted children. See page 12.

Common Traits of Introverts and Extroverts

In general, extroverts:	*In general, introverts:*
Learn and think by talking	Process ideas by thinking
Have intense needs to share ideas	May not want to tell ideas
Like activities	Have intense needs for privacy
Like variety	Stay with one project for a long time
Crave company	Crave time alone
Are quick to answer	Think reflectively before answering
Welcome interruptions	Resent interruptions
Show feelings	Mask feelings; hide what is important
Want many friends	Want one or few best friends, may feel lonely with others
Are spontaneous; learn by trial and error	Want to understand concepts and situations before experiencing them

- Correct children privately to avoid humiliating or hurting them and your relationship.
- Occasionally, arrange some independent learning projects for children to do on their own, or use computers in place of discussion or group activities.

Peer Relationships

With eyes sparkling and words punctuated with flailing arms, Kyle eagerly approached a small group of children in the dramatic play area. "Hey!" he announced. "Let's pretend we're dolphins and talk to each other in signals. I've got the code all figured out! Four beeps mean there's danger approaching and three short hums mean 'I see something to eat.' And dolphins change colors like chameleons—we can use these different clothes to camouflage—"

"You're weird, Kyle," Josie interrupted. "We don't want to play dolphins. We're having a pretend birthday party."

Deflated, Kyle moved to a corner and began to play "dolphins" by himself.

It's widely accepted that by the age of five or six, gifted children are quite aware of being different. Sometimes they—and the other children—think these differences mean that something is wrong with them. A child might wonder, "Why do things bother me that don't bother other children?" "Why do I have so many questions? Maybe I'm not as smart as the other kids—they don't ask questions."

Regardless of age, the more intelligent a person is, the more problems he or she often has in finding truly congenial companions. Although many gifted children manage quite well socially, as intelligence increases, so does the potential for social difficulty. Gifted children's relatively rare characteristics create some separateness from their age peers. These bright young children may have more trouble finding friends who can fully relate to them and thus may have fewer opportunities to experience understanding and empathy.

Who is a peer and in what setting? Young gifted children tend to select older playmates. Because gifted children are developmentally more advanced, their personalities may be more similar to those of older children than to those of children their age. Although a young gifted child may have older friends outside of school, we may be concerned that the student doesn't seem to have any real friends in class.

Feeling estranged in the classroom is a source of stress for young gifted children. Here are some factors that can complicate peer relationships:

- Gifted children make up intricate rules for games and create complex play. They gravitate to children who also crave complicated play, and sometimes alienate other children.
- Gifted children often come across as "bossy" because they can be extremely creative and want to organize the play to suit their many ideas.
- Gifted children realize that they can sometimes see, feel, know, and do things others can't. This can be frightening and alienating.

What can you do to help a gifted child make friends in your classroom? Here are some suggestions:

Reduce competition. Most gifted children desperately want to fit in. Refrain from suggesting that a bright child is better at something than his classmates. Avoid routinely using his work or skill mastery as a model. When you do give recognition, praise other children's work at the same time.

Help the child form relationships based on activities. This might mean that you team the child with one child for computer sharing, another for an art project, and another for math games.

Ask questions. Ask the gifted student: "What do you look for in a friend?" "What are some ways you might try to make friends?"

Use role plays. Role-play social situations with the child. Doing this lets him experience the impact of his own behaviors and express his feelings about other children's behavior. Children can act out all the roles in a specific misbehavior situation and create other ways to respond.

Play situational charades. It's important that this student learn to read nonverbal cues and become aware of his own social messages. Otherwise, he will continue to feel that he has no

control over how others treat him. For example, you might have children mime greeting someone in a friendly way, snubbing someone, taking care of someone who is hurt, or making fun of someone, and then discuss how they feel about this behavior.

Watch silent videos. Help children become aware of body language by showing part of a video without the sound. Then stop the machine and ask children to interpret what they've seen: "What's happening here?" "What is each character feeling?"

Be a true friend to the child. Model the best qualities of friendship, teaching respect and understanding as a basis for a healthy relationship.

The Need for Empathy

Four-year-old Renee wailed that she had lost Brown Bear. Wanting to soothe Renee, her teacher told her, "Just go play with something else and Brown Bear will show up when you least expect it." Renee replied, "Then I least expect it right now!"

This example illustrates an important point: Platitudes don't help! In this situation, Renee's response told the teacher that she didn't want to have her feelings brushed aside. She wanted empathy.

When students feel that their teachers have high empathy for them, significant benefits result: Academic achievement, positive self-concept, and attendance go up. So do positive peer relationships in the classroom. In addition, children also commit less vandalism and have fewer discipline problems. This has powerful implications in working with gifted children.

Empathy isn't just a nice idea; it's constructive energy. There are many ways to convey empathy, but perhaps the most important is by *listening.* To do this, you must offer the child your full attention. As you listen, focus on what the child is saying as if nothing else at that moment matters as much as her thoughts and feelings.

Rather than respond by trying to "fix" the problem for the child, work to understand what the situation means to her. Show your interest by nodding and offering short words of understanding: "I see." "Uh-huh." Repeat and paraphrase what you hear without adding your own ideas; this helps the child know whether she's expressing herself clearly. If possible, use the child's own words. If you need to paraphrase, use a tentative tone of voice: "It sound like you're pretty confused. Are you?" "It sounds like that really hurt you. Am I right?" Ask for clarification and amplification: "I'd like to know how you felt about that." "What were some of the ways you were feeling when he said that?" "What are you feeling now?"

You want to help the child recognize her feelings, understand them, and know that they're acceptable: "It seems that you're furious with Nadia." Restrain yourself from offering advice or making comparisons to other children. Focus your attention on gathering information and feelings and understanding what they signify to the child. If the student can identify her feelings, she can do something about them. "I'm mad" might mean that the child feels left out or embarrassed because she was shunned on the playground. Later, you can guide her to try constructive solutions to this lonely situation. But you must first earn her trust through your sincere interest and understanding.

Your goal is to help the student understand herself and gain confidence to look for ways to solve her problems. Ask questions that encourage her to try new behaviors: "What would you like Nadia to do?" "What could you say to her about that?" Be careful not to let the child feel that you're taking sides, or that you blame her or the other children for anything.

You may want to arrange some private time with this child. A few intimate minutes each day can send a powerful message and allow you to offer the student real support.

Self-Understanding and Self-Acceptance

After a father attended a talk on characteristics of giftedness, he approached the speaker and divulged, "Thank you for curing me. I always thought I was crazy. I felt that no one else saw and felt the way I did. Now I know there was nothing wrong with me."

This man's frank remarks remind us of what it can be like for some bright, creative children. So often, no one explains what being gifted is all about. As a teacher, you can help children recognize, accept, and value their differences. Self-understanding is a basis for self-esteem, for wise decision making, and for wholesome social and emotional relationships.

Gifted kids know and feel they're different. As with all children, their only frame of reference may be themselves. It can be difficult for them to understand how or why other students don't see things the way they do. One five-year-old put this poignantly when she said, "I understand others better than they understand me."

Many of the strategies we've suggested for addressing stress, sensitivity, control issues, perfectionism, underachievement, coping skills, introversion, peer relationships, and empathy will help you guide your students toward self-understanding and self-acceptance. You'll find many additional suggestions in Judy Galbraith's *The Gifted Kids Survival Guide (For Ages 10 and Under)* and James Delisle's *Gifted Kids Speak Out.* These two sensitive books reflect gifted children's thoughts, feelings, and eccentricities and offer models that balance the need to fit in and belong with self-esteem and integrity.

Helping All Children Appreciate Differences

Sharing differences in an affirming atmosphere can enable *all* of your students to get to know themselves and their classmates. Use a variety of means to guide children in doing this: small-group and large-group activities; writing, drawing, and reading experiences; and role plays with puppets, dolls, stuffed animals, or toy figures. Following are some suggestions to get you started.

Points of Pride: On long sections of butcher paper (sliced in half lengthwise), ask students to draw or cut and paste illustrations of "points of pride." These might include personal, social, or academic accomplishments; ways they've helped a friend, the classroom, or the earth; or something new they've attempted to do. Ask each child to explain the meaning of his picture.

All I Want to Be: This activity helps infuse meaning and purpose in classroom tasks. Ask children to brainstorm "all they want to be" from the present into the far future: basketball player, rockhound, gardener, teacher, parent, scout leader. Invite children to draw, write, or role-play the possibilities that they foresee in their own lives.

Temperature Reading: When children are in small groups, "take their temperature." On a scale from one ("as sad as I can be") to ten ("so happy I could burst"), ask students how they'd measure their present temperature. They can explain why if they choose. You can start. This helps children accept the range of feelings in themselves and others.

I Like Myself When. . . : Ask children to explain what behaviors they use when they like themselves. Then discuss with them what they can do to like themselves more of the time. Ask what they can do to help others feel good about themselves, too.

My Pictures: Ask each child to bring several photographs or pictures cut from magazines to school in an envelope. These can be of anything they choose. Group children in pairs and have partners share and tell each other about their pictures.

Tell Me About You: Again working in pairs, have students interview each other and then describe their partner to the class, sharing several facts they have learned.

Lots 'n' Lots: Give sentence starters and have the entire class come up with as many ideas as they can. You may want to write each sentence starter on the board, along with the various endings children provide. Here are some you might want to use:

• The thing I like best about my class is. . .
• I like it when children do this:
• I don't like it when children do this:
• The best thing I could do for myself is. . .
• I am very happy that. . . .

How It Feels to Be Happy: Ask children how it feels to be happy. Where do they feel it? How do they know? What can they do to help other children feel happier?

Common Courtesy: Many times, self-esteem is based in knowing what to do. Get a book on manners or other social skills for young children and go over one situation a week. Let children role-play these in little scenes. The lessons in *Taking Part*, a program developed by Gwendolyn Cartledge and James Kleefield, offer an excellent means for teaching and reinforcing social skills in young children.

———

There are many more ways you can help children get to know each other, appreciate the ways in which they are different, and grow in respect for others and self-esteem. For example, you can invite children to read, tell, or act out stories that let them experience different points of view. A simpler—and very effective—strategy is to use students' first and last names as spelling words. Every day, try to give each child ten seconds of personal attention. Welcome or leave the child with a greeting, a smile, a pat on the back, and eye contact. You'll find many additional simple but wonderful ideas in *100 Ways to Enhance Self-Concept in the Classroom* by Jack Canfield and Harold C. Wells.

Considering Early Entrance and Acceleration

The school principal was at a loss for a simple answer to a problem. Marisa, a highly gifted child, had entered kindergarten a year early. Now, after finishing first grade at age five, she was languishing in a grade-level curriculum that held no challenge for her. Marisa tested three to five grade levels above the norm in reading, math, and reasoning skills. She was small, however, and during class she was shy, withdrawn, and reluctant to contribute. Her advanced intellectual abilities found no company in the classroom, and on the playground she was at a disadvantage in size and coordination.

"Marisa's much happier in first grade than she was in kindergarten, but I'm reluctant to advance her another grade," the principal explained to the child's father. "In first grade, she has the advantage of being among children near her age. Although she's far ahead of them academically, she'll relate to them more comfortably socially and emotionally than she would older children. If we put her ahead one more grade, the curriculum still won't be significantly more challenging—and she'll have all the

developmental disadvantages of being several years younger than her classmates. If we advanced your daughter to a grade based on her test scores, she'd be in fifth grade at age six!"

Early entry to kindergarten and grade acceleration in elementary school are considered standard tools for responding to the needs of young high-ability children. Those options are clearly appropriate in many instances, and the children find a comfortable niche for intellectual, social, and emotional growth.

However, the complexities of giftedness defy simplistic options. The idea of putting a six-year-old in a fifth-grade classroom because that's where her test scores place her is disturbing. Equally troubling is the notion that we might force a young gifted child to wait an extra year before starting kindergarten simply because his birthday misses an arbitrary deadline by a few weeks or months. Regardless of when a child starts kindergarten or what grade the child skips, every gifted student continues to have special needs that require accommodation in the classroom.

We have test scores and grades to tell us that very bright children usually flourish academically after grade acceleration. But what about the social and emotional effects? How might children suffer from grade skipping? Because of their asynchronous development, young gifted children won't fit perfectly into one grade. Nonetheless, although some people think of early entrance and grade skipping as pushing the child, "lockstep" grade placement can *decelerate* and *detain*. We need to focus on the social and emotional effects of *restraining* a child from learning. Contrary to popular belief, when acceleration is done carefully, most gifted children thrive—academically, socially, and emotionally.

Conversely, children who are held back tend to lose ground in all three areas. For children who are required to receive instruction at a level significantly below their ability level, many problems can ensue. Children often develop poor study habits, grow apathetic, lose motivation, or become maladjusted. They may resent "putting in their time." Even in the best situations, these children may retreat into their internal world of imagination or devise some negative external means of intellectual stimulation and challenge. Consequently, they may be mislabeled as children who can't focus or pay attention.

Early Entrance

Early entrance to kindergarten or first grade may be the best acceleration option for young gifted children. This allows for the child's intelligence to be better accommodated and for a peer group to be established. It saves the student the later disruption of skipping a grade. By being more academically challenged in the earliest grade, a bright child is likely to have fewer of the emotional problems that typically result from facing academic challenges after years of "coasting" along. Early entrance can set the stage for many young gifted children to continue to thrive and excel throughout their school experience, to participate in more activities, to feel secure within a peer group when they express their ideas, and to experience more interdependence and cooperation.

Acceleration

When you recognize an extremely bright child in your classroom, you might wonder whether he would benefit from acceleration. Your role in making this recommendation is extremely important. As you begin to work with any young gifted student, keep in mind that you're in a unique position to see the child "in action" in the classroom setting. No test can evaluate the social or emotional status of your student as well as your firsthand experience and observations. With this insight, you may decide to suggest that a child would be a strong candidate for acceleration, or that the current grade-level assignment is the most appropriate.

As the teacher, you can be an essential advocate for gifted children in your classroom. Use your knowledge and observations to suggest an accurate assessment of the child's abilities to determine his intellectual and academic levels. Tests used must include tasks several grades above the current class level. The child's development should be above the average for the grade he will move into. (For additional information on testing and assessment, see Chapter 7, "Assessing and Documenting Development," beginning on page 121.)

Discover whether the child prefers older playmates. Since there are more opportunities outside the classroom for the child to be with older children, ask the child's parent about this. Socially and emotionally, many young gifted children are far more appropriately matched with older children.

Ask parents for samples of the child's drawings, writings, and other projects done at home or outside of school. Discuss with the parents how these reflect the child's feelings or attitudes toward learning and working with other children.

Determine if the child's fine and gross motor skills are reasonably adequate for the grade he will enter. Although you don't want the child to be unduly frustrated, the lack of a specific skill (such as using a scissors or coloring within the lines) isn't a sufficient reason to deny acceleration or early entrance. Gifted children can usually learn creative ways to compensate for temporary deficits.

If you feel that acceleration might be an option for the child, explore the idea with the parents to add their perspective to your own.* Then bring your observations to the attention of your school principal or other designated administrator.

———

For early entrance or acceleration to succeed, everyone involved must be invested in the process and optimistic about the outcome. Specifically:

• The *child* must be consulted and must welcome the idea.
• The receiving *teacher* must be carefully selected for qualities of flexibility and enthusiasm; have positive attitudes toward the acceleration; be willing to help the child adjust to the new situation; and demonstrate that she or he welcomes the child into the class (other students in the class will reflect the teacher's attitude).
• The *parent* must want this placement adjustment; be willing and able to cooperate with the teacher to arrange tutoring for the child in academic areas where there might be a learning gap; and communicate closely with the teacher about the child's reactions at home.
• The *administration* must coordinate the process and support the child, the teacher, and the parents.

Beyond these considerations, everyone involved must build an ongoing system of evaluation. Expect to make changes and adapt your plan. Acceleration is an initial step, not a panacea. You'll need to keep making adjustments in the pace, depth, and complexity of the child's classroom experience.

Questions and Answers

"Won't children be frustrated if we push them ahead?"

For young gifted children, frustration is more likely to be a result of having to endure waiting for classmates to grasp new material. Under this circumstance, the classroom becomes an obstacle to bright children's learning. When acceleration is done carefully, taking into consideration all aspects of a child's needs and characteristics, it's a valuable option.

"Isn't it good for a bright child's self-esteem to be the best in the class?"

The top of the class can be a very vulnerable place. The child may begin to feel that she's always expected to be "the best." She may believe it's her job to help her classmates and that it's futile to ask others for advice in turn. And when a child is at the very top, she's likely to have fewer opportunities to learn. The class may limit her opportunities to make a real effort that will allow her to experience pride and success.

Conclusion

So often, the "measure" of a gifted student—even one who is very young—comes down to test scores or demonstrated achievement. When you become an advocate for your gifted student's social and emotional growth, you help the student develop the mental "software" needed to use information in worthwhile endeavors and to find satisfaction in doing so. In focusing on children's social and emotional needs, you also establish a broader, healthier perspective from which caring adults can chart a more sensitive and successful individualized educational experience for each child.

---

* For additional information on working with parents, see "Enlisting Parents as Colleagues" in Chapter 1, pages 13–14, and Chapter 9, "Building Partnerships with Parents," pages 149–164.

References and Resources

Canfield, Jack, and Harold C. Wells. *100 Ways to Enhance Self-Concept in the Classroom: A Handbook for Teachers and Parents.* Englewood Cliffs, NJ: Prentice-Hall, 1976. A classic, friendly guide that will inspire you.

Cartledge, Gwendolyn, and James Kleefield. *Taking Part: Introducing Social Skills to Children.* Circle Pines, MN: American Guidance Service, 1991. This program for children in preschool through third grade provides more than 30 lessons with activities to build social skills such as listening, respecting the property of others, resolving conflicts, and communicating nonverbally. Includes stick puppets and a teacher's manual.

Clark, Barbara. *Optimizing Learning: The Integrative Education Model in the Classroom.* Columbus, OH: Merrill Publishing Co., 1986. A great leader in gifted education shows how and why to integrate control (physical, chosen, and perceived), cognitive processes, intuition, and more in a responsive learning environment.

Delisle, Deb, and Jim Delisle. *Growing Good Kids: 28 Activities to Enhance Self-Awareness, Compassion, and Leadership.* Minneapolis, MN: Free Spirit Publishing Inc., 1996. Creative and fun activities build students' skills in problem solving, decision making, cooperative learning, divergent thinking, communicating, and more while promoting self-awareness, tolerance, character development, and service to others.

Delisle, James R. *Guiding the Social and Emotional Development of Gifted Youth: A Practical Guide for Educators and Counselors.* New York: Longman, 1992. An essential resource that's very useful in the areas of self-concept, school achievement, and invitational education; specific adjustment concerns of gifted students; strategies, activities, materials, and conditions to promote self-control and achievement; and more.

Dreyer, Sharon Spredemann. *The Bookfinder: A Guide to Children's Literature about the Needs and Problems of Youth Aged 2–15,* vols. 1–5. Circle Pines, MN: American Guidance Service, 1977–1994. A resource tool that includes a subject index to match children with books they'll want to read or have read to them. Includes age interest range and synopsis of every book. Later volumes are also available on CD-ROM. Write to AGS, 4201 Woodland Road, Circle Pines, MN 55014-1796. Toll-free phone: 1-800-328-2560.

Galbraith, Judy. *The Gifted Kids Survival Guide (For Ages 10 & Under).* Minneapolis, MN: Free Spirit Publishing Inc., 1984. This lively book helps young gifted children understand and cope with the benefits, demands, and stresses of being gifted—including teasing, stress, loneliness, and boredom.

Goldstein, Arnold P., and Gerald Y. Michaels. *Empathy: Developmental Training and Consequence.* Hillside, NJ: Lawrence Erlbaum, 1985. How and why to be more empathetic.

Goleman, Daniel. *Emotional Intelligence: Why It Can Matter More than IQ.* New York: Bantam Books, 1995. Goleman argues convincingly that how we use our intelligence is more important than how much intelligence we have. Provocative reading for teachers and parents alike.

Heacox, Diane. *Up from Underachievement.* Minneapolis, MN: Free Spirit Publishing Inc., 1991. Outlines how teachers, students, and parents can work together on an action plan for student success. Includes reproducible handout masters.

Janos, Paul M., and Nancy M. Robinson. "Psychosocial Development in Intellectually Gifted Children." In *The Gifted and Talented: Developmental Perspectives,* F.D. Horowitz and M. O'Brien, eds. Washington, DC: The American Psychological Association, 1985, pp. 149-195. One of many useful, insightful, research-based chapters in a superlative anthology on giftedness.

Katz, Elinor. *Affective Education: Self Concept and the Gifted Student.* Boulder, CO: Open Space Communications, 1994. A concise overview of gifted children's self-concept related to models of intelligence, motivation, achievement, and other home and school issues.

Kurcinka, Mary Sheedy. *Raising Your Spirited Child: A Guide for Parents Whose Child Is More Intense, Sensitive, Perceptive, Persistent, Energetic.* New York: HarperCollins, 1991. A valuable, practical, and popular resource for teachers and parents. Includes hundreds of specific suggestions to help children monitor themselves and develop self-control.

Lawrence, Gordon. *People Types and Tiger Stripes.* Gainesville, FL: Center for Applications of Psychological Type, Inc., 1993. A practical, easy-to-understand explanation of personality types. Several chapters relate types to successful teaching and classroom issues such as motivation, curriculum, and learning and teaching styles.

Myers, Isabel Briggs, and Peter B. Myers. *Gifts Differing: Understanding Personality Type.* Palo Alto: Davies-Black Publishing, 1995. A look at personality types, with sections focused on teaching and learning.

Payne, Lauren Murphy, and Claudia Rohling. *Just Because I Am: A Child's Book of Affirmation* and *A Leader's Guide to Just Because I Am.* Minneapolis, MN:

Free Spirit Publishing Inc., 1994. The *Leader's Guide* reinforces the messages of the child's picture book with activities, questions, and reproducible parent handouts. Together these books are a complete beginning course on fostering self-esteem in preschool, early elementary school, child-care settings, and the home.

Roeper, Annemarie. *Educating Children for Life: The Modern Learning Community.* Monroe, NY: Trillium Press, 1990. Roeper lovingly inspires us to nurture children in developing responsibility, interdependence, and positive behaviors and attitudes along with their unique qualities.

Schmitz, Connie C., and Judy Galbraith. *Managing the Social and Emotional Needs of the Gifted: A Teacher's Survival Guide.* Minneapolis: Free Spirit Publishing Inc., 1985. A practical guide to understanding and supporting the social and emotional growth of gifted and talented youth. Also useful for enlisting parent cooperation.

Silverman, Linda Kreger. "A Developmental Model for Counseling the Gifted." In *Counseling the Gifted and Talented,* Linda Kreger Silverman, ed. Denver: Love Publishing Co., 1993. pp. 51-78. One of many sensitively written chapters in a comprehensive resource depicting the intricate, complex characteristics and needs of gifted children. Essential reading.

Webb, James T., Elizabeth A. Meckstroth, and Stephanie S. Tolan. *Guiding the Gifted Child: A Practical Resource for Parents and Teachers,* rev. ed. Scottsdale, AZ: Gifted Psychology Press, forthcoming. A primer on understanding and nurturing gifted children that includes chapters on motivation, discipline, peer and sibling relations, stress management, and depression. The original edition won the American Psychological Association's Best Book Award.

My Problem-Solving Plan

For Students

My Name: _____

Start by doing steps 1–5.

1. This is the problem:

2. This is what happened and how each person (including me) feels:

3. These are all the ideas I can think of for solving the problem:

4. These are my BEST ideas and what might happen if I try them:

IDEAS	WHAT MIGHT HAPPEN
_____	_____
_____	_____
_____	_____
_____	_____

➡

MY PROBLEM-SOLVING PLAN (CONTINUED)

5. I'll try this idea:

    I'll try my idea at least _____ times a day until _____ (date).
    Then I'll see how it's going.

Try your idea until the date you chose in step 5. Then do step 6.

6. My idea worked (*circle one*): **GREAT**   **NOT SO GREAT**

    Here's what happened:

    Here's what I learned:

    Here's what I'll do next time:

If your problem still isn't solved, look back at your ideas in step 4. Is there something else you can try? Ask your teacher for another copy of this handout. Keep working on your problem!

7. Here's what I'll do next:

11

Meeting the Needs of Children from Diverse Populations

Ming Li rarely says a word, although she seems to understand what's going on. In class, she's painfully shy. When her teacher tries to draw her into an activity, Ming averts her gaze and turns to her solitary play. At five, she successfully completes pages of two- and three-digit addition and subtraction problems on her own during free time. But she barely participates in her reading group's projects. Then, at recess, Ming cuts loose, becoming a streak of shrieking energy. Her teacher feels mystified. How will she ever get to know this child?

Although today considerable energy goes into identifying and serving gifted children from ethnically and culturally diverse backgrounds, many gifted children from minority cultures, as well as those from other minority groups, are still falling through the cracks. One reason for this may be because many of the "clues" to giftedness we typically look for are rooted in the expressions and behaviors of the majority culture.

Casting a Wide Net

Many minority groups—African-Americans, Hispanics, and Native Americans, for example— are underrepresented in gifted programs. We can begin addressing this discrepancy by expanding our understanding of cultural differences and similarities. As you consider the ideas in this chapter, you'll want to keep these facts in mind:

- Giftedness exists in all human groups in roughly the same proportions.
- Culture and environment strongly influence development of certain skills and familiarity and comfort with certain activities.
- Standardized tests are not the only—or even the most—useful means to find gifted children.
- The expression of giftedness varies among cultures. High-level abilities may be demonstrated through behaviors that are characteristic of a minority cultural group and therefore may not be recognized in mainstream society.

Apart from ethnic and social distinctions, children from underserved populations may be different from the majority culture in other ways. They may be poor. They may live in substandard housing. English may not be the primary language in their families; in some cases, adults in the family may not speak any English at all. Outside of school, the children may have little or no opportunity to interact with other children from the majority culture. The more these conditions overlap, the less likely the gifted child (a minority within a minority) in these circumstances will be served. The situation is made more complex by issues examined in earlier chapters, including the following:

- confusing, vague definitions of giftedness
- gifted programs that emphasize measurable academic achievement
- biased identification procedures
- limited, competing funds and resources.

Gifted children exist in every racial, cultural, and economic situation. Yet, in some groups, these children are usually underidentified and underserved—often because the *expressions* of giftedness vary so greatly from culture to culture. Whatever a child's background may be, the young gifted student requires appropriate educational intervention to prevent his skills and abilities from being lost to himself and to the rest of us.

A Variety of Needs Considered

There are more varieties of cultural groups than we could possibly discuss in a single chapter. What we have done here is to point out and explore *some* of the issues related to identifying and nurturing giftedness in those children who come from ethnic minorities; are economically disadvantaged; live in rural areas; are girls; are "twice exceptional" (both gifted and learning disabled); are highly gifted; and have high energy.

Children from Ethnic Minorities

Among the many ethnic minorities in American society, those most broadly represented include people who are Native American, Hispanic, Southeast Asian, and African American, as well as those who are new immigrants. Distinct customs and beliefs about behavior exist among families in each group. The following examples, although generalized, offer a glimpse at the kinds of differences that can impact children's school experiences.*

In most Native American cultures, decisions are made by the family or community group.

---

* Some of the material in this section about ethnic minority cultures is adapted from Judy Galbraith and Jim Delisle, *The Gifted Kids' Survival Guide (For Ages 11–18): Revised, Expanded, and Updated Edition* (Minneapolis, MN: Free Spirit Publishing Inc., 1996). Used with permission.

Children are raised to be interdependent, not independent. A gifted Native American child may not stand out in class as a leader or an individual performer—in fact, the child may strive *not* to stand out, but rather to cooperate with classmates and demur to the teacher and other adults.

Children from Puerto Rican families are generally taught to discuss problems and ideas in the family rather than to act on their own initiative. Many Mexican American and Southeast-Asian American children are taught to respect their elders and others in authority above themselves. Individual competition, independence, and self-direction are intentionally discouraged. Children raised in this philosophy may feel uncomfortable if they are singled out in school for individual performance or achievement.

African American culture includes survival strategies to deal with institutional racism and personal discrimination. Many African Americans adapt bicultural patterns so they can live in their traditional environment and at the same time manage conventions of the dominant culture. Some African American students use a distinct linguistic system with its own rules of grammar and pronunciation. Care must be taken that high-ability children don't go unrecognized because their language usage doesn't conform to standard English.

Recent immigrants typically face a spectrum of challenges, from finding housing and a means of income to managing day-to-day life within the framework of unfamiliar language and social expectations. At school, the talents of immigrant students who are highly able in math, science, or the arts may go unnoticed because of the school's or teacher's focus on their language difficulties.

Olga and Ivan, recent immigrants, came to their sponsor, bewildered. "We just don't know what to do about Mikael. He is so unhappy when he comes home from school. He says the math work is too easy and that the teacher doesn't understand when he tries to tell her. In Russia, school was so different. We just don't know what to do."

Look and Listen

Our conception of giftedness is growing increasingly diverse and now includes abilities and potential abilities far beyond academic performance. We cannot comprehensively describe the various forms of giftedness; neither do we want a definition of giftedness or intelligence to limit or impede any child's development. This is particularly true when looking at children from diverse populations. Your basic guidelines should be these:

1. Use the broadest definition of giftedness to include diverse abilities.
2. Find and serve as many young children with high *potential* as possible.

The idea is to recognize exceptional needs and abilities however they occur. An astute, sensitive teacher can be more effective than a standardized test in recognizing exceptional abilities. But when looking for gifted children from various minority categories, we have to be aware of our own biases. If, for example, a teacher has invested considerable time and effort in developing grammatically correct speech and writing, he might overlook the gifted child whose language use seems awkward to him. The teacher needs to look beyond *how* the child is speaking and focus on *what* the child is saying.

Giftedness emerges when you blend innate potential with experiences that evoke higher-level cognitive and affective processes. Children who are culturally different or economically disadvantaged may need an extra boost. By applying the concepts of multiple intelligences and different learning styles discussed in Chapters 1 and 2, you can cast a wide net and allow gifted minority children to be better served. You can also identify these children through some of the following strategies:

- Use checklists. We provide several in this book: the "Checklist of My Child's Strengths" (for parents—pages 22–23) and the "Student Observation Forms" (for teachers—pages 131–138). Consider every possibility of exceptional skill when seeking to discover a child's outstanding abilities.
- Find a child's "best performance." Look for any sign of exceptional, even isolated, performance that could represent unidentified abilities. If you find one outstanding ability, such as memory for music, you can begin to invite a child's confidence by creating opportunities for her to use that talent. A single encouraging experience can often produce a ripple effect on the

child's self-assurance and on the competence he begins to show in other directions.
- Consider "processing" behaviors, such as risk taking and the ability to hypothesize and improvise.
- Ask other teachers.
- Trust your hunches. If you suspect that a child has exceptional abilities, your hunch will probably be reliable.
- Make classroom observations, especially during multicultural-based activities.
- Interview the child to gain insight into her thinking, aspirations, home activities, and sense of self.
- Solicit the parent's views about the child's talents, abilities, and expressions of creative and critical thinking. Chapters 1, 2, and 9 discuss ways to communicate with parents and include several letters and forms to facilitate this process.
- Keep parents informed. Parent involvement is essential in finding and serving very young minority gifted children. If you keep parents informed and look for ways they can help, you are likely to empower them with a sense of being able to contribute. They'll be invested and more interested in cooperating with you to reinforce your classroom activities.

Language and cultural differences can keep parents away and can distance teachers from discovering children's exceptional abilities. One important and very effective way to bridge this gap is by working with your school or district to establish a "cultural liaison," a contact person for parents who are not comfortable speaking English. Unless you invite and facilitate parent participation from those who feel the most estranged, you won't be able to fully assimilate their children in your classroom.

Foster a Multicultural Consciousness

Although children from minority cultures may not conform to the majority group, it's important to realize that their expressions can be healthy and appropriate to their culture. Children of cultural minorities are often raised with different problem-solving strategies, different attitudes toward education, different degrees of adaptation to the majority culture, and different languages and language styles. We can't generalize about these children, but we can appreciate the culture from which a child emerges, because this is a factor in how the child does or doesn't exhibit exceptional abilities.

Cultural differences can mask a child's exceptional abilities, particularly if we assess those abilities only from the vantage of the dominant culture. Culture is more than arts and crafts, music, dance, food, dress, and holidays. It includes behavior and values that provide meaning and security.

When you foster a multicultural consciousness—in yourself and in your students—you enable children to identify themselves as citizens of the world. In integrating multicultural awareness in your classroom, you also provide an arena for children of diverse cultures to more comfortably exhibit their exceptional abilities. Following are some ways you can celebrate cultural differences:

• Read richly illustrated stories of various cultures. You will find multicultural resources in the "References and Resources" sections throughout this book and in Appendix B beginning on page 198. Your school librarian or media specialist can also recommend books to help your students explore various cultures. Select some that you especially like, and you'll convey appreciation and acceptance by your own heartfelt enthusiasm.
• Discuss alternative cultural views of the same story, as suggested in "Flexibility: Alternative Histories" (pages 63–67) and "Creative Divergence: Alternative Fairy Tales" (pages 86–88).
• Create ethnic or folk crafts and arts; use music, dance, and song. While culture is more than art and music, experiencing the art and music of various cultures helps children appreciate differences and expands their creativity.
• Invite students from different cultural backgrounds to present aspects of their culture. For example, ask them to tell about a special custom or a favorite food or to teach the class a phrase in their language. If children once lived somewhere else, ask them what they miss most about their old home and what they like best about their new one.
• Use the culture exploration activities suggested in "Originality: Creating Culture" (pages

67–72), in which children observe their own and other people's cultures and then imagine and create their own original cultures with unique geographies, histories, customs, and artifacts.

Economically Disadvantaged Children

Poverty consistently excludes children from being identified as gifted. Economic deprivation can impact any child. It affects maternal and child health and social functioning, both of which may relate to school performance.

To function well in their home or community, economically disadvantaged children may develop abilities that are different from other children's. For example, instead of learning information and skills that require a good deal of parents' time and money, some economically disadvantaged children may be particularly astute in understanding other people's needs and feelings, responsible in carrying out instructions, or creative when it comes to solving problems. It's important to remember that these children can also have the same potential for academic giftedness as economically advantaged children do. Often, the difference lies in the fact that the potential is underdeveloped. Whenever we suspect that a child is economically disadvantaged, we must attempt to intervene and provide appropriate additional educational opportunities. If a child seems to show a spark of interest in a particular activity, he may flourish with a little extra personal instruction, coaching, and encouragement from you.

Teachers of young children can be a decisive force against cumulative deficits in any child—especially in a child from a minority population. Without appropriate intervention, some socially or culturally disadvantaged children will exhibit a progressive decline in intelligence, scholastic achievement scores, or both.

Young Gifted Children in Rural Areas

Gifted children in sparsely populated areas can be difficult to find and serve because doing so requires exceptional effort, often by one teacher who is caring and astute. The scarcity of school personnel relative to the vast geographical distances involved makes identifying children with special talents and abilities a particularly challenging endeavor. Because resources to serve these gifted children are often rare, a teacher's influence is even more crucial and may be the *only* means to identify and serve these children.

The challenge of identifying rural gifted children is compounded when the population is bilingual. Parts of some standardized tests assess knowledge of mainstream language and culture. Don't rely on standardized tests alone. Nonverbal assessments, interviews, checklists, analyses of children's work, and anecdotal information from teachers and parents will also help you identify skills and potential. Children's adeptness in solving problems offers yet another window into their exceptional abilities.

Collaboration with adjacent districts can be of great help in both finding and serving gifted rural children. Materials, ideas, curricula, and expertise can all be shared. If you teach in a rural area, you might consider some of the following suggestions:

- Use satellite television instruction, video hookups, and the Internet.
- Share materials by creating educational video and audio tape exchange networks.
- Transport gifted children to a single location so they can interact with each other.

Gifted Girls

"I'm a boy!" declared Gina Marie at age six—causing her parents and teachers to wonder whether she needed therapy. Today, at 22, Gina Marie has excelled in almost every aspect of school and campus life at a highly selective university. She now has a choice of outstanding job offers and is a joyful, adventurous person. Why had Gina Marie once wished she was a boy?

Many gifted girls are on an obstacle course that leads them into well-documented gender discrepancies in self-esteem, course-taking patterns, test results, and eventual career status and earning power.* Studies continually remind us that we expect boys to be more self-reliant:

---

* Many of the study results discussed in this section are cited in American Association of University Women, *How Schools Shortchange Girls* (Washington, D.C.: AAUW Educational Foundation, 1991).

A baby dressed in blue is handed to a caregiver. As the baby wails, the caregiver bounces the child on her knees and explains, "He's just exercising his lungs." Later, the same baby dressed in pink is on the caregiver's lap and starts to cry. She cuddles and soothes the tiny child.

Studies also show that girls tend to *start out* ahead of boys. Compared to young boys of the same age, girls are likely to:

- be more robust
- read and count earlier
- score higher on IQ tests during preschool
- be ready for formal schooling at an earlier age
- outperform boys in most studies of early entrants to elementary school.

Even into second grade, gifted girls are more like gifted boys than like average girls in their interests, activities, and career aspirations. Young gifted girls differ from their male counterparts, however, in that they tend to be exceptionally socially aware and are more likely to be "teacher pleasers." They are usually better socially adjusted than average girls or gifted boys. Throughout elementary schools, gifted girls tend to score higher on achievement tests than gifted boys.

Despite these pluses, gifted girls see more disadvantages to being gifted than do their male peers. They have lower academic and social self-concepts than gifted boys. Parental attitudes toward their gifted children differ as well: Parents tend to be less invested and involved in gifted daughters than they are in gifted sons.

Gifted Girls Can Be Too Adaptable

In second grade, Caroline is reading at a level far beyond that of her classmates. She has no idea that more advanced reading material could be offered to her. After quickly finishing her reading work, she begins to entertain herself by guessing which page of her assignment has the most words on it and then counting the words on every page to see if she's correct. Because Caroline isn't disruptive, no one notices that she's no longer reading.

Gifted girls can be too well adjusted for their own good. Many are conditioned to be adaptable. Long before the third grade, socialization processes can subtly teach girls to hide their abilities.

For many girls, their giftedness goes "underground" as they work to blend in by conforming to what they see other girls being praised for. And, as age goes up, many girls' self-esteem and expectations ebb. While young gifted girls have high career aspirations and vivid career fantasies—to be astronauts or paleontologists, for example—by adolescence, the same girls have experienced more than a decade of socialization and have often "adjusted" their aspirations to lesser goals.

Young Girls' Abilities Can Go Unnoticed

Bryna was barely five when she started kindergarten, and she didn't seem fully "ready" yet. Instead of participating with the rest of the class, she either stayed in the library corner with her nose in a book or gazed out a window. The school staff decided that Bryna was still too immature for school and requested that she wait out another year. At home, Bryna just about exhausted her mom with all of her demands for attention. So Mom took Bryna to a psychologist for help. The psychologist administered an IQ test and found Bryna to be highly gifted, with a voracious craving for intellectual stimulation.

How did Bryna's talents go unrecognized? There are many possible reasons. Since most parents who are gifted underestimate their own abilities, they may have trouble acknowledging that their child is gifted—bright, yes, but not gifted. This is particularly so for preschool girls. Here again, the different expectations parents have for boys and girls could very likely have come into play. Boys tend to be raised hearing "Do!" and "Boys will be boys"; girls hear "Don't!" and "That's not ladylike." With daughters, parents spend more time cautioning them not to take risks. And for girls, the emphasis is on conformity rather than achievement. While boys are seen as leaders, parents and teachers are likely to describe girls' assertive behavior as "bossy." Girls are also more likely to *learn* to be helpless; their parents and teachers often intervene and help them, whereas with boys these adults are more likely to be encouraging and say, "You can do it!"

The problem of gifted girls neglecting to realize their potential is complex, and so is the task of guiding them. It's important to remember that these girls often become invisible and, if not invited, they won't show what they are capable of doing. Unintentionally, many well-meaning teachers still are likely to teach differently to the two genders. Often, teachers provide boys with detailed instructions for completing a complex task, but simply do the task for girls. At times, too, teachers accept answers when boys call them out without raising their hands, yet reprimand girls for this behavior. And it isn't unusual for teachers to criticize boys for lack of effort (and thus communicate that the boys have control over the results of their work) but to simply accept mediocre efforts from girls.

Girls and Boys Often Experience School Differently

Compared to boys, girls in the classroom:

- are called on about one-fourth as often
- are interrupted more often (while boys are allowed to continue speaking)
- are more often told that they are wrong (while boys are given hints to correct their answers)
- are allowed less time on computers and math manipulatives (and will more likely give these over to the boys)
- receive less eye contact from teachers
- receive less of the teacher's attention
- are more likely to be rewarded for neatness and good handwriting (while boys are rewarded for ideas and creativity)
- are often "overhelped," which leads them to become dependent and look for something external to transform their lives.

Without early recognition and support, giftedness in girls is often simply lost. Research clearly shows that, by the time they reach high school, gifted girls expect less of themselves than gifted boys—and others expect less of them.

Ways to Inspire Young Gifted Girls

The good news is that you, as a teacher, can be enormously effective in reversing negative stereotypes for girls. Key to maintaining hope and confidence for gifted girls is nurturing their belief that they can act effectively and make decisions independently. The period of preschool through kindergarten is critical in inspiring gifted girls. Here are several strategies for you to consider:

- Seek to identify gifted girls at a young age, to give them early opportunities to experience their exceptional abilities.
- Use portfolios and observations to assess children's abilities so you know what you are dealing with. School readiness tests alone often don't allow very bright children to demonstrate the extent of their abilities.
- Consider early entrance for highly able young girls.
- Find peers with similar abilities and interests, so gifted girls will feel safe to progress.
- Give young girls specific, positive feedback about their abilities—especially in math and science.
- Support young girls' effort and persistence.
- Help young girls see mistakes and "failures" as creative learning experiences.
- Demonstrate considerate, effective, assertive ways for girls to express themselves. Reward assertiveness.
- Integrate, rather than separate, girls and boys.
- Monitor and compare your classroom interactions with girls and with boys. Make it a point to call on girls as often as you call on boys, to give girls informative responses, and to resist "overhelping" girls by giving them answers.
- Stress goal setting and problem solving at a very young age. Make sure to encourage every girl to think for herself and grow in self-confidence.
- Reward exploration. Girls need external feedback. Recognize them with a nod, a smile, or a word when they *explore* as well as when they comply.
- Let a gifted girl know that you value her uniqueness. For example, you might tell a girl, privately, "You were the only one to think of that!"
- Encourage gifted girls to learn to struggle and persist.
- Provide role models through books, speakers, and films.
- Be alert to signs of boredom: poor class participation, daydreaming, or sadness.
- If a four- or five-year-old girl shows particularly high intelligence, recommend private or school testing for early admission to kindergarten or for special preschool gifted programs.
- Be aware of gender-role stereotyping in toys, games, computer programs, books, and other learning materials.

- Involve parents.
- Caution parents that they are likely to see their boys as more able than their girls and their girls as higher in social skills. Explain how these expectations can be a potent detriment.
- Stress to parents that all children run, climb, and spill things in school. Suggest that they send their daughters to school in clothes that are suitable for these activities.
- Be aware that many parents hinder their daughters with lower expectations. They are less likely to see their daughters as gifted and may not recommend them for gifted programs.

Twice Exceptional: Gifted Children with Learning Differences

Some young children have two seemingly contradictory sets of needs: They are gifted *and* learning disabled.* These double-labeled children are often at a double disadvantage. They may also be doubly at risk if their learning difficulty masks their giftedness or their giftedness masks their learning difficulty. Some of these "twice exceptional" children can appear to be average students and thus totally miss services they need. Clinical diagnosis is necessary to detect dual exceptionalities and discrepancies in abilities, such as visual or spatial strengths or auditory processing deficiencies.

Often, *deficiencies* in the gifted student with learning difficulties are more apparent than exceptional abilities. Although teachers need to focus on bringing up a deficiency, they also need to allow other ability areas to blossom. Children need *both* strategies to develop confidence and pride. It's as important to search for strengths as for weaknesses.

Teachers need to be especially sensitive to the potential for confusing children who have learning differences with underachievers, because their characteristics can be identical. Children's different ability levels can vary. However, if a student seems particularly frustrated with, challenged by, or uninterested in a

---

* Many schools and publications now use the term "learning differences" or "learning difficulties" instead of "learning disabilities." The words "disabled" and "disabilities" have negative connotations that can get in the way of students', teachers', and parents' ability to understand and remediate children's learning challenges.

task, or if you observe unusual discrepancies among particular ability function levels, you will want to consider a referral to your school's special education office for further investigation of possible learning difficulties.

Gifted children with physical disabilities can encounter a paradox, too: They are viewed as both inadequate (because of their disability) and competent (because of their giftedness). But while we work to understand and accommodate a disability, the competence must be our critical focus.

Teachers need to be aware that they may expect less of children with disabilities, and they should take care not to identify a child by a physical condition or ostracize the student because of it. Neither giftedness nor physical difficulties and learning differences alone define a child's character, needs, and abilities.

Highly Gifted Children

We pay great attention to increments of intelligence for children of below-average ability, and we adjust our expectations and programs to match their needs. However, we seem to consolidate highly intelligent children into a single group of "bright" or "gifted" students. If we recognize that some children have IQs in the extremely low range of 25, 40, and 55, we also need to help those who are just as unusual on the higher end. In fact, there's more variation in intelligence among highly gifted students than there is among those who are average or moderately gifted.

Highly gifted children seem to have minds like satellite dishes. These students are extra perceptive about people, issues, and ideas. They can be conscious of many things at once, make connections that are both unique and logical, and integrate and analyze relationships. Because exceedingly gifted children see many layers of meaning for any situation or idea, their responses in the classroom can differ markedly from the teacher's concept of the topic.

Complex thinking can also lead these children to be extremely precise and to require precision from others. For example, to a child who fully knows the difference between a *species* and a *variety,* it matters very much which term you use. Highly gifted children can feel outraged if they aren't taken seriously. You might find yourself drawn into arguments over things that seem insignificant to you but are highly significant to your exceptional student.

Traits of Highly Gifted Children

Keeping up with highly gifted students can be a tremendous challenge. In order to meet this challenge, it helps to understand some of the characteristics and abilities these students often exhibit:

A voracious appetite for intellectual stimulation and learning. Many highly gifted children learn in leaps. For example, a student may learn all the moves of chess in one game. A child may grasp an entire concept quickly; once the underlying pattern is mastered, it can be almost impossible for her to break it down into steps. Drill and practice can feel like torture to this child, whose natural tendency is to crave novelty and reject repetition and redundancy. If you have explained division and the child understands it, she will find it useless and even painful to be required to "show her work" repeatedly. A child with this level of ability might balk at homework that offers no novel learning value, or refuse to do more than one problem on a worksheet.

Multiple focusing. To meet his "minimal daily requirement" of intellectual stimulation, a highly gifted child may need to find ways to concurrently supplement the regular classroom "dosage"—perhaps by reading a book while you're explaining a concept, or by expanding a math computation while you're still teaching it.

Insatiable curiosity. The highly gifted child is characterized by intense curiosity, often asking questions such as: Why are some batteries rechargeable? How does sound come out from the tape player? How big is the universe?

Exceptional memory. Many extremely gifted children can pinpoint minute details and include them in elaborate explanations. What the child remembers, *you* may forget. In fact, you may need to explain what "forget" means and how "forgetting" happens. Otherwise the child might think that you're lying or pretending not to know and become angry!

Immersion. Astronomy is a favorite fascination for highly gifted kids; it's a subject that opens up infinite uses of math and physics. Other children are ravenous for information about geography, dinosaurs, or rocks. One child, for example, might be totally involved with the Olympics: She knows all the events, how they are judged, which countries and athletes are favored, and more. She's interested in the games' Greek origins, has moved from that to Greek letters (which she uses as codes), myths, and goddesses—and she wants to share it all. Highly gifted children often live with a series of passions, devouring all the experiments and information and people who are willing to listen about one subject and then, after they are satiated, moving on to rock-and-roll stars, steam trains, or fossils. These children may benefit from being allowed to integrate the class material into their current enchantment.

Empathy. Highly gifted students can be empathetic with just about anything or anyone. There are numerous reports of how these children can be intuitively perceptive. Many parents can't allow their very young highly gifted children to watch the news on TV because of the intensity with which children feel all the inhumanities they see. A gifted child may empathize with a tree being cut down and cry in sympathetic pain. He may worry that the letter he mails will be squashed and hurt in the mailbox or bag. In sports, a child might show something close to shame when his team wins and worry about how the other team feels. With an exceptionally gifted student, you may need to spend extra time dealing with perceived injustices. For example, you might arrange for a child to place her toy horses in a "corral" on the shelf rather than store them in a heap.

Vulnerability. Any potential adjustment for gifted children is amplified for the highly gifted child, who is often more vulnerable to social and emotional problems. Sources of this vulnerability include asynchronous development, alienation, lack of understanding, intense sensitivity, adult expectations, and inappropriate educational services. Children may experience social and intellectual rejection where none was intended. Their vivid imaginations often make it difficult for them to live up to their own expectations.

Social alienation. At school, many highly gifted four- or five-year-olds are seen as withdrawn, socially immature, or emotionally disturbed because they can't find mutual companions in their classroom. A highly gifted child may be chronologically age six, but mentally age ten. Such a child may not relate comfortably to classmates. Insisting that the student stay with her age mates can exacerbate this alienation. Usually, older children can congenially interact with younger ones about subjects that are of mutual interest.

Poor handwriting. Some extremely bright children seem to have almost a writing disability. Expressing what they know with a pencil in their hand is a tedious, frustrating chore. As a response to this frustration, these children may reduce the elaborate descriptions in their minds to a few words on paper, thus avoiding a focus on minutiae when they want to move ahead with other ideas and projects. A child might think to himself, "The enormous glacier obstructed the fjord's passage." Yet, faced with the obstacle of a slow-moving pencil, he'll choose to write simply, "The big ice sticks out." Creative teachers can look for alternative ways for these children to demonstrate what they think and know—for example, by using a computer, speaking into a tape recorder, or creating visual depictions that they then explain orally.

Energy. Highly gifted children may be exceptionally active if they are intellectually "starving."

Identifying Highly Gifted Children

We find highly gifted young students by comparing how their development exceeds what's expected of average children. Often, these exceptional children's abilities to verbalize and imagine—to reason abstractly, to construct meaning, and to understand deeply—are years ahead of their chronological age.

In seeking to recognize extreme giftedness, let the child show you what she can do. Provide ever more complicated problems to solve. Listen to the parents and let them tell you about their child outside the confines of the classroom. Recommend IQ testing and look for the areas or subtests with the highest scores as well as the full scale and composite scores. You can suggest that a *Stanford-Binet Intelligence Scale, Form L–M* be administered. It's the only standardized IQ test we have to measure young children's intelligence in the highest ranges.

What Next?

Although only about one in several hundred children might be considered highly gifted, these children, like all children, need appropriate learning experiences. Most of these unique students require an individually differentiated school program to accommodate qualities that are rare for their age peers. Expecting an extremely gifted student to conform to a regular classroom routine is as inappropriate as placing a moderately gifted child in a special education class for slow learners and asking him to slow down his learning to keep pace with the class. We must allow exceptionally gifted children to excel.

Much literature has demonstrated the possible problems that may ensue from requiring highly gifted students to endure instruction at a level significantly below their ability. These problems include poor study habits, apathy, lack of motivation, and maladjustment. Even in the best situations, children may retreat into their internal world of imagination, or devise some external means of intellectual stimulation and challenge. Consequently, they may be mislabeled as students who can't focus or pay attention. To eliminate potential problems, we need to provide highly gifted children academic challenges that are commensurate with their intellectual ability and academic achievement level.

Usually, there's no place in our schools for highly gifted children. That place needs to be created. When using the ideas presented in this book, you might need to go further and make unprecedented, radical adaptations. For example, it may be worthwhile to place a highly gifted child in a higher grade for a particular subject, such as math, so she can have the support of substantive interaction with intellectual peers. As the child's regular teacher, you might find that this eases your curriculum planning as well. Monitor the situation and expect to make continual adjustments.

Associate with other professionals and families who have experience with highly gifted children and acceleration.* One excellent resource is the Hollingworth Center for Highly Gifted Children, 827 Central Ave. #282, Dover, NH 60093. This center publishes a newsletter and offers valuable information about networking, conferences, services, and other organizations of interest to adults working with exceptionally gifted young children.

Prodigies

Prodigies need to be mentioned separately, if only to balance what the popular media often presents as "gifted children." Prodigies have a distinct, extreme form of giftedness that is sometimes exploited on television and in other ways. While a gifted child usually has great general ability, a prodigy usually has a more focused, specialized, and dominant ability—as well as a powerful drive and confidence to develop it in a nurturing environment. Prodigies are often younger than age ten, yet they perform at a the level of highly trained adults. Prodigies can excel in poetry, music, mathematics, chess, physics, gymnastics, or languages, to name a few areas. A child who is a prodigy may or may not have high academic abilities.

You'll need to be extremely flexible in working with a child prodigy. There's a precarious balance between what's appropriately responsible to the development of talent and what's confining or exploitative. Because prodigies sometimes need to leave class for performances or practices, you can cooperate with their unusual requirements by allowing some "give" in certain school demands. In some instances, you may want to excuse the young prodigy from supplemental work on certain subjects or projects and instead allow time for the intense focus required to develop special talents.

Children with High Energy

High energy often accompanies high intelligence. Highly intelligent children may seem to be always busy, distractible, and hungry for activity. In young gifted children, we may hear rapid, excessive, almost compulsive speech accompanied by animated gesturing with the entire body.

Teachers need to integrate gifted children's often intense, highly active physical needs. This is of special concern when a child's intellectual peers are older and more physically developed. In these situations, brighter children may feel physically inadequate and avoid playground games that demonstrate their relatively inferior psychomotor development.

Often, preschool and other early childhood experiences focus on "socializing" beginning

---

* For a discussion of acceleration, see "Considering Early Entrance and Acceleration" beginning on page 176.

students. Circle time can become excruciatingly constricting to small children with the urge to move. Sometimes, with gifted students who have a great deal of energy, circle-time compliance becomes an educational goal. Yet, paradoxically, being encouraged to move about—as long as others are not disrupted—can facilitate learning for active, gifted children.

In our classrooms, we can provide opportunities for appropriate release of high energy. One way to do this is by adapting our behavior expectations in order to harness children's energy in constructive ways. For example:

- We can allow children to read while standing up.
- We can let children quietly manipulate a plaything to release energy while they are listening in a group.
- We can arrange for active preschoolers to have alternatives to naps. In one school we know of, a gifted program for three-, four-, and five-year-old children is scheduled during rest time, with learning station activities that offer many possibilities for children to use physical energy.
- We can teach children relaxation techniques (taking a deep breath, counting to ten, visualizing a peaceful place) that can help them gain self-control.

There's a long social history of expecting boys to be active and girls to be compliant. It's damaging to expect that girls should be more sedate than boys.

Many young gifted children are misdiagnosed as having attention deficit disorder (ADD or ADHD). Gifted education consultant Sharon Lind has developed a useful perspective on highly active children.* She suggests that, before referring a child for ADD placement, teachers should gain more information about the child.

Lind's exploratory approach might reward you with more cooperation. She suggests that you need to look for ways to modify the environment in order to more appropriately meet the learning styles and abilities of the child. This student might need a curriculum that is on a level more commensurate with her abilities. To feel accepted, she may need to be placed with intellectual peers. It may be helpful to simply ask her to explain to you why she needs to move about or doesn't complete the work you assign. You can monitor her behavior and try to determine what activity precedes a bout of disruptiveness. And because gifted children are often capable of multiple focusing, you might observe the student to see if she's capable of following instructions even if she appears not to be listening. Ask yourself, too, if disruptions could be attention-getting devices. If this seems to be the case, make an effort to give the child more attention for positive behavior.

Questions and Answers

"Some of the children in my class are very different from the students I usually teach. There's so much I don't know about these children! How can I tell if I'm really bringing out the best in a child?"

There are times when it's almost impossible to know what's really best for a child. This is especially true when working with diverse populations. There are so many variations in cultural philosophies and childrearing practices that family preferences might be at odds with your initial determination. As teachers, we can try to accommodate different needs and remain open to reevaluating and adjusting our programs. We can continue to learn more about our students and how we can cultivate their enthusiasm for learning. As always, your best guides are to observe keenly, ask the child, and collaborate with parents.

Conclusion

The vast majority of educators today are committed to becoming more aware of and sensitive to children's varying needs, characteristics, and abilities. As we continue to work with gifted children, we must keep in mind that no *one* suggestion can serve them all; no *single* idea is universally appropriate. As you encounter diverse populations in your own classroom, your best, most effective aproach is to stay open, interested, and flexible. Help your students learn to do this, too. And always remember your goal: to give *every* child the opportunity to learn, to grow, and to develop his or her potential.

---

* Lind, Sharon. "Are We Mislabeling Over-Excitable Children?" *Understanding Our Gifted* 5:5A (1993), pp. 1–10.

References and Resources

American Association of University Women. *How Schools Shortchange Girls.* Washington, DC: AAUW Educational Foundation, 1991. Nearly every page includes examples of how we expect less of girls and they expect less of themselves.

Birely, Marlene. *Crossover Children: A Sourcebook for Helping Children Who Are Gifted and Learning Disabled,* 2d ed. Reston, VA: The Council for Exceptional Children, 1995. Contains a wealth of information to assist teachers and parents of "twice exceptional" children.

Borland, James H., and Lisa Wright. "Identifying Young, Potentially Gifted, Economically Disadvantaged Students." *Gifted Child Quarterly* 38:4 (1994), pp. 164-171. A concise description and procedure to find gifted kindergarten students in urban schools using site-appropriate methods: observation, dynamic assessment, and the concept of best performance.

Dreyer, Sharon Spredemann. *The Bookfinder: A Guide to Children's Literature about the Needs and Problems of Youth Aged 2–15,* vols. 1–5. Circle Pines, MN: American Guidance Service, 1977–1994. A wonderful resource tool that includes a comprehensive subject index to match children with books they'll want to read. Includes age interest range and synopsis of every book. Later volumes are also available on CD-ROM. Write to AGS, 4201 Woodland Road, Circle Pines, MN 55014-1796. Toll-free phone: 1-800-328-2560.

ERIC Clearinghouse on Disabilities and Gifted Education: 1-800-328-0272. Call ERIC to receive great free information on many specific topics regarding diverse populations and other aspects of gifted education.

The Hollingworth Center for Highly Gifted Children, 827 Central Ave. #282, Dover, NH 60093. This center publishes a newsletter and offers valuable information about networking, conferences, services, and other organizations of interest to adults working with exceptionally gifted young children.

Kerr, Barbara. *Smart Girls Two: A New Psychology of Girls, Women, and Giftedness.* Dayton, OH: Ohio Psychology Press, 1994. A wealth of information about meeting the needs of gifted girls. Includes many ideas focused on specific topics such as minorities, extraordinary talents, programs, and young gifted children.

Lind, Sharon. "Are We Mislabeling Over-Excitable Children?" *Understanding Our Gifted* 5:5A (1993), pp. 1-10. An essential perspective to consider in identifying children who might not match the expected behavior profile. Lind offers many alternative suggestions for responding to a child's giftedness and to aberrant behaviors.

Richert, E. Susanne. "Rampant Problems and Promising Practices in Identification." In *Handbook of Gifted Education*, Nicholas Colangelo and Gary A. Davis, eds. Boston: Allyn & Bacon, 1991, pp. 81-96. A provocative perspective on the pitfalls involved in identifying gifted children, with sound ideas for programs and identification practices in your school. Richert's article is one of many reasons to have the *Handbook of Gifted Education*—an extensive collection of the writings of many respected experts in the field of gifted education—on your reference shelf.

Silverman, Linda Kreger. "Invisible Gifted, Invisible Handicaps." *Roeper Review* 12 (September 1989), pp. 1, 37-42. A succinct, useful guide to learning disabilities in gifted children and how to serve them in the classroom. Covers topics including underachievement and learning disabilities, spatial strengths and sequential weaknesses, auditory sequential processing dysfunction, guidelines for identifying gifted physically disabled children, and 24 specific teaching strategies for success.

———. "Social Development, Leadership, and Gender Issues." In *Counseling the Gifted and Talented*, Linda Kreger Silverman, ed. Denver: Love Publishing Co., 1993. pp. 291-327. This chapter is a sensitive inquiry into and explanation of social and gender issues in an essential, comprehensive counseling guide.

Walker, Barbara K. *Laughing Together: Giggles and Grins from Around the Globe.* Illustrated by Simms Taback. Minneapolis, MN: Free Spirit Publishing Inc., 1992. A delightful book that promotes global cultural awareness by sharing humor from almost 100 countries and political and ethnic groups. Includes ideas for using the book in the classroom and at home. Published in cooperation with the U.S. Committee for UNICEF.

Conclusion

When teachers feel and impart enthusiasm for discovering new ideas and activities, young children just naturally follow. The intent of this book is to help you foster a creative classroom environment in which learning is interactive, process oriented, and nurturing to young children. Just as a poem comes alive when it is read aloud, the activities and suggestions we've developed will come alive for you as you try them out in your classroom. The ideas will enhance your work with all your students. They can also provide a baseline of support for the unique needs of the young gifted children in your charge, their parents, and you.

We believe that the most exciting and dynamic teaching in the world goes on in preschool and early elementary classrooms. No one is more sensitive to new ideas than the pre-primary and primary teachers who are drawn to work creatively with young children and who have preserved their own sense of wonder and joy in learning. We know, too, that as one of those teachers, you welcome exhilarating challenges that will spark fresh inspiration in you and in all of your students.

This book is designed to be that spark: to enable you and each student in your classroom to individualize a new level of critical and imaginative thinking—to take greater risks, to dare more, and to attempt more. Young children love to stretch beyond the limits of conventional knowledge. Their natural responsiveness to creative catalysts and hands-on, participatory activities will ignite their enthusiasm, extending their discovery and inventiveness in new ways.

The impact of this book will arise from how you use it to expand your own repertoire of teaching strategies and understandings. Our hope is that it will provide many opportunities for exploring new ways to support the development of young gifted students and for translating this knowledge into your daily teaching experience.

Let *Teaching Young Gifted Children in the Regular Classroom* be a springboard for you. We encourage you to experiment and improvise with the book's insights and strategies, adapting them to the unique needs, interests, and talents of the children in your classroom. As you do this, many of your own ideas will emerge. Teaching and learning will take on a new dimension—one that fosters a stimulating climate of thinking and discovering, creating and originating.

We'd like to hear about how you use the activities and about any new ideas our book generates for you. Please write to us at:

Free Spirit Publishing Inc.
400 First Avenue North, Suite 616
Minneapolis, MN 55401.

An adventure awaits us all!

Appendix A: Tests for Identifying Young Gifted Children

Following are descriptions of some tests that can be useful in identifying young gifted children. To acquire or use any of these tests, please consult with your school or district psychologist. Certain training qualifications may be required to order, administer, and interpret the tests.

Note: Nearly all tests have some bias toward the majority culture. When a description is preceded by an asterisk (*), this indicates that the test is relatively less dependent on acculturation and English language acquisition, and is likely to be more appropriate for children from minority cultures.

* *Cartoon Conservation Scales.* Grades K–6. Can be used in any language, individually or in small groups. Measures intellectual development using a neo-Piagetian approach. No special training is needed by the examiner; takes about 25 minutes to administer.

Differential Ability Scales (DAS). Ages 2.6–7.11. Individually administered test measures overall cognitive ability as well as specific abilities and achievement levels. Includes 17 subtests and offers out-of-level testing for younger children. Achievement tests take 15–25 minutes; the full cognitive battery requires 45–65 minutes.

* *Fischer Comprehensive Assessment of Giftedness Scale.* Grades preschool–high school. Examines observable classroom and out-of-school behaviors in response to environment. Ranks children's applied motivation, interest, behavior, and creative

output as compared with classmates, not national norms. Assesses 44 characteristics including areas of precocious development, applied motivation, creative output, and aesthetic perceptions. The view this test provides broadens and deepens the scope for finding gifted children.

* *Goodenough-Harris Drawing Test.* Ages 3–15. Brief, nonverbal test of intellectual ability. Can be administered either individually or in a group. Involves perception, abstraction, and generalization. Evaluation measures the complexity of the child's concept formation. Administration and scoring take little training; testing time required is usually less than 10 minutes.

* *Kaufman Assessment Battery for Children (K–ABC).* Ages 2.5–12.5. Assesses mental-processing and problem-solving abilities with minimized use of language and academic experiences. Includes 16 subtests grouped in three scales: Sequential Processing, Simultaneous Processing, and Achievement. Since the *K–ABC* has ceiling limitations that allow children to score no more than two standard deviations above the mean, gifted children tend to score lower than they would on the *Stanford-Binet* and *Wechsler* tests. Administration time is 35–85 minutes.

* *McCarthy Scales of Children's Abilities.* Ages 2.6–8.6. Measures verbal, perceptual-performance, quantitative, general cognitive, memory, and motor abilities. Best used for initial screening; not recommended for assessing gifted

children. Individually administered by a trained examiner in 45–60 minutes.

Otis-Lennon Mental Abilities Test. Grades K–12. Group test appropriate for initial screening, though may show lower scores than individual IQ tests. Assesses cognitive abilities related to success in school learning. Eleven verbal and ten nonverbal abilities tested include categories of Verbal Comprehension, Verbal Reasoning, Pictorial Reasoning, Figural Reasoning, and Quantitative Reasoning.

Peabody Picture Vocabulary Test–Revised (PPVT–R). Ages 2.5–adult. Measures receptive English vocabulary. Useful for assessing the English vocabulary in non-English-speaking children, but not for general gifted identification.

* *Raven's Coloured Progressive Matrices.* Ages 5.6–11.6. Measures nonverbal or abstract reasoning and general ability to perceive and think clearly. A good measure of general intellectual functioning, though scores have a low correlation with academic performance. Easily individually administered in 10–25 minutes by an examiner with no special training.

Screening Assessment for Gifted Elementary Students–Primary (SAGES–P). Ages 5–8. Group-administered instrument to identify students for gifted programs that emphasize aptitude and achievement at either the screening level or the final selection stage. Subtests are Reasoning and General Information.

Slosson Intelligence Test. Ages 2–27 years. Brief, individually administered intelligence test that is highly dependent on language. Best used as an initial screening device. Assesses mathematical reasoning, vocabulary, auditory memory, and information. Scores are correlated with the *Stanford-Binet Intelligence Scale, Form L–M.* Can be administered by a briefly trained examiner in 10–30 minutes.

Stanford-Binet Intelligence Scale, Form L–M. Ages 2–adult. This is the preceding edition of the *Stanford-Binet Intelligence Scale, Fourth Edition,* and is the only instrument available to assess children in the highest ranges of intelligence. Can be calculated to derive IQ scores above 200.

* *Stanford-Binet Intelligence Scale, Fourth Edition.* Ages 2–adult. Individually administered IQ test

useful for identifying gifted children. Has sufficient ceiling to accommodate quantifying abilities in most young gifted children; has 12 subtests to identify specific strengths and weaknesses.

* *System of Multicultural Pluralistic Assessment (SOMPA).* Ages 5–12. Measures cognitive, perceptual-motor, and adaptive behavior of black, white, and Hispanic American children. Aims to be racially and culturally nondiscriminatory, but needs to be interpreted with caution. Administration is individual and requires 2½–3 hours by a trained examiner.

* *Test of Early Mathematics Ability.* Ages 3.0–8.11. Measures formal and informal concepts and skills through progressive probes or questions that allow exploration of the child's mathematical thinking skills.

* *Torrance Test of Creative Thinking.* Grades K–12. Measures creative, productive thinking in verbal and figural dimensions. Also scores for fluency, flexibility, originality, and some elaboration. Useful with minority or culturally disadvantaged young children; for other children, informal observation assessment might be adequate instead.

* *Wechsler Intelligence Scale for Children–Third Edition (WISC–III).* Ages 6.0–6.11. Widely used to assess gifted children. Provides 12 subtests, three IQ scores, and four index scores for identification of relative strengths. The Performance Scales of all the Wechsler tests can be used with less language and cultural bias. Individually administered in about 1½ hours.

* *Wechsler Intelligence Scale for Children–Revised (WISC–R).* Ages 6.6–16.6. There is some argument for continuing to use the *WISC–R* rather than the *WISC–III* to assess gifted children because the former has less "point loading" for speed factors in the performance items. *WISC–R* is also available in a Spanish edition normed on 2,200 Puerto Rican children.

* *Wechsler Preschool and Primary Scale of Intelligence–Revised (WPPSI–R).* Ages 3–7.3. Widely accepted to assess young gifted children. Particularly useful because it assesses 12 different abilities to identify specific strengths and relative weaknesses. Individually administered by a highly trained examiner; takes approximately 1½ hours.

Appendix B: More Resources for Teachers

Additional books and materials for use with gifted primary-age children, divided into six major subject areas. For help in finding videos to purchase, call Video Finders, 1-800-343-4727, or PBS Video, 1-800-344-3337. For help in finding audios, call The Public Radio MusicSource, 1-800-75MUSIC (1-800-756-8742).

Art, Music, Dance, and Theater

Barratt-Dragan, Patricia. *The Kids Arts and Crafts Book.* Concord, CA: Nitty Gritty Productions, 1975. Suggests a wide variety of craft projects in different media that children can do without adult supervision.

Beethoven Lives Upstairs. Produced by Eros Financial Investments Inc. in association with Classical Productions for Children Inc., 1992. Set in 19th-century Vienna, this video tells the story of an eccentric boarder (Beethoven) who turns a young boy's home upside down. Includes more than 25 excerpts from the composer's best-loved works. 52 minutes.

Blizzard, Gladys S. *Come Look with Me: World at Play.* Charlottesville, VA: Thomasson-Grant, 1993. Drawing on paintings focused on the general theme of people at play, this book asks open-ended questions and offers brief backgrounds on the artists and their work.

Corsi, Jerome R. Leonardo Da Vinci: *A Three-Dimensional Study.* Rohnert Park, CA:

Pomegranate Artbooks, 1995. Presented in three dimensions along with an informative text, Da Vinci's most magnificent conceptualizations take on new life for children.

Delafosse, Claude, and Gallimard Jeunesse. *Landscapes.* New York: Scholastic, 1993. A "First Discovery Art Book," this intriguing little volume enables young readers to notice painters' unique styles in a series of famous landscapes.
———. *Paintings.* New York: Scholastic, 1993. A "First Discovery Art Book" with brightly painted transparent pages introduces great works of art to the youngest readers in a playful, accessible way.
———. *Portraits.* New York: Scholastic, 1993. A "First Discovery Art Book," similar to *Paintings* in design, this book focuses on famous portraits and draws the young child into the world of artistic representation.

George, Richard. *Roald Dahl's James and the Giant Peach: A Play.* Hammondsworth, England: Puffin Books, 1983. A giant peach takes an orphaned boy to the land of his dreams. Suggested for reader's (chamber) theater.

Hayes, Ann. *Meet the Marching Smithereens.* New York: Harcourt Brace & Co., 1995. A rhythmic text offers facts about the marching band and its instruments, while endearing animal musicians keep the parade moving in sparkling style.

———. *Meet the Orchestra.* New York: Harcourt Brace & Co., 1991. An unusual introduction to the orchestra describes the instruments—strings, brass, woodwinds, and percussion—and offers interesting information about them while animal musicians prepare for a performance.

Hearn, Lafcadio. *The Boy Who Drew Cats.* San Marino, CA: The Huntington Library and Art Gallery, 1972. In a magnificent union of words and pictures, this old Japanese fairy tale tells the story of a child who is joyfully single-minded in the exercise of his talents.

Herbert, Susan. *The Cat's History of Western Art.* New York: Little, Brown & Co., 1994. Thirty-one delightful color illustrations depict a "catty" twist to well-known surveys of Western art. Includes masterful images with annotated notes by an eminent art historian.

Herman, Gail Neary, and Patricia Hollingsworth. *Kinetic Kaleidoscope: Exploring Movement and Energy in the Visual Arts.* Tucson, AZ: Zephyr Press, 1992. This pioneering work provides a conceptual base for kinesthetic teaching and learning, and includes many activities that will stimulate creative and imaginative thinking in young children.

Jeunesse, Gallimard. *Musical Instruments.* New York: Scholastic Publishers, 1994. One of the Scholastic "Voyages of Discovery" books, this one focuses on the performing arts.
———. *Paint and Painting.* New York: Scholastic, 1994. A "Voyages of Discovery" book that deals with visual arts.

Kids' Art. A fine-arts newsletter for children. Write to Kids' Art, P.O. Box 274, Mount Shasta, CA 96067.

King-Smith, Dick. *Pigs Might Fly.* New York: Viking Press, 1982. A piglet runt learns to swim and ends up a hero. Suggested for reader's (chamber) theater.

Locker, Thomas. *The Boy Who Held Back the Sea.* New York: Dial Books, 1987. The retelling of this old Dutch tale by Lenny Hort is masterfully illustrated by Locker. A wonderful way to integrate literature and the art of the Dutch Masters.

———. *Miranda's Smile.* New York: Dial Books, 1994. A charming story, illustrated by the author, about an artist-father who wants to capture his daughter's smile in a portrait. When she loses a tooth, he has to find another way to continue his work.
———. *The Young Artist.* New York: Dial Books, 1989. An exquisite book in which Locker, an artist, writes about the life of a young painter. The story is accompanied by many luminous paintings.

Martin, Mary, and Steven Zorn. *Masterpieces.* Philadelphia: Running Press, 1990. One of the most original coloring books on the market features 60 famous paintings and many facts about the artists, their styles, and all the ways they broke the rules of their day to create their art.

Micklethwait, Lucy. *I Spy Two Eyes: Numbers in Art.* New York: Greenwillow Books, 1993. No ordinary counting book, this volume contains magnificent works of art featuring a variety of artists dating from the 15th century to the present. A great deal to explore and discuss.

Namioka, Lensey. *Yang the Youngest and His Terrible Ear.* Boston: Little, Brown & Co,, 1992. The youngest member of a family of new immigrants faces giving a violin performance to attract students for his father.

Patterns in the Wild. Washington, DC: National Wildlife Federation, 1992. Through a series of striking photos by the world's leading nature photographers, this book presents a celebration of geometric patterns. The text explains the reasons for the patterns—from the huge spiral of a galaxy to the minute, delicate, and colorful design of a butterfly's wing.

Richmond, Robin. *Children in Art.* Nashville, TN: Ideals Children's Books, 1992. Brings together artists' renderings of children from all time periods and places; provides biographical information and teaches young readers about the artists' techniques and styles.

Sibbett, Ed, Jr. *Butterfly Stained Glass Coloring Book.* New York: Dover Publications Inc., 1985. Sixteen lovely butterfly designs printed on both sides of translucent paper. Children can cut colored tissue paper and paste it down as though inserting colored glass, or color with crayons, felt-tip pens, acrylics, or watercolors.

Stanley, Diane. *The Gentleman and the Kitchen Maid.* Illustrated by Dennis Nolan. New York: Dial Books for Young Readers, 1994. This truly original art book tells the story of a young art student who notices in two museum paintings a growing love between a gentleman and kitchen maid. Sadly, the lovers are frozen and immobile—until the students find a solution to their problem.

Thomas, David. *J.M.W. Turner.* London: The Medici Society Ltd., 1979. Though designed for adults, this small volume is an excellent teacher's resource on Turner and his work. Provides a good deal of background information as well as examples of the artist's most exquisite paintings.

Venezia, Mike. *Monet.* Chicago: Children's Press, 1990. Part of the "Getting to Know the World's Greatest Artists" series—individual books that focus on different famous artists. Beautifully written and illustrated.
———. *Pierre Auguste Renoir.* New York: Children's Press, 1996. Another lovely book in the "Getting to Know the World's Greatest Artists" series.

Warren, Sandra. *Arlie the Alligator.* Strongsville, OH: Arlie Enterprises, 1992. A story-song picture book about a curious baby alligator and his adventures with people on the beach. Includes beautiful songs and sheet music.

Welton, Jude. *Eyewitness Art Book: Impressionism.* London: Dorling Kindersley, 1993. Re-creates and explores the world of impressionism as it evolved through a group of pioneering artists. Examines the social changes that inspired this art form, the lives the artists led, and the kinds of materials they used. Published in association with the Art Institute of Chicago.

Wild California. Produced by Sea Studios, 1989. This video combines music and footage of the California wilderness to create unique images and impressions. An ideal catalyst for creative activities. 40 minutes.

Wildlife Symphony. Produced by the Reader's Digest Association, Inc., 1993. In this video, music from *Swan Lake, The Magic Flute, Firebird Suite,* and more provide a rich background for the animals that frolic across the globe's various landscapes. 48 minutes.

Environment and Ecology

Audubon. A rich and useful bimonthly magazine that investigates a wide range of ecological and environmental topics around the globe. Write to Audubon Magazine, P.O. Box 5471, Pittsfield, MA 01203-5471.

The Biggest Bears! Produced by David Zatz, Broadcast Services of Alaska, 1993. Narrated by a five-year-old boy, this video leads young children on a romp through Alaska's wildlands to explore the daily activities of bears and their cubs. 30 minutes. Call Broadcast Services of Alaska, toll-free telephone: 1-800-OK-BEARS (1-800-652-3277).

Birder's World. A great aid to any study on birds, this monthly magazine provides information and hundreds of beautiful photographs on the fine art of birding, as well as regular reports on endangered species and rare bird sightings. Write to Birder's World Magazine, P.O. Box 1347, Elmhurst, IL 60126-9980.

Cherry, Lynne. *The Armadillo from Amarillo.* San Diego, CA: Harcourt Brace & Co., 1994. Gives children a lesson in geography and ecology through the unique lens of a curious armadillo and a helpful eagle who agrees to fly him around.

Butterflies. Produced by the Ida Cason Callaway Foundation, 1990. Designed for students, teachers, and families, this short video reveals the mystery and wonder of butterflies in all their phases. 15 minutes. Write to Callaway Gardens, Education Department, Pine Mountain, GA 31822-2000.

Defenders. Bimonthly magazine of an organization called Defenders of Wildlife. Covers a range of current issues relating to endangered species and environmental conditions. Write to Defenders Magazine, 1244 19th Street NW, Washington, DC 20036.

Discovering Wolves: A Nature Activity Book. Illustrated by Cary Hunkel. Middleton, WI: Dog-Eared Publications, 1991. An adventurous journey into the world of wolves, this volume offers 18 fun, thought-provoking activities that encourage critical thinking on the subject of the wolf. Explores habitat and daily living habits, popular myths about the species, and the threats to its survival. Produced in cooperation with the Timber Wolf Alliance.

Elephant. Produced by BBC Wildvision and BBC Lionheart Television, 1994. One of many in the "Eyewitness Video Series," this video invites children of all ages into the world of elephants, showing how these magnificent animals live, grow, and care for themselves in the wild. 35 minutes.

George, Jean Craighead. *Missing Gator of Gumbo Limbo.* New York: HarperCollins, 1992. The author leads young children through an ecological mystery in a Florida rain forest.

HSUS News. Magazine published quarterly by the Humane Society of the United States. Focuses primarily on issues of people's inhumanity or negligence toward domestic and wild animals. Write to HSUS News, 2100 L Street NW, Washington, DC 20037-1525.

International Wildlife. This bimonthly report is similar in theme to *National Wildlife* magazine—stressing the need for responsible management of the earth's fragile ecosystems—but with a more international focus. Write to the National Wildlife Federation, P.O. Box 777, Mount Morris, IL 61054-8276.

Jane Goodall: My Life with the Chimpanzees. Produced by the National Geographic Society, 1990. An engaging video portrait of Goodall's remarkable experiences and her lifelong study of chimpanzees. Useful for children and adults interested in animals, the environment, and ecology. 60 minutes.

Jewels of the Caribbean Sea. Produced by the National Geographic Society, 1994. This video reveals the aquatic wilderness beneath the sea, giving children close-up visions of rare and fantastic creatures. 60 minutes.

Kessler, Cristina. *All the King's Animals: The Return of Endangered Wildlife to Swaziland.* Honesdale, PA: Boyds Mills Press, 1995. Jam-packed with color photographs. The author-photographer does a masterful job of relating a true story about conservation efforts little known in the U.S.

Luenn, Nancy. *Mother Earth.* New York: Simon & Schuster, 1992. A timely introduction to ecology and the importance of conservation, presented in a way that makes it attractive even for the youngest students.

Mainstream. A useful source for sensitizing children to the need for more humane treatment of animals, this quarterly magazine focuses on animal life close to home (common and exotic pets, the fur trade, etc.) and offers narratives, photographs, and activities designed for children and families. Write to Mainstream Magazine, P.O. Box 22505, Sacramento, CA 95822.

Mattson, Mark. *Environmental Atlas of the United States.* New York: Scholastic, 1993. A very useful resource for designing activities on environment, the book is easy to use and divides its sections according to main themes such as forests, garbage, and water.

National Humane Education Society Quarterly Journal. This source reports on what is happening nationwide to help or hurt animals. Write to the National Humane Education Society, 521-A East Market Street, Leesburg, VA 20176.

National Wildlife. A well-balanced, bimonthly report designed to increase global awareness of the need for proper use and management of earth's resources—soil, air, water, forests, minerals, and plant and animal life. Write to the National Wildlife Federation, P.O. Box 777, Mount Morris, IL 61054-8276.

Nature Conservancy. A unique bimonthly magazine that focuses on the preservation of rare species through habitat protection. Very useful for classes on various animal habitats. Write to Nature Conservancy Magazine, P.O. Box 79181, Baltimore, MD 21279-0181.

Rainforest Voices. Produced by Nature Science Network, 1990. Filmed in the lush Costa Rican rain forests, this video explores a range of intriguing environments within this colorful and fascinating ecosystem. 48 minutes. Write to the Nature Science Network, 108 High Street, Carrboro, NC 27510.

Really Wild Animals. Produced by the National Geographic Society, 1994. Takes children on a magic carpet with "Spin," National Geographic's animated globe-on-the-go, to explore some amazing animals as well as ancient stories and legends. 40 minutes.

Robinson, Sandra Chisholm. *The Wonder of Wolves: A Story and Activities.* Illustrated by Gail Kohler Opsahl. Denver, CO: Denver Museum of Natural History, 1989. A moving tale about the special bond between wolves and the Nuu-chah-nulth people of Vancouver's west coast. Filled with activities designed to inform young children and adults about one of the most misunderstood animals. Beautifully conceived and presented.

Schimmel, Schim. *Dear Children of the Earth.* Minocqua, WI: NorthWord Press, 1994. Schimmel combines beautiful acrylic paintings, lyrics, and stories to write a loving letter to the children of earth from Mother Earth, calling for conservation and protection.

Schlank, Carol Hilgartner, and Barbara Metzger. *A Clean Sea: The Rachel Carson Story.* Culver City, CA: Cascade Pass, 1994. The story of Carson's life as a marine biologist and the world's first environmentalist.

Temple, Lannis, ed. *Dear World: How Children around the World Feel About Our Environment.* New York: Random House, 1993. A wonderful and moving collection of quotes and drawings by kids from around the world on the subject of our environment and the threats it currently faces.

World of the Sea Otters. Produced by Stanley M. Minasian, 1985. A charming video that immerses children in the teeming environment of the Pacific Coast and its creatures. 30 minutes. Write to the Marine Mammal Fund, Fort Mason Center, San Francisco, CA 94123.

Language Arts

Biography and Autobiography

Bedard, Michael. *Emily.* Illustrated by Barbara Cooney. New York: Doubleday Books for Young Readers, 1992. A sensitively written tale about a young girl who manages to meet Emily Dickinson and enter the poet's extraordinary world.

Gleiter, Jan, and Kathleen Thompson. *Pocahontas.* Chicago: Rand McNally & Co., 1985. A succinct and enjoyable telling of the story of Pocahontas—from her perspective.

Greenfield, Eloise. *Mary McLeod Bethune.* Illustrated by Jerry Pinkney. New York: Harper Collins, 1977. An inspiring account, this volume relates the monumental achievements of a black educator. Pinkney's illustrations are outstanding.

Johnston, Johanna. *They Led the Way: 14 American Women.* New York: Scholastic., 1973. A very informative but simply told story of 14 women who made significant contributions to women's rights.

Kovacs, Deborah, and James Preller. *Meet the Authors and Illustrators,* vols. 1 and 2. New York: Scholastic, 1991. A useful reference for learning about the world of authors and illustrators, this source contains biographical information that will intrigue and inspire both you and your class.

McGovern, Ann. *The Secret Soldier: The Story of Deborah Sampson.* New York: Four Winds Press, 1975. A woman disguises herself as a man during the American Revolutionary War.
———. *Shark Lady: The True Adventures of Eugenie Clark.* New York: Four Winds Press, 1978. The story of an ichthyologist who first became interested in the study of fish when visiting aquariums at the age of nine.

Pinkney, Andrea Davis. *Dear Benjamin Banneker.* Illustrated by Brian Pinkney. San Diego, CA: Harcourt Brace, 1994. This inspiring story about Benjamin Banneker, a free black man during the time of slavery, tells of his accomplishments as an astronomer, a mathematician, and the author of the first published almanac by an African American man. Also describes Banneker's extraordinary correspondence with Secretary of State Thomas Jefferson, pleading on behalf of his people.

Roberts, Jack L. *Nelson Mandela: Determined to Be Free.* Brookfield, CT: Millbrook Press, 1995. This volume in the excellent "Gateway Biography" series for grades 3–5 narrates the epic journey of one of the most inspiring social and political leaders of our time.

Fiction and Nonfiction

Ada, Alma Flor. *Dear Peter Rabbit.* New York: Maxwell Macmillan International, 1994. In this delightful behind-the-scenes adventure, Ada interconnects famous characters from some of the best-loved nursery stories.

Anno, Mitsumasa. *Anno's Journey.* New York: Philomel Books, 1978. A beautifully illustrated, wordless book that invites young children into the villages and countryside of an earlier, horse-and-buggy time and encourages them to create their own stories.

Baylor, Byrd. *The Desert Is Theirs.* New York: Charles Scribner's Sons, 1975. A beautiful story about the closeness of people to their land. Describes the hawks, deer, and pack rats; the plants; and the Desert People who call the earth their mother. A Caldecott Honor Book.

Cannon, Janell. *Stellaluna.* New York: Harcourt Brace & Co., 1993. A touching story about a baby fruit bat who falls headfirst into a bird's nest and is raised like a bird. Exquisite illustrations.

Cooney, Barbara. *Island Boy.* New York: Puffin Books, 1988. The story of a young pioneer boy's life on an island with his family.

Flack, Jerry D. *Mystery and Detection: Thinking and Problem Solving with the Sleuths.* Englewood, CO: Teacher Ideas Press, 1990. Part of the "Gifted Treasury" series, this volume is an imaginative approach to the study and teaching of critical thinking and problem solving.

Gantschev, Ivan. *The Volcano.* London: Neugebauer Press, 1981. Beautifully illustrated by the author, this book tells of a troublemaking crab named Brok who tries to destroy a volcano.

Graham, Bob. *Rose Meets Mr. Wintergarten.* Cambridge, MA: Candlewick Press, 1992. Bright illustrations and a humorous text convey the language and emotions of childhood as readers watch Rose overcome neighborhood gossip to offer friendship to the mysterious man next door.

Gwynne, Fred. *A Chocolate Moose for Dinner.* New York: Simon & Schuster Books for Young Readers, 1976. A very literal young lady tries to understand the phrases of the adult world.

Hamilton, Virginia. *When Birds Could Talk and Bats Could Sing.* Illustrated by Barry Moser. New York: The Blue Sky Press, 1996. Based on African American folk tales told in the South during the plantation era, this book by an author whose own grandfather escaped slavery is lively and entertaining—a testament to the survival of the human spirit.

Herriot, James. *Oscar, Cat-About-Town.* New York: St. Martin's Press, 1990. A warm story about a good-natured stray cat left at the veterinarian's to be nursed back to health and his adventures after moving in with a family.

Howe, James. *I Wish I Were a Butterfly.* Illustrated by Ed Young. New York: Harcourt Brace & Co., 1987. Rich and colorful illustrations enhance a story about a cricket who wishes to be a butterfly until he discovers that crickets make beautiful music.

Jonas, Ann. *Reflections.* New York: Greenwillow Books, 1987. This black-and-white picture book chronicles a child's busy day using backward and upside-down visualization.
———. *Round Trip.* New York: Greenwillow Books, 1983. Another delightful "upside-down and backward" book that depicts a journey from the country to New York City and back again.

Kesselman, Wendy. *Sand in My Shoes.* Illustrated by Ronald Himler. New York: Hyperion Books for Children, 1995. Through a series of evocative coastline images and lyrical text, this book leads children to the final moments of summer and treasured memories of the sea.

Latting-Ehlers, Laurie. *Canoeing.* Illustrated by Ivan Gantschev. Natick, MA: Picture Book Studio, 1986. The author's prose poem combines with the artist's lush artwork to evoke the thrill of canoeing.

Lawhead, Stephen R. *The Tale of Jeremy Vole.* New York: Avon Books, 1993. Narrates the amusing adventures of several animals who live along the river.

Legge, David. *Bamboozled.* New York: Scholastic, 1994. A heartwarming tale of the tender relationship between a grandfather and granddaughter.

MacLachlan, Patricia. *Sarah, Plain and Tall.* New York: Harper Trophy, 1985. When their father invites a mail-order bride to come live with them in their prairie home, Caleb and Anna are captivated by their new mother and hope that she will stay. A touching tale of early pioneer America.

Martin, Bill Jr., and John Archambault. *Knots on a Counting Rope.* New York: Henry Holt & Co., 1987. This beautifully illustrated story of love, hope, and courage uses the counting rope as a metaphor for the passage of time and for a boy's emerging confidence in facing his greatest challenge—his blindness.

Monsell, Mary Elise. *Underwear!* Illustrated by Lynn Munsinger. Morton Grove, IL: Albert Whitman & Co., 1988. A humorous tale of a zebra and orangutan who love to wear underwear—all colors, prints, and styles—and who bring a little humor to a grumpy buffalo. Filled with charming illustrations.

Potok, Chaim. *The Tree of Here.* Illustrated by Tony Auth. New York: Alfred A. Knopf, 1993. In an imaginative conversation between a boy and a tree, the author tells an unforgettable story about saying goodbye and starting over.

Tales of Beatrix Potter. Produced by EMI Films Productions Ltd., 1994. The delightful Beatrix Potter characters come to life in this video, an imaginative musical interpretation of Potter's tales choreographed by Sir Frederick Ashton, composed and scored by John Lanchbery, and danced by members of London's Royal Ballet. 87 minutes. Write to Republic Pictures Corporation, 12636 Beatrice Street, Los Angeles CA 90066-0930.

Teague, Mark. *Pigsty.* New York: Scholastic, 1994. A young boy resists cleaning his room until a number of unkempt pigs move in and wreak havoc. A delightfully humorous story.

Thompson, Julee Dickerson. *Dance of the Rain Gods.* Trenton, NJ: Africa World Press, 1994. With rich and vibrant illustrations, an African American folk tale brings to life the magic of a rainstorm.

Trichnor, Richard, and Jenny Smith. *A Spark in the Dark.* Nevada City, CA: Dawn Publications, 1994. Colorful illustrations by the authors enrich this transcendent story of how the world was created. Will inspire creative responses in young readers.

Udry, Janice May. *What Mary Jo Shared.* Illustrated by Elizabeth Sayles. New York: Scholastic, 1991. Soft, poetic illustrations reinforce this tender tale about a young girl who looks for something special to share with her class.

Warren, Sandra. *The Great Bridge Lowering.* Monroe, NY: Trillium Press, 1987. Packed with activities to stimulate original thought in young children, this storybook is a catalyst for creative thinking.
———. *If I Were a Road.* Monroe, NY: Trillium Press, 1987. Like *The Great Bridge Lowering,* this book entices young children into creative work in a unique and appealing way.

Winthrop, Elizabeth. *The Castle in the Attic.* New York: Holiday House, 1994. A magical adventure beautifully told.

Yolen, Jane. *Piggins and the Royal Wedding.* Illustrated by Jane Dyer. San Diego, CA: Harcourt Brace Jovanovich, 1988. A charming story, vividly told and illustrated, of Piggins the pig—a proper butler and a gracious puzzle-solver.

Young Authors Guide to Publishers. 2d ed. Westerville, OH: Raspberry Publications, 1994. Includes the best publishing opportunities available for today's young authors, K–12.

Poetry

Creative Kids Magazine. A bimonthly magazine for creative children. Write to Prufrock Press, PO Box 8813, Waco, TX 76714-8813, or call 1-800-998-2208.

Dakos, Kalli. *If You're Not Here Please Raise Your Hand: Poems about School.* New York: Four Winds Press, 1990. Poems about the elementary school experience.

Frank, Josette. *Snow Toward Evening: A Year in a River Valley.* Illustrated by Thomas Locker. New York: Dial Books, 1990. Nature poems, selected by Josette Frank and illustrated by Locker, focus on the beauty and wonder of nature's seasonal transformations.

Johnson, Mildred D. *This Is What Children Should Do: A Rhyming Advice Poem to Help Young Children Succeed.* Chicago: MDJ Publications, 1993. A short series of verses to inspire young students to get the most out of school. Includes instructions for presenting the material to children.

Koch, Kenneth. *Rose, Where Did You Get that Red? Teaching Great Poetry to Children.* New York: Random House, 1973. A wonderful source for teaching children to write poetry.
———. *Wishes, Lies, and Dreams.* New York: Chelsea House Publishers, 1970. Koch and New York's Public School District 61 share their poetry.

Lee, Dennis. *The Ice Cream Store: Poems.* New York: Margaret K. McElderry Books, 1992. A lively collection of poems about colorful people, creatures, and places that young children will love.

Prelutsky, Jack. *The Dragons Are Singing Tonight.* New York: Greenwillow Books, 1993. A whimsical collection of poems about dragons.
———. *Something Big Has Been Here.* New York: Greenwillow Books, 1990. An illustrated collection of humorous poems on a variety of topics. Guaranteed to tickle the fancy of young children.

Schwartz, Alvin. *And the Green Grass Grew All Around: Folk Poetry from Everyone.* New York: HarperCollins, 1992. A rich selection of poems from around the world. Includes a useful index and bibliography.

Silverstein, Shel. *A Light in the Attic.* New York: Harper & Row, 1981. A delightful collection of poems and drawings by one of America's best-loved poets for children.
———. *Where the Sidewalk Ends: The Poems and Drawings of Shel Silverstein.* New York: Harper & Row, 1974. Poems and illustrations by this popular children's poet. Includes an index.

Steele, Lani. *Primarily Poetry: Poetry Lessons for Grades K–3.* Illustrated by Jean Thornley. San Luis Obispo, CA: Dandy Lion Publications, 1989. A rich and whimsical source for exposing young children to the wonderful world of poetry, this book offers a series of creative activities to help children generate ideas and write their own poems.

Viorst, Judith. *Sad Underwear and Other Complications: More Poems for Children and Their Parents.* New York: Atheneum Books for Young Readers, 1995. This collection of poems examines a wide variety of feelings from a child's point of view.

Who Has Seen the Wind? An Illustrated Collection of Poetry for Young People. New York: Rizzoli International Publications, 1991. Published for the Museum of Fine Arts in Boston, this is a delightful book of poetry classics illustrated with masterpieces from the museum's collection.

Mathematics

Clement, Rod. *Counting on Frank.* Milwaukee, WI: Gareth Stevens Publishing, 1991. A hilarious approach to counting and figuring, this book features the unconventional Frank and his unusual (yet accurate) calculations. In an entirely unexpected way, Frank makes math real and interesting. (For example, did you know that a ball-point pen draws a line 7,000 feet long before the ink runs out?)

Greenes, Carole. *Math Games: Sparkling Activities for Early Childhood Classrooms.* Allen, TX: DLM Teaching Resources, 1989. Contains 140 classroom activities that present mathematical concepts for primary students and provide opportunities to learn by doing.

Instructor. This magazine is a complete teaching resource, covering a wide range of topics from math manipulatives to emotional intelligence. Write to Scholastic, 555 Broadway, New York, NY 10012. The magazine is also on the Internet.

Lasky, Kathryn. *The Librarian Who Measured the Earth.* Illustrated by Kevin Hawkes. Boston: Little, Brown & Co., 1994. More than two thousand years ago, a young man wanted to figure out how he could measure the circumference of the earth without traveling the distance. His answer came within two hundred miles of present-day calculations! A true story.

Stickels, Terry. *Think-ercises: Math and Word Puzzles to Exercise Your Brain.* Pacific Grove, CA: Critical Thinking Press & Software, 1995. Presents a series of puzzles in order of mathematical difficulty. A nonintimidating exploration of critical thinking that emphasizes the joy and fun of learning.

Science

Adshead, Paul. *Puzzle Island.* Martinez, CA: Discovery Toys, 1990. This delightful alphabet puzzler includes a great many biological and environmental facts for young readers.

Ashby, Ruth. *Jane Goodall's Animal World: Sea Otters.* New York: Macmillan Publishing Co., 1990. Introduces young readers to the wonderful world of the capricious and charming sea otter. One book in a series.

Barber, Antonia. *The Monkey and the Panda.* New York: Macmillan Books for Young Readers, 1995. Who is better, the monkey or the panda? Here's a fable that cleverly addresses the issue of jealousy in a way that will enchant young people.

Bender, Lionel. *Inventions.* New York: Knopf, 1991. Students can explore such inventions as the wheel, gears, levers, clocks, telephones, and rocket engines. One in a series of "Eyewitness Books."

Benson, Laura Lee. *This Is Our Earth.* Watertown, ME: Charlesbridge Publishing, 1994. A simple, but grand, lilting verse with short, easy-to-read prose text gives the reader an introduction to earth and life sciences.

Branley, Franklyn M. *What the Moon Is Like.* Illustrated by True Kelley. New York: HarperCollins, 1986. An inviting introduction to the wonders of the moon—one that young children will eagerly grasp and that will inspire further interest and inquiry.

Carle, Eric. *A House for Hermit Crab.* New York: Scholastic, 1987. The author is the creator of many beloved books about animals, birds, and insects, but he says that he feels particularly fond of the hermit crab, the hero of this book.
———. *The Tiny Seed.* New York: Crowell, 1970. Charmingly narrates a flowering plant's life cycle through the seasons.

Cornell, Joseph. *Sharing the Joy of Nature: Nature Activities for All Ages.* Nevada City, CA: Dawn Publications, 1989. This sequel to the author's *Sharing Nature with Children* is a rich collection of new games and activities for both adults and children. Organized in thematic sequences that inspire awe in nature's many wonders.

The Cousteau Society. *Otters.* New York: Simon & Schuster, 1993. Simple, factual, and exquisitely photographed, this little book unravels the daily living habits of that personable population of sea otters who bob about in the waves of the northwestern American coast.
———. *Whales.* New York: Simon & Schuster, 1993. A little book with breathtaking photographs of the great whales and their majestic movements through the air and underwater. Offers the young reader basic facts and vivid visual impressions.

Donahue, Mike. *The Grandpa Tree.* Niwot, CO: Roberts Rinehart, 1988. This tale of a life cycle takes young readers from a tree's beginning as a sapling to its demise on the forest floor.

Fromer, Julie. *Jane Goodall Living with the Chimps.* Frederick, MD: Twenty-First Century Books, 1992. Describes how Goodall's discoveries about chimpanzees changed how we think about animals, ourselves, and our place in nature. Part of the "Earth Keepers" series.

George, Jean Craighead. *Julie of the Wolves.* Prince Frederick, MD: Recorded Books, 1993. Three sound cassettes (4 hours, 30 minutes) tell of a 13-year-old Eskimo girl lost on Alaska's North Slope and befriended by a wolf pack.

Gibbons, Gail. *Caves and Caverns.* San Diego, CA: Harcourt Brace & Co., 1993. An engaging and fascinating journey into the scientific mysteries of caves and caverns—the unusual formations and unusual creatures that lurk inside them. Designed especially for young children.

Grambling, Lois G. *Can I Have a Stegosaurus, Mom? Can I? Please?* Illustrated by H.B. Lewis. Mahwah, NJ: BridgeWater Books, 1995. Enlivened by dynamic illustrations, this unusual tale for dinosaur fans has a surprise ending.

Haber, Louis. *Black Pioneers of Science and Inventions.* New York: Harcourt, Brace & World, 1970. A fine introduction to the scientific contributions of African Americans, this source contains useful information and a bibliography for classroom use.

Herbert, Don. *Mr. Wizard's Supermarket Science.* New York: Random House, 1980. Useful as a general science source, this volume gives directions for 100 simple experiments. Includes pertinent information on scientific principles involved.

Incredible Edibles: Science You Can Eat! Akron, OH: National Invention Center, 1991. This collection of fun and creative activities for children in grades 1–6 guides them to discover scientific principles using ordinary food products.

Integrating Science, Technology, and Mathematics: Products for K–6. Enfield, CT: LEGO Dacta, 1995. This very useful catalog offers a wide range of materials from the educational division of the LEGO Group.

Jenkins, Steve. *Biggest, Strongest, Fastest.* New York: Ticknor & Fields Books for Young Readers, 1995. Illustrated with striking cut-paper collages, this book offers a vivid tour of the world of animal life.

Julivert, Angels. *The Fascinating World of Butterflies and Moths.* New York: Barron's Publishers, 1991. Introduces readers to the physical characteristics, habits, and natural environments of various kinds of butterflies.

Leon, Vicki. *Seals and Sea Lions: An Affectionate Portrait.* San Luis Obispo, CA: Blake Publishing, 1988. Describes conditions, activities, and daily living habits of *pinnipeds*—seals, sea lions, and elephant seals. Superbly photographed by several different photographers.

Resnick, Jane P. *Wolves and Coyotes.* Chicago: KidsBooks, 1995. Part of the "Eye On Nature" series, this volume has much to teach young children about the lives and daily survival habits of wolves and coyotes.

Robinson, Sandra Chisholm. *Sea Otter River Otter.* Illustrated by Gail Kohler Opsahl and Marjorie C. Leggitt. Niwot, CO: Roberts Rinehart, 1993. Offers stories and projects that are well structured and beautifully illustrated. Delightful, instructive, and easy to read.

Simon, Seymour. *Volcanoes.* New York: Mulberry Paperback Book, 1988. A leading science writer for children, Simon invites the young reader on an impressive tour of some of the most fascinating volcano activity around the world.

Sipiera, Paul P. *I Can Be an Oceanographer.* Chicago: Children's Press, 1987. A wonderful, highly readable introduction to oceanography for young readers. Uses images of both female and male oceanographers in photographs and illustrations.

Smith, Jamie C. *What Color Is Newton's Apple? Inquiry Science for Young Children.* Monroe, NY: Trillium Press, 1988. Physics and chemistry for young children presented in four levels: toddler, nursery, kindergarten, and primary.

Smithsonian Review. A useful, extremely well-investigated source for a wide variety of subjects, from desert habitats to orchestras to acupuncture. Includes vivid photographs. Write to Smithsonian Review, P.O. Box 55583, Boulder, CO 80321-5583.

Sterling, May Ellen. *Thematic Unit: Ecology. Huntington Beach,* CA: Teacher Created Materials, 1991. A useful and practical unit—reproducible and effective for any primary class studying ecology.

Stokes, Donald, Lillian Stokes, and Ernest Williams. *The Butterfly Book: An Easy Guide to Butterfly Gardening, Identification, and Behavior.* Boston: Little, Brown & Co., 1991. This engaging and accessible guide includes over 140 stunning color photographs of butterflies in all of their life stages. Brings fun, adventure, and learning to the intriguing process of starting a butterfly garden.

Taylor, Barbara. *Rain Forest.* Photographed by Frank Greenaway. New York: Dorling Kindersley, 1992. Designed for young readers, this book gives children a closer look at the exotic creatures of the rain forest and their daily living habits.

Taylor, Kim. *Butterfly.* New York: Dorling Kindersley, 1992. This little book for the very young child introduces the evolution of a caterpillar into a butterfly. Superbly illustrated with a simple yet imaginative text. A "See How They Grow" book.

Willis, Jeanne. *Earthlets*. New York: E.P. Dutton, 1989. Professor Xargle's class of extraterrestrials learns about physical characteristics and behavior of the human body.

Social Studies

Global and Multicultural

Aardema, Verna. *Bringing the Rain to Kapiti Plain: A Nandi Tale*. Illustrated by Beatriz Vidal. New York: The Dial Press, 1981. A lovely African tale, originating in Kenya, about a young man who devises a way to beckon the rains to his dry land.

Altman, Linda Jacobs. *Amelia's Road*. New York: Lee & Low Books, 1993. A poignant look at a migrant farm family through the eyes of a little girl. An excellent catalyst for discussion.

Ballard, Robert D. *The Lost Wreck of the Isis*. New York: Scholastic/Madison Press, 1990. Dr. Ballard visits the Mediterranean to explore a Roman shipwreck site and investigate an active underwater volcano. Includes a bibliography.

Brewer, Chris, and Linda Grinde, eds. *Many People, Many Ways*. Tucson, AZ: Zephyr Press, 1995. Geared for grades 4–8 but adaptable to younger ages, this book offers a lively, comprehensive, and thoughtfully sequenced presentation of cultures around the world. Includes a wide range of activities and a useful listing of video and audio recordings, books, and other aides related to each country.

Durrell, Ann, and Marilyn Sachs, eds. *The Big Book for Peace*. New York: Dutton Children's Books, 1990. Seventeen stories sensitively depict the wisdom of peace and the foolishness of war.

Exploring Realistic Fiction. New York: Scholastic, 1992. A literature and writing workshop booklet that presents three short stories. Can serve as a catalyst for creative writing.

Goble, Paul. *The Girl Who Loved Wild Horses*. New York: Aladdin Books, 1978. Though a young girl loves her family, she prefers running wild and free with the horses and finally becomes one of them. A retelling of a Native American story.

Kids Explore Kenya. Produced by Learning Matters, Inc. In this video, children embark on a safari to make a movie and discover the rich culture, history, and customs of this intriguing country. 30 minutes. Write to Learning Matters, Inc., P.O. Box 6589, Portland, OR 97228, or call toll-free 1-800-540-9487.

Joosse, Barbara M. Mama, *Do You Love Me?* Illustrated by Barbara Lavallee. San Francisco: Chronicle Books, 1991. An Alaskan child tests the limits of her own independence and of her mother's love—which proves to be unconditional and everlasting. Tenderly told and richly illustrated.

Mattox, Cheryl Warren. *Shake It to the One That You Love the Best*. Nashville, TN: Warren-Mattox Productions, 1989. Drawing from African, African American, Creole, and Caribbean cultures, this music cassette and songbook offer imaginative arrangements covering a broad spectrum of styles: jazz, reggae, gospel, rhythm and blues, and classical.

Menzel, Peter. *Material World: A Global Family Portrait*. San Francisco: Sierra Club Books, 1994. To create this exquisite volume, 16 of the world's foremost photographers traveled to 30 nations. There they lived with families and created family portraits in vivid and sensitive detail. A unique and moving panorama of the human condition around the globe.

Miles, Miska. *Annie and the Old One*. Illustrated by Peter Parnall. Boston: Little, Brown & Co., 1971. A simply but poetically told story of a young Navajo girl and her special relationship with her ancient grandmother, who taught her how to weave.

Munsch, Robert, and Saoussan Askar. *From Far Away*. Illustrated by Michael Martchenko. Toronto: Annick Press, 1995. Developed from a series of actual letters between a young Lebanese girl and the authors, this book chronicles the personal journey every foreign child must make when adjusting to a new world.

National Women's History Project. *101 Wonderful Ways to Celebrate Women's History*. Windsor, CA: National Women's History Project, 1986. Seeks to promote a multicultural awareness of women's history in schools and communities nationwide; presents a wide range of activities for children of all grades, along with extensive lists of resources and materials to enhance and develop units.

Risby, Bonnie, and Robby Risby. *Map Activities for Primary Students.* San Luis Obispo. CA: Dandy Lion Publications, 1994. This hands-on activity book for grades 2–4 integrates reading comprehension, math skills (using a scale drawing), and problem solving.

Scullar, Sue. *The Great Round-the-World Balloon Race.* New York: Dutton Children's Books, 1991. Tells the story of Harriet Shaw and her niece and nephew as they set out on a round-the-world balloon race.

Sheldon, Dyan. *Under the Moon.* Illustrated by Gary Blythe. New York: Dial Books for Young Readers, 1993. After finding an arrowhead, a young girl takes an imaginary journey into the past, where Native Americans lived in a land as yet untouched by others.

Snyder, Dianne. *The Boy of the Three-Year Nap.* Illustrated by Allen Say. Boston: Houghton Mifflin Co., 1988. This Japanese tale is rich and evocative, transporting the young reader into a world of suspense and adventure. A Caldecott Honor book.

Steiner, Barbara. *Whale Brother.* Illustrated by Gretchen Will Mayo. New York: Walker & Co., 1988. Omu is a young boy who wants to learn how to carve like Padloq, a great artist in his community. Omu must learn how to give his carvings life, and an experience with a whale shows him how to do this.

Stevens, Carla. *Lily and Miss Liberty.* New York: Scholastic, 1992. A fictional story of a young girl who makes and sells crowns to raise money for mounting the Statue of Liberty, France's gift to the United States.

Wade, Rahima Carole. *Joining Hands.* Tucson, AZ: Zephyr Press, 1991. Shows how to establish a caring classroom community in which school, social, and academic life can be woven together to provide meaningful educational experiences for children. A thoughtfully assembled guide.

History and Geography

Bartok, Mira, and Christine Ronan. *Indians of the Great Plains.* Glenview, IL: GoodYear Books, 1996. A good resource on history and culture for young children. One of the "Big World Read Along" series.

Blos, Joan W. *A Gathering of Days.* New York: Charles Scribner's Sons, 1979. A young girl in the 1800s is forced to face life with a new stepmother. A provocative story told in the form of vivid journal entries.

Bunting, Eve. *Dandelions.* Illustrated by Greg Shed. San Diego, CA: Harcourt Brace & Co., 1995. Rich, atmospheric pictures enhance this beautifully told story of the trials and accomplishments of a pioneer family who leaves home to settle in Nebraska.

Christiansen, Candace. *Calico and the Tin Horns.* Illustrated by Thomas Locker. New York: Dial Books, 1992. In this fascinating tale of early America, set in the Hudson River Valley, a young girl helps fight to save her family's farm and their right to own it. Based on a true story.

Clifford, Mary Louise. *When the Great Canoes Came.* Illustrated by Joyce Haynes. Gretna, LA: Pelican Publishing Co., 1993. A fictionalized re-creation of events between 1560 and 1686 in what became the state of Virginia, told from the perspective of the Powhatan Indians. A good historical source.

Dorris, Michael. *Morning Girl.* New York: Hyperion Books for Children, 1992. Describes life on an island before the first Europeans arrived.

Hildebrandt, Greg, and Tim Hildebrandt. *In Search of King Tut's Tomb: A Hide-and-Seek Puzzle Book.* Illustrated by the Brothers Hildebrandt. Martinez, CA: Unicorn Publishing House, 1993. Invites students to journey back in time, explore clues on their own, and experience the thrill of unraveling the tomb's many secrets. Available through the distributor, Discovery Toys; to order, call toll-free 1-800-426-4777.

Knight, James E. *Jamestown: New World Adventure.* Mahwah, NJ: Troll Associates, 1982. Through black-and-white sketches and the text of three years of diary entries, two English children learn the story of their grandfather's experiences as one of the original Jamestown colonists of 1607.

Penner, Lucille Recht. *Eating the Plates.* New York: Macmillan, 1991. Highlights Pilgrim eating habits, customs, and manners in the first colony at New Plymouth; includes biographical references.

Starkey, Dinah. *Atlas of Exploration.* New York: Scholastic Reference, 1993. A colorful and helpful quick reference through the ages of exploration, from ancient Egypt to space explorations of today. Includes well-illustrated maps of explorers' routes.

Varley, Carol, and Lisa Miles. *The Usborne Geography Encyclopedia.* London: Usborne Publishing, 1993. This vividly illustrated and fact-filled guide to the world we live in explores all the major topics of geography, including rocks and minerals, weather and climate, population, industry, and the environment.

Appendix C: Sources for Gifted Education Materials

The sources listed here provide useful information and materials to support young gifted children's learning, growth, and development, including magazines on gifted education, teaching materials (reproducibles, manipulatives, games, activities, units, etc.), multicultural resources, posters, books, tapes, and videos. We've provided addresses, phone numbers, and, where available, email addresses and Web sites so you can write or call for catalogs.

American Guidance Service
4201 Woodland Road
Circle Pines, MN 55014-1796
Toll-free telephone: 1-800-328-2560
email: ags@skypoint.com
Web site: http://www.agsnet.com

Apple Publishing
W. 6050 Apple Road
Watertown, WI 53098-3937
Toll-free telephone: 1-800-475-1118

Art Image Publications Inc.
P.O. Box 568
Champlain, NY 12919
Toll-free telephone: 1-800-361-2598

The Association for the Gifted
Council for Exceptional Children (CEC)
1920 Association Drive
Reston, VA 22091-1589
Toll-free telephone: 1-800-486-5773

A.W. Peller
Bright Ideas for the Gifted and Talented Catalog
210 Sixth Avenue, P.O. Box 106
Hawthorne, NJ 07507
Toll-free telephone: 1-800-451-7450

California Association for the Gifted
426 Escuela Avenue, Suite 19
Mountain View, CA 94040
Telephone: (415) 965-0653

The Center for Gifted
National-Louis University
2840 Sheridan Road
Evanston, IL 60201-1796
Telephone: (847) 251-2661

Challenge Magazine: Reaching and Teaching the Gifted Child
Good Apple
P.O. Box 2649
Columbus, OH 43216
Toll-free telephone: 1-800-321-3106

Cobblestone Magazine
Cobblestone Publishing, Inc.
7 School Street
Peterborough, NH 03458
Telephone: (603) 924-7209

Council for Exceptional Children (CEC)
1920 Association Drive
Reston, VA 22091-1589
Toll-free telephone: 1-800-486-5773

Creative Classroom Magazine
P.O. Box 53148
Boulder, CO 80322
Toll-free telephone: 1-800-274-1364

Creative Education Foundation
Torrance Center for Creative Studies
University of Georgia
323 Aderhold Hall
Athens, GA 30602-7146
Telephone: (706) 542-5104

Creative Learning Press
P.O. Box 320
Mansfield Center, CT 06250
Telephone: (860) 429-8118

Creative Publications
5623 W. 115th Street
Worth, IL 60482
Toll-free telephone: 1-800-624-0822

Critical Thinking Books and Software
P.O. Box 448
Pacific Grove, CA 93950
Toll-free telephone: 1-800-458-4849

Curriculum Associates, Inc.
P.O. Box 2001
N. Billerica, MA 01862-0901
Toll-free telephone: 1-800-225-0248

Dale Seymour Publications
P.O. Box 5026
White Plains, NY 10602
Toll-free telephone: 1-800-872-1100

Dandy Lion Publications
3563 Sueldo, Suite L
San Luis Obispo, CA 93401
Toll-free telephone: 1-800-776-8032

Educational Assessment Service, Inc.
W. 6050 Apple Road
Watertown, WI 53098-3937
Toll-free telephone: 1-800-795-7466

Educational Teaching Aids
620 Lakeview Parkway
Vernon Hills, IL 60061
Toll-free telephone: 1-800-445-5985

Engine-Uity, Ltd.
P.O. Box 9610
Phoenix, AZ 85068
Toll-free telephone: 1-800-877-8718

ERIC Clearinghouse on Disabilities and Gifted Education
1920 Association Drive
Reston, VA 22091-1589
Toll-free telephone: 1-800-328-0272

Essmont Publishing
P.O. Box 186
Brandon, VT 05733-0186
Toll-free telephone: 1-800-337-6525

Free Spirit Publishing Inc.
400 First Avenue North, Suite 616
Minneapolis, MN 55401-1730
Toll-free telephone: 1-800-735-7323
email: help4kids@freespirit.com

Gifted Child Society, Inc.
190 Rock Road
Glen Rock, NJ 07452-1736
Telephone: (201) 444-6530
Web site: http://www.gifted.org/

Gifted Child Today Publishing, Inc.
P.O. Box 6448
Mobile, AL 36660
Toll-free telephone: 1-800-476-8711

Gifted Education Press Quarterly Magazine
10201 Yuma Court
P.O. Box 1586
Manassas, VA 20109
Telephone: (703) 369-5017

Gifted Psychology Press
P.O. Box 5057
Scottsdale, AZ 85261
Telephone: (602) 368-7862

Hollingworth Center for Highly Gifted Children
827 Central Avenue #282
Dover, NH 60093
Telephone: (207) 655-3767

Illinois Association for Gifted Children
550 Frontage Road
Northfield, IL 60093
Telephone: (847) 501-6151

Interact
1825 Gillespie Way #101
El Cajon, CA 92020-1095
Toll-free telephone: 1-800-359-0961

IRI SkyLight Training and Publishing
2626 South Clearbrook Drive
Arlington Heights, IL 60067
Toll-free telephone: 1-800-348-4474

Mindware
2720 Patton Road
Roseville, MN 55113
Toll-free telephone: 1-800-999-0398

National Association for the Education of Young Children (NAEYC)
1509 16th Street NW
Washington, DC 20036-1426
Toll-free telephone: 1-800-424-2460
email: membership@naeyc.org

National Association for Gifted Children (NAGC)
1707 L Street NW, Suite 550
Washington, DC 20036
Telephone: (202) 785-4268
Web site: http://www.nagc.org/

National Council of Teachers of Mathematics (NCTM)
1906 Association Drive
Reston, VA 22091-1593
Telephone: (703) 620-9840
Web site: http://www.nctm.org/

National Resource Center for the Gifted and Talented (NRC/GT)
University of Connecticut
362 Fairfield Road, U-7
Storrs, CT 06269-2007
Telephone: (860) 486-4676
Web site: http://www.ucc.uconn.edu/
wwwgt/nrcgt.html

National Women's History Project
7738 Bell Road
Windsor, CA 95492-8518
Toll-free telephone: 1-800-691-8888
email: NWHP@aol.com
Web site: http://www.nwhp.org/

New Moon: The Magazine for Girls and Their Dreams
P.O. Box 3587
Duluth, MN 55803-3587
Telephone: (218) 728-5507
Web site: http://www.newmoon.duluth.mn.us/

Open Space Communications, Inc.
P.O. Box 18268
Boulder, CO 80308-8268
Toll-free telephone: 1-800-494-6178

Parents of Gifted and Talented Learning-Disabled Children
2420 Eccleston Street
Silver Spring, MD 20902
Telephone: (301) 986-1422

Phi Delta Kappa
P.O. Box 789
Bloomington, IN 47402-9961
Toll-free telephone: 1-800-766-1156

Pieces of Learning
Division of Creative Learning Consultants Inc.
1610 Brook Lynn Drive
Beavercreek, OH 45432-1906
Toll-free telephone: 1-800-729-5137

Prufrock Press
P.O. Box 8813
Waco, TX 76714-8813
Toll-free telephone: 1-800-998-2208

Resource Center for Redesigning Education
P.O. Box 298
Brandon, VT 05733-0298
Toll-free telephone: 1-800-639-4122

Roeper City and Country School
P.O. Box 329
Bloomfield Hills, MI 48303-0329
Telephone: (810) 642-1500

Royal Fireworks Press
P.O. Box 399
Unionville, NY 10988
Telephone: (914) 726-3333

Skipping Stones Magazine
P.O. Box 3939
Eugene, OR 97403-0939
Telephone: (541) 342-4956

Teacher Created Materials
6421 Industry Way
Westminster, CA 92683
Toll-free telephone: 1-800-662-4321

Thinking Caps
P.O. Box 26239
Phoenix, AZ 85068
Telephone: (602) 870-1527

Tin Man Press
P.O. Box 219
Stanwood, WA 98292
Toll-free telephone: 1-800-676-0459

Zephyr Press
Box 66006
Tucson, AZ 85728-6006
Telephone: (520) 322-5090

Bibliography

Alvino, J. Parents' *Guide to Raising a Gifted Child: Recognizing and Developing Your Child's Potential*. New York: Ballantine Books, 1985.

American Association of University Women. *How Schools Shortchange Girls*. Washington, DC: AAUW Educational Foundation, 1991.

Armstrong, Thomas. *Multiple Intelligences in the Classroom*. Alexandria, VA: ASCD, 1994.

Bartell, Janet. Primary Teacher, Middlefork School, Northfield, IL. Valuable assistance in curriculum development.

Beecher, Margaret. *Developing the Gifts and Talents of All Students in the Regular Classroom*. Mansfield Center, CT: Creative Learning Press, 1995.

Belgrad, Susan. "Greater Gifts Than These." *Illinois Council for the Gifted Journal* 11 (1992): 47-48.

Bredekamp, Sue, and Carol Copple, eds. *Developmentally Appropriate Practice in Early Childhood Programs*, rev. ed. Washington, DC: National Association for the Education of Young Children, 1997.

Carbo, Marie, Rita Dunn, and Kenneth Dunn. *Teaching Students to Read Through Their Individual Learning Styles*. Needham Heights, MA: Allyn & Bacon, 1991.

Center for Talented Youth (CTY) Publications and Resources, ed. *Identifying and Cultivating Talent in Preschool and Elementary School Children*. Baltimore: Johns Hopkins University, 1992.

Clark, Barbara. *Growing Up Gifted: Developing the Potential of Children at Home and at School*, 4th ed. New York: Maxwell Macmillan International, 1992.
———. *Optimizing Learning: The Integrative Education Model in the Classroom*. Columbus, OH: Merrill Publishing Co., 1986.

Cohen, Leonora M., Ann C. Burgess, and Tara K. Busick. *Teaching Gifted Kindergarten and Primary Children in the Regular Classroom: Meeting the Mandate*. Eugene, OR: Oregon School Study Council, 1990.

Colangelo, Nicholas, and Gary A. Davis, eds. *Handbook of Gifted Education*. Boston: Allyn & Bacon, 1991.

Cook, Carole, and Jody Carlisle. *Challenges for Children: Creative Activities for Gifted and Talented Primary Students*. West Nyack, NY: The Center for Applied Research in Education, Inc., 1985.

Cox, June, Neil Daniel, and Bruce Boston. *Educating Able Learners: Programs and Promising Practices*. Austin, TX: University of Texas Press, 1985.

Crabbe, Anne, and Pat Hoelscher. "Teaching Thinking Early." *Journal for the Illinois Council of the Gifted* 11 (1992): 45-46.

Daniel, Neil, and June Cox. *Flexible Pacing for Able Learners*. Reston, VA: Council for Exceptional Children, 1988.

Davis, Gary A., and Sylvia B. Rimm. *Education of the Gifted and Talented*, 3d ed. Boston: Allyn & Bacon, 1994.

Delisle, James R. *Gifted Kids Speak Out*. Minneapolis, MN: Free Spirit Publishing Inc., 1987.
———. *Guiding the Social and Emotional Development of Gifted Youth: A Practical Guide for Educators and Counselors*. New York: Longman, 1992.

Eby, Judy W., and Joan Franklin Smutny. *A Thoughtful Overview of Gifted Education*. While Plains, NY: Longman, 1990.

Eckert, Sharon, and Judy Leimbach. *Primarily Math: A Problem Solving Approach*. San Luis Obispo, CA: Dandy Lion Publications, 1993.

Ehrlich, Virginia Z. *Gifted Children: A Guide for Parents and Teachers*. Englewood Cliffs, NJ: Prentice-Hall, 1982.

Ellis, Julie L., and John M. Willinsky, eds. *Girls, Women, and Giftedness*. Monroe, NY: Trillium Press, 1990.

Feldhusen, Hazel. *Individualized Teaching of Gifted Children in Regular Classrooms*. East Aurora, NY: D.O.K. Publishers, 1986.

Feldhusen, John, Joyce VanTassel-Baska, and Ken Seeley, eds. *Excellence in Educating the Gifted*. Denver, CO: Love Publishing Co., 1989.

Feldman, David Henry, and Lynn T. Goldsmith. *Nature's Gambit: Child Prodigies and the Development of Human Potential*. New York: Teachers College Press, 1991.

Fisher, Maurice. "Early Childhood Education for the Gifted: The Need for Intense Study and Observation." *Journal for the Illinois Council of the Gifted* 11 (1992): 6-9.

Fogarty, Robin. *Integrate the Curricula*. Palatine, IL: IRI/SkyLight Publishing, 1991.

Fogarty, Robin, and Kay Opeka. *Start Them Thinking: A Handbook of Classroom Strategies for the Early Years*. Palatine, IL: The IRI Group, Inc., 1988.

Fogarty, Robin, and Judy Stoehr. *The Mindful School: Integrating Curricula with Multiple Intelligences*. Palatine, IL: IRI/SkyLight Training and Publishing, 1995.

Frazier, Kay. "Identifying Gifted Preschool and Kindergarten Children." *Challenge: Reaching and Teaching the Gifted Child* 32 (1988): 12-17.

Galbraith, Judy. *The Gifted Kids Survival Guide (For Ages 10 & Under)*. Minneapolis, MN: Free Spirit Publishing Inc., 1984.

Gallagher, James, and Shelagh A. Gallagher. *Teaching the Gifted Child*, 4th ed. Boston: Allyn & Bacon, 1994.

Gardner, Howard. "Are There Additional Intelligences? The Case for Naturalist, Spiritual, and Existential Intelligences." In *Education, Information, and Transformation*, J. Kane, ed. Englewood Cliffs, NJ: Prentice-Hall, forthcoming.
———. *Frames of Mind: The Theory of Multiple Intelligence*, 10th ed. New York: Basic Books, 1993.

Gellman, E.S. *School Testing: What Parents and Educators Need to Know*. Westport, CT: Praeger Publishers, 1995.

Godfrey, Gwen. *Resource Guide for Parents, Teachers, and Advocates of Gifted Children*. Morton Grove, IL: National Association for the Fostering of Intelligence, 1995.

Goleman, Daniel. *Emotional Intelligence: Why It Can Matter More than IQ*. New York: Bantam Books, 1995.

Halsted, Judith W. *Guiding Gifted Readers from Preschool through High School: A Handbook for Parents, Teachers, Counselors, and Librarians*. Columbus, OH: Ohio Psychology Publishing, 1988.

Hegeman, Kathryn. *Gifted Children in the Regular Classroom*. Monroe, NY: Trillium Press, 1987.

Howley, Aimee, Craig B. Howley, and Edwin D. Pendarvis. *Teaching Gifted Children: Principles and Strategies*. Boston: Little, Brown and Co., 1986.

Johnson, Nancy. *Active Questioning*. Beavercreek, OH: Pieces of Learning, 1995.
———. *Look Closer: Visual Thinking Skills and Activities*. Beavercreek, OH: Pieces of Learning, 1996.

Kaplan, Susan. "The ABC's of Curriculum for Gifted Five-Year-Olds: Alphabet, Blocks, and Chess?" *Journal for the Illinois Council of the Gifted* 11 (1992): 43-44.

Karnes, Merle B., ed. *The Underserved: Our Gifted Young Children*. Reston, VA: Council for Exceptional Children, 1983.

Katz, Elinor. *Affective Education: Self Concept and the Gifted Student*. Boulder, CO: Open Space Communications, 1994.

Keirouz, Kathryn S. "Concerns of Parents of Gifted Children: A Research Review." *Gifted Child Quarterly* 34:2 (1990): 56-63.

Kerr, Barbara A. *Smart Girls, Gifted Women*. Columbus, OH: Ohio Psychology Publishing, 1985.
———. *Smart Girls Two: A New Psychology of Girls, Women, and Giftedness*. Dayton, OH: Ohio Psychology Press, 1994.

Kingore, Bertie. *Portfolios: Enriching and Assessing All Students, Identifying the Gifted, Grades K–6*. Des Moines, IA: Leadership Publishers, 1993.
———. "Portfolios for Young Children." *Understanding Our Gifted* 7:3 (1995): 1, 10-12.

Kitano, Margie. "Counseling Gifted Preschoolers." *Gifted Child Today* (July/August 1986): 20-25.
———. "Young Gifted Children: Strategies for Preschool Teachers." *Young Children* (May 1982): 14-24.

Kitano, Margie, and Darrell Kirby. *Gifted Education*. Boston: Little, Brown & Co., 1986.

Knopper, Dorothy. *Parent Education: Parents as Partners*. Boulder, CO: Open Space Communications, 1995.

Kruse, Janice. *Classroom Activities in Thinking Skills*. Philadelphia: Research for Better Schools, 1988.

Kulik, James, and Chen-Lin Kulik. "Ability Grouping and Gifted Students." In *Handbook of Gifted Education*, Nicholas Colangelo and Gary A. Davis, eds. Boston: Allyn & Bacon, 1991.

Landau, Erika. *The Courage to Be Gifted*. Unionville, NY: Trillium Press, 1990.

Lazear, David. *Multiple Intelligence Approaches to Assessment: Solving the Assessment Conundrum*. Tucson, AZ: Zephyr Press, 1994.

———. *Seven Pathways of Learning: Teaching Students and Parents About Multiple Intelligences.* Tucson, AZ: Zephyr Press, 1994.

———. *Seven Ways of Knowing: Teaching for Multiple Intelligences.* Palatine, IL: IRI SkyLight Publishing, 1991.

Leimbach, Judy. *Primarily Thinking.* San Luis Obispo, CA: Dandy Lion Publications, 1991.

Leimbach, Judy, and Sharon Eckert. *Primary Book Reporter: Independent Reading for Young Learners.* San Luis Obispo, CA: Dandy Lion Publications, 1996.

Maltby, Florence. *Gifted Children and Teachers in the Primary School.* London: Falmer Press, 1984.

Marland, Sidney, Jr. *Education of the Gifted and Talented: Report to the Congress of the United States by the U.S. Commissioner of Education.* Washington, DC: U.S. Government Printing Office, 1972.

Massalski, Dorothy. "The Whole Child and the Gift— Nurturing Our Very Young Gifted Students." *Journal for the Illinois Council of the Gifted* 11 (1992): 33-34.

McCluskey, Ken W., and Keith Walker. *The Doubtful Gift: Strategies for Educating Gifted Children in the Regular Classroom.* Kingston, ON: R.P. Frye, 1986.

Meckstroth, Elizabeth A. "Guiding the Parents of Gifted Children." *In Counseling Gifted and Talented Children: A Guide for Teachers, Counselors, and Parents,* Roberta M. Milgram, ed. Norwood, NJ: Ablex Publishing, 1991, 95-120.

———. "Paradigm Shifts into Giftedness." *Roeper Review* 15:2 (1992): 91-92.

Milgram, Roberta M., ed. *Teaching Gifted and Talented Learners in Regular Classrooms.* Springfield, IL: C.C. Thomas, 1989.

Milios, Rita. *Imagi-size: Activities to Exercise Your Students' Imaginations.* Dayton, OH: Pieces of Learning, 1993.

Miller, Bernard S., and M. Price, eds. *The Gifted Child, the Family, and the Community.* New York: Walker and Co., 1981.

Mithaug, Dennis E. *Self-Determined Kids: Raising Satisfied and Successful Children.* Lexington, MA: Lexington Books, 1991.

Myers, Robert E., and E. Paul Torrance. *What Next? Futuristic Scenarios for Creative Problem Solving.* Tucson, AZ: Zephyr Press, 1994.

National Council of Teachers of Mathematics. *Curriculum and Evaluation Standards for School Mathematics.* Reston, VA: National Council of Teachers of Mathematics, 1989.

Parke, Beverly N. *Gifted Students in Regular Classrooms.* Boston: Allyn & Bacon, 1989.

Parke, Beverly N., and Phyllis S. Ness. "Curricular Decision-Making for the Education of Young Gifted Children." *Gifted Child Quarterly* 32:1 (1988): 196-199.

Parker, Jeanette Plauche. *Instructional Strategies for Teaching the Gifted.* Boston: Allyn & Bacon, 1989.

Payne, Lauren Murphy, and Claudia Rohling. *Just Because I Am: A Child's Book of Affirmation.* Minneapolis, MN: Free Spirit Publishing Inc., 1994.

———. *A Leader's Guide to Just Because I Am: A Child's Book of Affirmation.* Minneapolis, MN: Free Spirit Publishing Inc., 1994.

Piirto, Jane. *Talented Children and Adults: Their Development and Education.* New York: Macmillan College Publishing Co., 1994.

———. *Understanding Those Who Create.* Dayton, OH: Ohio Psychology Publishing, 1992.

Rimm, Sylvia. *How to Parent So Children Will Learn.* Watertown, WI: Apple Publishing Co., 1983.

———. *Keys to Parenting the Gifted Child.* New York: Barron's Educational Series, 1995.

———. *Underachievement Syndrome: Causes and Cures.* Watertown, WI: Apple Publishing Co., 1986.

Robinson, Ann. "Cooperation or Exploitation: The Arguments Against Cooperative Learning for Talented Students." *Journal for the Education of the Gifted* 14(1): 9-27.

Roedell, Wendy C., Nancy Jackson, and Halbert B. Robinson. *Gifted Young Children.* New York: Teachers College Press, 1980.

Roeper, Annemarie. "Characteristics of Gifted Children and How Parents and Teachers Can Cope with Them." *Journal for the Illinois Council of the Gifted* 11 (1992): 31-32.

———. *Educating Children for Life: The Modern Learning Community.* Monroe, NY: Trillium Press, 1990.

Rogers, Karen. *The Relationship of Grouping Practices to the Education of the Gifted and Talented Learner: Research-Based Decision Making.* Storrs, CT: National Research Center on the Gifted and Talented, 1991.

Samara, John, and Jim Curry, eds. *Developing Units for Primary Students.* Bowling Green, KY: KAGE Publications, 1994.

Saunders, Jacqulyn, and Pamela Espeland. *Bringing Out the Best: A Resource Guide for Parents of Young Gifted Children.* Minneapolis, MN: Free Spirit Publishing Inc., 1991.

Schmitz, Connie, and Judy Galbraith. *Managing the Social and Emotional Needs of the Gifted: A Teacher's Survival Guide.* Minneapolis, MN: Free Spirit Publishing Inc., 1985.

Schwartz, Lita Linzer. *Why Give "Gifts" to the Gifted? Investing in a National Resource.* Thousand Oaks, CA: Corwin Press, 1994.

Shaklee, Beverly. "Creating Positive Learning Environments: Young Gifted Children at Home and in School." *Understanding Our Gifted* 7:3 (1995): 1, 8-9.

Shaklee, Beverly, and Jane Rohrer. "Early Assessment of Exceptional Potential." *Journal for the Illinois Council of the Gifted* 11 (1992): 22-24.

Silverman, Linda Kreger. "The Gifted Individual." In *Counseling the Gifted and Talented,* Linda Kreger Silverman, ed. Denver: Love Publishing Co., 1993, 3-28.

Sisk, Dorothy. *Creative Teaching of the Gifted.* New York: McGraw-Hill, 1987.

Skromme, Arnold. *The 7-Ability Plan: A Plan for Identifying and Maximizing Our Children's Best Abilities.* Moline, IL: Self-Confidence Press, 1989.

Smutny, Joan Franklin. "Early Gifts, Early School Recognition." *Understanding Our Gifted* 7:3 (1995): 1, 13-16.
———. "Enhancing Linguistic Gifts of the Young." *Understanding Our Gifted* 8:4 (1996): 1, 12-15.
———, ed. *The Young Gifted Child: Potential and Promise, an Anthology.* Cresskill, NJ: Hampton Press, 1997.

Smutny, Joan Franklin, and Rita Haynes Blocksom. *Education of the Gifted: Programs and Perspectives.* Bloomington, IN: Phi Delta Kappa Foundation, 1990.

Smutny, Joan Franklin, Kathleen Veenker, and Stephen Veenker. *Your Gifted Child: How to Recognize and Develop the Special Talents in Your Child from Birth to Age Seven.* New York: Ballantine Books, 1989.

Snowden, Peggy L. "Education of Young Gifted Children." *Journal for the Illinois Council of the Gifted* 11 (1992): 51-60.

Sternberg, Robert J. *Beyond IQ: A Triarchic Theory of Human Intelligence.* New York: Cambridge University Press, 1985.

Taylor, Roger. *Reshaping the Curriculum: Integrate, Differentiate, Compact, and Think.* Oakbrook, IL: Curriculum Design for Excellence, 1991.

Tolan, Steven S. *A Time to Fly Free.* New York: Aladdin Books, 1990.

Torrance, E. Paul. *Creativity: Just Wanting to Know.* Pretoria, South Africa: Benedic Books, 1994.
———. "Growing Up Creatively Gifted: A 22-Year Longitudinal Study." *The Creative Child and Adult Quarterly* 5 (3): 148-159.
———. *The Search for Satori and Creativity.* Buffalo, NY: Creative Education Foundation, 1979.
———. "Testing the Creativity of Preschool Children." In *The Faces and Forms of Creativity.* Ventura, CA: Ventura County Superintendent of Schools Office, 1981, 65-80.

Torrance, E. Paul, and H. Tammy Safter. *Incubation Model of Teaching: Getting Beyond Aha!* Buffalo, NY: Bearly Limited, 1990.

Treffinger, Donald J. *Encouraging Creative Learning for the Gifted and Talented: A Handbook of Methods and Techniques.* Los Angeles: National/State Leadership Training Institute on the Gifted and Talented, 1980.

Treffinger, Donald, Robert Hohn, and John Feldhusen. *Reach Each You Teach.* East Aurora, NY: D.O.K. Publishers, 1979.

Udall, Anne J., and Joan E. Daniels. *Creating the Thoughtful Classroom: Strategies to Promote Student Thinking.* Tucson, AZ: Zephyr Press, 1991.

U.S. Department of Education, Office of Educational Research and Improvement. *National Excellence: A Case for Developing America's Talent.* Washington, DC: U.S. Government Printing Office, 1993.

Van De Walle, John A. *Elementary School Mathematics: Teaching Developmentally,* 2d ed. White Plains, NY: Longman, 1994.

VanTassel-Baska, Joyce, Dana T. Johnson, and Linda Neal Boyce, eds. *Developing Verbal Talent: Ideas and Strategies for Teachers of Elementary and Middle School Students.* Boston: Allyn & Bacon, 1996.

Walker, Sally Yahnke. *The Survival Guide for Parents of Gifted Kids: How to Understand, Live With, and Stick Up for Your Gifted Child.* Minneapolis, MN: Free Spirit Publishing Inc., 1991.

Webb, James T., and Patricia A. Kleine. "Assessing Gifted and Talented Children." In *Testing Young Children,* J.L. Culbertson and D.J. Willis, eds. Austin, TX: Pro-ed., 1993.

Webb, James T., Elizabeth A. Meckstroth, and Stephanie S. Tolan. *Guiding the Gifted Child: A Practical Source for Parents and Teachers,* rev. ed. Scottsdale, AZ: Gifted Psychology Publishing, forthcoming.

West, Thomas G. *In the Mind's Eye: Visual Thinkers, Gifted People with Learning Difficulties, Computer Images, and the Ironies of Creativity.* Buffalo, NY: Prometheus Books, 1991.

Whitmore, Joanne Rand. *Giftedness, Conflict and Underachievement.* Boston: Allyn & Bacon, 1980.

Willis, Scott. "Teaching Young Children: Educators Seek 'Developmental Appropriateness.'" *Curriculum Update* (November 1993): 1-8.

Winebrenner, Susan. *Teaching Gifted Kids in the Regular Classroom.* Minneapolis, MN: Free Spirit Publishing Inc., 1992.
———. *Teaching Kids with Learning Difficulties in the Regular Classroom.* Minneapolis, MN: Free Spirit Publishing Inc., 1996.

Index

About the Authors

Founder of The Center for Gifted at National-Louis University, **Joan Franklin Smutny, M.A.,** teaches creative writing to children in her programs and gifted education to graduate students. Her extensive works in the field are often published and/or cited in professional literature, and she presents at local and national seminars, on television and on radio. She is co-chair of membership and of the special schools and programs division for the National Association for Gifted Children, editor for the *IAGC Journal* and *Understanding Our Gifted,* and contributing editor for *Roeper Review: A Journal on Gifted Education.* She has coauthored three books—*A Thoughtful Overview of Gifted Education* (with Judy W. Eby; Longman, 1990); *Your Gifted Child: How to Recognize and Develop the Special Talents in Your Child from Birth to Age Seven* (with Kathleen Veenker and Stephen Veenker; Ballantine Books, 1989); and *Education of the Gifted: Programs and Perspectives* (with Rita Haynes Blocksom; Phi Delta Kappa, 1990)—and was editor for *The Young Gifted Child: Potential and Promise, an Anthology* (Hampton Press, 1997). In 1996, Joan won the NAGC Distinguished Service Award for outstanding contribution to the field of gifted education.

Sally Yahnke Walker, Ph.D., is a consultant, educator, and published author in the field of gifted education. An influential advocate for gifted children, she has piloted programs and coordinated many efforts to create a broad-based level of support for talented students in public school districts. As a consultant for KIDS (Kishwaukee Intermediate Delivery System) with the Regional Office of Education, Sally has provided inservice training, chaired a State Task Force on Early Identification and Intervention of Young Gifted, actively promoted greater networking among educators, and facilitated workshops for parents of gifted children. She has written several informative and useful articles on gifted children for teachers and parents, as well as *The Survival Guide for Parents of Gifted Kids: How to Understand, Live With, and Stick Up for Your Gifted Child* (Free Spirit Publishing, 1991), winner of a Parents' Choice Award, and *Making Memories: A Parent Home Portfolio* with Lori Whitman (Pieces of Learning, 1997).

Elizabeth A. Meckstroth, M.Ed., M.S.W., has been active in the field of gifted education since 1979. She coordinated the development of Supporting the Emotional Needs of the Gifted Children and Adults program (SENG). She is a coauthor of *Guiding the Gifted Child: A Practical Source for Parents and Educators* (with James T. Webb and Stephanie S. Tolan; Gifted Psychology Press, rev. ed. forthcoming), which won the American Psychological Association's Best Book Award. In addition, Betty has written numerous book chapters and articles and has served as the "Parenting" column contributor for *Understanding Our Gifted.* She also served on the Executive Committee of the Counseling and Guidance Division of the National Association for Gifted Children. Betty earned her M.Ed. from the University of Dayton, her certificate in analytical psychology from the C.G. Jung Institute of Chicago, and her M.S.W. in clinical social work from Loyola University in Chicago. She is especially interested in assessment and support for highly gifted children, and she concentrates her work on psychotherapy, assessment, and consulting.